T0326373

UNDERSTANDING
CLASS

UNDERSTANDING CLASS

ERIK OLIN WRIGHT

VERSO

London • New York

For my brother, Woody Wright,
and father-in-law, Robert L. Kahn, with love
and admiration

First published by Verso 2015
© Erik Olin Wright 2015

1 3 5 7 9 10 8 6 4 2

Verso
UK: 6 Meard Street, London W1F 0EG
US: 388 Atlantic Ave, Brooklyn, NY 11217
www.versobooks.com

Verso is the imprint of New Left Books

ISBN-13: 978-1-78168-945-5 (PB)
ISBN-13: 978-1-78168-920-2 (HC)
eISBN-13: 978-1-78168-921-9 (US)
eISBN-13: 978-1-78168-922-6 (UK)

British Library Cataloguing in Publication Data
A catalogue record for this book is available from the British Library

Library of Congress Cataloging-in-Publication Data

Wright, Erik Olin.
Understanding class / Erik Olin Wright.
pages cm
Includes index.
ISBN 978-1-78168-945-5 (paperback) — ISBN 978-1-78168-920-2 (hardback)
— ISBN 978-1-78168-921-9 (ebk)
1. Social classes. 2. Marxian school of sociology. I. Title.
HT609.W7134 2015
305.5—dc23
2015012843

Typeset in Sabon by Hewer Text UK Ltd, Edinburgh, Scotland
Printed in the United States

CONTENTS

PREFACE

The essays assembled in this book were written between 1995 and 2015. They involve three agendas: interrogating the approaches to class analysis of specific writers working in a variety of theoretical traditions; developing general frameworks of class analysis that can help integrate the insights of different theoretical traditions; and analyzing the problem of class conflict and class compromise in contemporary capitalism.

Most of the chapters in this book are concerned with the first of these agendas, exploring in detail theoretical issues in the work of a range of writers who specify the concept of class in different ways: Max Weber, Charles Tilly, Aage Sørensen, Michael Mann, David Grusky and Kim Weeden, Thomas Piketty, Jan Pakulski and Malcolm Waters, and Guy Standing. My own approach to class is firmly embedded in the Marxist tradition, while none of these writers adopts a Marxist approach and some are overtly hostile to Marxism. Often in encounters between Marxist and non-Marxist approaches to some problem the basic stance is one of combat, each side trying to defeat the arguments of the other. While there may be circumstances in intellectual debates where vanquishing an opponent is appropriate, in these essays my goal is to figure out what is most useful and interesting rather than mainly to point out what is wrong with a particular theorist's work. One might call this virtue-centered critique rather than flaw-centered critique. Of course, it is necessary to clarify gaps and silences in particular bodies of work, to illuminate salient differences between approaches, and sometimes to identify more serious theoretical flaws. But all of this is still in the service of clarifying and appropriating what is valuable rather than simply discrediting the ideas of rival approaches.

It is one thing to recognize that there are valuable insights to be appropriated from even hostile theoretical traditions; it is another to try to systematically integrate those insights into a broader framework. This is the second task of this book—proposing general strategies for integrating key ideas from Marxist and non-Marxist currents of class analysis. My approach to accomplishing this comes out of a longstanding preoccupation in my work with constructing conceptual typologies as a way of clarifying the theoretical differences between my arguments and those of others grappling with the same problems. For example, in my early empirical work on class structure I used a typology in the form of a branching diagram of alternative ways of defining class as a way of identifying the specificity of the Marxist concept.

Varieties of Concepts of Class

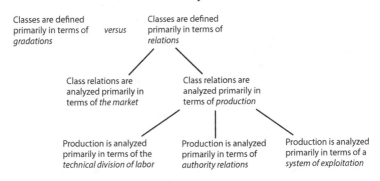

Source: Erik Olin Wright, *Class Structure and Income Determination*, New York: Academic Press, 1979, p. 5.

My initial purpose in constructing this kind of typology was to draw clear lines of demarcation between alternative theories and concepts and then argue for the virtue of my preferred option. More recently, however, it has become clear to me that there is an alternative way of using such typologies. To the extent that a typology of theories identifies the distinct mechanisms that are the focus of different theories, it might be possible to integrate at least some of the different approaches to class into a more general framework of analysis organized around the interconnections among these different mechanisms. Rather than mainly see alternative approaches as competing with each other, perhaps they could potentially be seen as complementary.

My first effort at doing this was the edited book, *Approaches to Class Analysis* (Cambridge University Press, 2005). The book included essays by six sociologists working within different theoretical approaches to class analysis. Each contributor was instructed to write an essay elaborating the theoretical foundations of a particular approach to class analysis. The title of the concluding chapter posed the question "If Class Is the Answer, What Is the Question?" The basic idea was that different strands of class analysis were anchored in different kinds of questions, and this helped explain why the concept of class was defined in different ways. The last sentence of the book loosely evoked Marx's famous passage about a society without class divisions in which it was possible to hunt in the morning, to fish in the afternoon, rear cattle in the evening, criticize after dinner: "One can be a Weberian for the study of class mobility, a Bourdieusian for the study of class determinants of lifestyles, and a Marxian for the critique of capitalism."

The next logical step was to try to integrate the mechanisms connected to these different questions into a more comprehensive framework. Three chapters in this book try to do this in different ways. Chapter 1, "From Grand Paradigm Battles to Pragmatist Realism," originally published in 2009 in *New Left Review*, constructs an integrative model for class analysis by arguing that the different broad traditions of class analysis are anchored in three different clusters of causal mechanisms: stratification approaches to class define class in terms of individual attributes and conditions; Weberian approaches define class in terms of a variety of mechanisms of opportunity hoarding; and Marxist approaches define class in terms of mechanisms of exploitation and domination. Each of these causal mechanisms plays a key role in particular streams of causal processes. The task of the essay was to clarify these focal mechanisms and then try to integrate them into a broader explanatory model of class analysis. The key device of this integration was a series of diagrams connecting the micro-level of class effects tied to attributes of individuals with the more macro-level effects generated by the nature of structural positions within the market and production.

In the initial plan for this book, chapter 1 was to be the only chapter in which a general framework of analysis was presented. As it turned out, a second, complementary way of integrating different traditions of class analysis emerged as I worked on one of the new essays for the book, the discussion in chapter 6 of David Grusky and Kim Weeden's work on "micro-classes." Their analysis posed a particular challenge for me. While I admired the rigorous empirical work in the series of papers written by these two American sociologists, my basic reaction was that their research had very little to do with *class* analysis. The core idea of their work is that if class is identified as causally significant positions within the system of production, then class should be defined as fine-grained occupational categories. These are the categories, they argue, that are salient to people's lives as participants in an economic structure. They refer to these as "micro-classes" in contrast to the "big classes" of the Marxist and Weberian traditions. This means that in a country like the United States there are hundreds, perhaps thousands, of distinct classes.

My initial reaction to Grusky and Weeden's arguments was to simply say that they involved a misuse of the word "class." This suggested writing a kind of methodological chapter on the problem of words and concepts, but that seemed out of place with the basic strategy of the book, which was to find what was most useful in a variety of approaches. I then tried to connect the Grusky-Weeden concept of micro-class to the framework elaborated in chapter 1, but it just did not fit and my efforts at trying to make it fit seemed contrived. This again led me to consider arguing that what Grusky and Weeden were doing was not any variety of class analysis, in spite of the terms they used. If I removed their work from the domain of class analysis, I would not have to worry about the fact that it did not fit into my effort at a general synthesis. This suggested dropping the idea of the chapter altogether.

After several weeks of working on the chapter without making any real headway, a solution came to me unexpectedly when I recalled the analytical framework for the analysis of the state and power by Robert Alford and Roger Friedland in their book *The Powers of Theory: Capitalism, the State, and Democracy* (Cambridge University Press, 1985). In that book, Alford and Friedland use the metaphor of a game to distinguish three levels of power and conflict: at the *systemic* level of power, conflict is over what game to play (capitalism versus socialism); at the *institutional* level of power, conflict is over the rules of the game (over what kind of capitalism); and at the *situational* level of power, conflict is over the moves in the game (how to best realize interests under fixed rules). What occurred to me was that different approaches to class analysis could be seen as anchoring the definition of class in terms of one or another of these levels of power and conflict: Marxist class concepts are defined at the systemic level of the game; Weberian class categories are defined at the institutional level of the rules of the game; and the Grusky-Weeden model of micro-classes defines class exclusively at the situational level of moves within fixed rules in a single game. I examine this game metaphor in detail in chapter 6, so I won't sketch the argument now; the important point here is that this insight unlocked the chapter for me. As a result, chapter 6 contains an extended discussion of a second general strategy for connecting different traditions of class analysis within a broader framework.

One other chapter contains an integrative framework for connecting different approaches to class analysis. The chapter on Michael Mann's approach to class is built around a three-fold distinction in clusters of concepts used in class analysis: class relations, class location, and class structure; class structuration and class formation; and collective class actors. The first of these concerns the structural positions filled by individuals; the second concerns the nature of social relations within classes rooted in communities and social networks; the third focuses on class-based organizations engaged in struggles. Some theorists, like Michael Mann, insist that class is only meaningful when it exists as a collective actor, while others focus almost exclusively on the structural meaning of class, and some consider the dense interactions of class formation as the necessary condition for a social category to be a class. I argue that a fully developed class analysis investigates the interconnections among all three of these clusters.

The third general agenda of the book shifts attention from the problem of the diverse meanings of the concept of class and how these meanings can be brought into alignment to the problem of how to understand the macro-problem of configurations of class struggle and balances of power in contemporary capitalism. All three of the chapters that engage this problem take the basic parameters of Marxist class analysis as given and then propose a way of understanding the effects of the institutional conditions and balance of power of contemporary capitalism on patterns of class struggle and class compromise. In terms of the general model proposed in chapter 6, the analysis in these chapters defines class in the traditional Marxist way at the systemic level of the game itself and then, using this definition, explores the problem of different configurations of class struggle at the level of the rules of the game and moves in the game. The chapters thus show how the Marxist concept of class, while specified at the systemic level of power and conflict, can be deployed in explanatory models at the other levels.

Erik Olin Wright
Madison, Wisconsin
February 2015

FROM GRAND PARADIGM BATTLES TO PRAGMATIST REALISM: TOWARDS AN INTEGRATED CLASS ANALYSIS

When I began writing about class in the mid-1970s, I saw Marxism as a comprehensive paradigm confronting positivist social science.[1] I argued that Marxism had distinctive epistemological premises and distinctive methodological approaches that were fundamentally opposed to the prevailing practices of mainstream social science. While I argued that this battle should be engaged on empirical as well as theoretical terrain, I viewed Marxism and mainstream sociology as foundationally distinct and incommensurable warring paradigms. Looking back in the mid-1980s at this earlier work, I wrote: "I originally had visions of glorious paradigm battles, with lances drawn and the valiant Marxist knight unseating the bourgeois rival in a dramatic quantitative joust. What is more, the fantasy saw the vanquished admitting defeat and changing horses as a result."[2]

Nearly four decades have passed since this early work on class. In the intervening period I have rethought the underlying logic of my approach to class analysis a number of times.[3] While I continue to work within the Marxist tradition, I no longer feel that the most useful way of thinking about Marxism is as a comprehensive paradigm that is incommensurate with "bourgeois" sociology.[4] Rather,

---

1 An early statement of my views on Marxism and mainstream social science can be found in the methodological introduction to *Class, Crisis and the State*, London: New Left Books, 1978.

2 "Reflections on Classes," *Berkeley Journal of Sociology*, 1987, reprinted in Erik Olin Wright, *The Debate on Classes*, London: Verso, 1989, 76.

3 The principle publications in which I have discussed these metatheoretical issues are *Class, Crisis and the State*; *Classes*, London: Verso, 1985; *The Debate on Classes* London: Verso, 1989; *Class Counts: Comparative Studies in Class Analysis*, Cambridge University Press, 1997; and *Approaches to Class Analysis*, Cambridge: Cambridge University Press, 2005.

4 I prefer to use the expression "Marxist tradition" rather than "Marx*ism*"

I see different theoretical traditions as identifying different kinds of causal processes or mechanisms, which they claim have explanatory power for particular agendas. These different traditions have scientific value to the extent that these claims are justified. The different mechanisms elaborated by different theoretical traditions intersect and interact in the world, generating the things we observe. The Marxist tradition is a valuable and interesting body of ideas because it successfully identifies real mechanisms that matter for a wide range of important problems, but it does not constitute a full-blown "paradigm" capable of comprehensively explaining all things social or subsuming all social mechanisms under a unified framework. It also does not have a monopoly on the capacity to identify real mechanisms, and thus in practice sociological research by Marxists should combine distinctive Marxist-identified mechanisms with whatever other causal processes seem pertinent to the tasks at hand. What might be called "pragmatist realism" has replaced the Grand Battle of Paradigms.

Pragmatist realism does not imply simply dissolving Marxism into some amorphous "sociology" or social science. Marxism remains distinctive in organizing its agenda around a set of fundamental questions and problems which other theoretical traditions either ignore or marginalize. It is distinctive in its normative commitments to class emancipation. And it is distinctive in identifying a specific set of interconnected causal processes relevant to those questions and emancipatory ideals. These elements constitute the anchors for a distinctive intellectual tradition of emancipatory social science, but they are not the basis for an exclusionary paradigm.[5]

In this chapter I explore some of the implications of this pragmatist realism for class analysis. In my theoretical work in the late 1970s and early 1980s, I argued for the general superiority of the Marxist concept of class over its main sociological rivals—especially Weberian concepts of class and class within mainstream stratification research. It now seems to me more appropriate to see these different ways of talking about class as each identifying different clusters of causal processes at work in shaping the micro and macro aspects of economically rooted inequality in capitalist societies. For some questions and problems, one or another of these

---

precisely because the latter suggests something more like a comprehensive paradigm.

5   For a discussion of this way of thinking about Marxism as an intellectual tradition, see Erik Olin Wright, *Interrogating Inequality,* London: Verso, 1994, especially part 3.

clusters of mechanisms may be more important, but all are relevant to a full sociological understanding of economic inequality and its consequences. Each of these approaches to class analysis is incomplete if it ignores the others. I continue to feel that Marxist class analysis is superior to the other traditions for a range of questions that I feel are of central importance, especially questions about the nature of capitalism, its harms and contradictions, and the possibilities of its transformation. But even for these core Marxist questions, the other traditions of class analysis have something to offer.

For simplicity in this discussion, I focus on three clusters of class-relevant causal processes, each associated with different strands of sociological theory and approaches to class analysis. The first identifies class with the attributes and material conditions of the lives of individuals. The second focuses on the ways in which social positions give some people control over economic resources of various sorts while excluding others from access to those resources. And the third identifies class, above all, with the ways in which economic positions give some people control over the lives and activities of others. I call these three approaches the *individual-attributes* approach to class, the *opportunity-hoarding* approach, and the *domination and exploitation* approach. The first is associated with the stratification tradition, the second with the Weberian tradition, and the third with the Marxist tradition.[6]

CLASS AS INDIVIDUAL ATTRIBUTES

Among both sociologists and the lay public, the principal way that most people understand the concept of class is in terms of individual attributes and life conditions. People have all sorts of attributes, including sex, age, race, religion, intelligence, education, geographical location, and so on. Some of these attributes they have from birth, some they acquire but once acquired are very stable, and some are quite dependent on a person's specific social situation at any point in time and may accordingly change. These attributes are consequential for various things we might want to explain, from health to voting behavior to childrearing practices. People can also be characterized by the material conditions in which they live: squalid apartments, pleasant houses in the suburbs, or mansions in

---

6 Not all currents of class analysis fall neatly into these three theoretical clusters. In chapter 6 below I will discuss one additional approach to class which is rooted in disaggregated occupational categories.

gated communities; dire poverty, adequate income, or extravagant wealth; insecure access to health services or excellent health insurance and access to high-quality services. "Class," then, is a way of talking about the connection between individual attributes and these material life conditions: class identifies those economically important attributes of people that shape their opportunities and choices in a market economy and thus their material conditions of life. Class should neither be identified simply with the individual attributes nor with the material conditions of life of people, but with the interconnections between these two.

The key individual attribute that is part of class in economically developed societies within this approach is education, but some sociologists also include somewhat more elusive attributes such as cultural resources, social connections, and even individual motivations.[7] All of these deeply shape the opportunities people face and thus the income they can acquire in the market, the kind of housing they can expect to have, the quality of the health care they are likely to get, and much more.

When these different attributes of individuals and material conditions of life broadly cluster together, these clusters are called "classes." The "middle class," within this approach to the study of class, identifies people who are more or less in the broad middle of the economy and society: they have enough education and money to participate fully in some vaguely defined "mainstream" way of life. "Upper class" identifies people whose wealth, high income, social connections, and valuable talents enable them to live their lives apart from "ordinary" people. The "lower class" identifies people who lack the necessary educational and cultural resources to live securely above the poverty line. And finally, the "underclass" identifies people who live in extreme poverty, marginalized from the mainstream of American society by a lack of basic education and skills needed for stable employment.

While most research within the individual-attributes approach discusses class using loose gradational terms like upper, middle and lower class, there are some currents that attempt to specify an array of more qualitatively distinguished categories. A good example is the work of Mike Savage and his colleagues in their analysis of what has come to be known as the "Great British Class Survey."[8] Along the

---

7   Pierre Bourdieu is the leading contemporary sociologist who systematically includes a range of cultural elements in an expanded list of class-relevant individual attributes.

8   Mike Savage, et. al, "A New Model of Social Class? Findings from the BBC's Great British Class Survey Experiment," *Sociology* 47(2), 219–250. 2013.

lines of the work of Pierre Bourdieu, they define the abstract concept of class in terms of three dimensions of economically relevant resources which individuals possess: economic capital, cultural capital, and social capital. They then ask the empirical question: how many classes can be empirically distinguished based on the ways in which indicators of these three dimensions of individual attributes cluster together? Their answer, using fairly sophisticated inductive statistical strategies, is that there are seven classes in Britain today: elite; established middle class; technical middle class; new affluent workers; traditional working class; emergent service workers; and precariat.

In the individual-attributes approach to class, the central concern of sociologists has been to understand how people acquire the attributes that place them in one class or another. For most people in the countries where sociologists live, economic status and rewards are mainly acquired through employment in paid jobs, so the central thrust of much research in this tradition is on the process by which people acquire the cultural, motivational, and educational resources that affect their occupations in the labor market. Because the conditions of life in childhood are clearly of considerable importance in these processes, this tradition of class analysis devotes a great deal of attention to what is sometimes called "class background"—the class character of the family settings in which these key attributes are acquired. The causal logic of these kinds of class processes is illustrated in a stripped-down form in Figure 1.1.

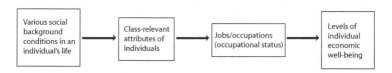

Figure 1.1. The Individual-Attributes Approach to Class and Inequality

Skills, education, and motivations are, of course, very important determinants of an individual's economic prospects. What is missing in this approach to class, however, is any serious consideration of the *inequalities in the positions themselves* that people occupy. Education shapes the kinds of jobs people get, but how should we conceptualize the nature of the jobs that people fill by virtue of their education? Why are some jobs "better" than others? Why do some jobs confer on their incumbents a great deal of power while others do not? Rather than focusing exclusively on the process by which individuals are sorted into positions, the other two approaches to class analysis begin by analyzing the nature of the positions themselves into which people are sorted.

CLASS AS OPPORTUNITY HOARDING

The problem of "opportunity hoarding" is closely associated with the work of Max Weber.[9] The idea is that if a job is to confer on its occupants high income and special advantages it is important that the incumbents of those jobs have various means of excluding other people from access to the jobs. This is also sometimes referred to as a process of *social closure*, the process whereby access to a position becomes reserved for some people and closed off to others. One way of achieving social closure is by creating requirements for filling the job that are very costly for people to meet. Educational credentials often have this character: high levels of education generate high income in part because of significant restrictions on the supply of highly educated people. Admissions procedures, tuition costs, risk aversion to large loans by low-income people, and a range of other factors all block access to higher education for many people, and these barriers benefit those in jobs that require higher education. If a massive effort was made to improve the educational level of those with less education, this program would itself lower the value of education for those who already have it, since its value depends to a significant extent on its scarcity. The opportunity-hoarding mechanism is illustrated in Figure 1.2.

Figure 1.2. The Opportunity-Hoarding Approach to Class and Inequality

---

9   Among American sociologists, the term "opportunity hoarding" was used most explicitly by Charles Tilly, especially in his book *Durable Inequality* (Berkeley: University of California Press, 1999). Tilly's approach is discussed in depth in chapter 3 below. Bourdieu's work on fields and forms of capital also revolves around processes of opportunity hoarding.

Some might object to this description of educational credentials by arguing that education also affects earnings by enhancing a person's productivity. Economists argue that education creates "human capital," which makes people more productive, and this higher productivity makes employers willing to pay them higher wages. While some of the higher earnings that accompany higher education reflect productivity differences, this is only part of the story. Equally important are the ways in which the process of acquiring education excludes people through various mechanisms and thus restricts the supply of people available to take these jobs. A simple thought experiment shows how this works: imagine that the United States had open borders and let anyone with a medical degree or engineering degree or computer science degree anywhere in the world come to the United States and practice their profession. The massive increase in the supply of people with these credentials would undermine the earning capacity of holders of the credentials even though their actual knowledge and skills, and thus their productivity, would not be diminished. Citizenship rights are a special, and potent, form of "license" to sell one's labor in a labor market.

Credentialing and licensing are particularly important mechanisms for opportunity hoarding, but many other institutional devices have been used in various times and places to restrict access to given types of jobs: color bars excluded racial minorities from many jobs in the United States, especially (but not only) in the South until the 1960s; marriage bars and gender exclusions restricted access to certain jobs for women until well into the twentieth century in most developed capitalist countries; religion, cultural style, manners, accent—all of these have constituted mechanisms of exclusion.

Perhaps the most important exclusionary mechanism that protects the privileges and advantages of people in certain jobs in a capitalist society is private property rights in the means of production. Private property rights are the pivotal form of exclusion that determines access to the "job" of capitalist employer. If workers were to attempt to take over a factory and run it themselves they would be violating this process of closure by challenging their exclusion from control over the means of production. The capacity of owners to acquire profits depends upon their defense of this exclusion, which we call "property rights." The core class division within both Weberian and Marxian traditions of sociology between capitalists and workers can therefore be understood as reflecting a specific form of opportunity hoarding enforced by the legal rules of property rights.

Exclusionary mechanisms that shape class structures within the opportunity-hoarding approach do not operate only in the most privileged parts of the class structure. Labor unions can also function as an exclusionary mechanism by protecting the incumbents of jobs from competition by outsiders. This does not mean that on balance unions contribute to increasing inequality, since they may also act politically to reduce inequalities and they may effectively reduce inequalities generated by other mechanisms of exclusion, especially mechanisms connected to private ownership of the means of production. Still, to the extent that unions create barriers to entry to certain jobs, they do create a form of social closure that improves the material conditions of life of their members.

Sociologists who adopt the opportunity-hoarding approach to class generally identify three broad class categories in American society: capitalists, defined by private property rights in the ownership of means of production; the middle class, defined by mechanisms of exclusion over the acquisition of education and skills; and the working class, defined by their exclusion from both higher educational credentials and capital. That segment of the working class that is protected by unions is either seen as a privileged stratum within the working class, or, sometimes, as a component of the middle class.

The critical difference between the opportunity-hoarding mechanisms of class and the individual attribute mechanisms is this: opportunity hoarding means that the economic advantages people get from being in a privileged class position are *causally connected* to the disadvantages of people excluded from those class positions. In the case of the mechanisms connected to individual attributes, advantages and disadvantages are independent of each other, generated by processes attached to individuals. To state this in a simple way, in the case of opportunity-hoarding mechanisms, the rich are rich in part *because* the poor are poor; the rich do things to secure their wealth that contribute to the disadvantages poor people face in the world. In the case of simple individual attributes, the rich are rich because they have favorable attributes; the poor are poor because they lack these attributes; and there is no systematic causal connection between these facts. In this view, eliminating poverty by improving the relevant attributes of the poor—by improving their education, cultural level, and human capital—would in no way harm the affluent. Where opportunity-hoarding mechanisms are important, in contrast, eliminating poverty by removing the mechanisms of exclusion potentially undermines the advantages of the affluent within the existing system.

CLASS AS EXPLOITATION AND DOMINATION

Class as exploitation and domination is the most controversial way of thinking about class.[10] Most sociologists ignore this set of mechanisms when talking about class, and some explicitly deny their relevance. These mechanisms of class analysis are associated most strongly with the Marxist tradition of sociology, but some sociologists more influenced by Weber also include exploitation and domination in their conception of class.[11]

"Domination" and, especially, "exploitation" are contentious words in sociology because they generally imply a moral judgment rather than being simply a neutral description. Many sociologists try to avoid such terms because of this normative content.[12] I feel, however, that they are important and accurately identify certain key issues in understanding class. Both domination and exploitation refer to ways in which people control the lives of others. "Domination" refers to the ability to control the *activities* of others. "Exploitation" refers to the acquisition of economic benefits from the laboring activity of those who are dominated. All exploitation, therefore, implies some kind of domination, but not all domination involves exploitation. Prison guards, for example, dominate prisoners but do not necessarily exploit them.

In relations of exploitation and domination it is not the case that one group simply benefits by restricting access to certain kinds of

---

10 For the present purposes it is useful to see domination and exploitation as closely linked mechanisms. For some explanatory purposes one or the other of these mechanisms would be more salient.

11 Weber, of course, develops an elaborate general discussion of domination, power, and authority, but mostly in the context of his analyses of organizations and the state, not his specification of the concept of class; and he completely ignores the problem of exploitation. See chapter 2 for an extended discussion of these issues in Weber's class analysis.

12 John Goldthorpe explicitly objects to the concept of exploitation on these grounds. In a footnote to an article in the *American Journal of Sociology* commenting on Aage Sørenson's rent-based concept of class, Goldthorpe says of the concept of exploitation that it is "a word I would myself gladly see disappear from the sociological lexicon." He adds, by way of clarification, "Its function in Marxist thought was to allow a fusion of normative and positive claims in a way that I would find unacceptable." And he concludes: "If invoking exploitation is no more than a way of flagging the presence of structurally opposed class interests that lead to zero-sum conflicts, then its use is innocuous but scarcely necessary." "Commentary on Sørenson," *American Journal of Sociology* 105: 6, May 2000, 1574.

resources or positions. In addition, the exploiting/dominating group is able to control the laboring effort of another for its own advantage. Consider the following classic contrasting cases: In the first case, large landowners seize control of common grazing lands, exclude peasants from access to this land, and reap economic advantages from their exclusive control of it for their own use. In the second case, the same landlords seize control of the grazing lands, exclude the peasants, but then bring some of those peasants back onto the land as agricultural laborers. In this second case, in addition to gaining advantage from controlling access to the land (opportunity hoarding) the landowner also dominates and exploits the labor of the farmworkers. This is a stronger form of relational interdependency than in the case of simple exclusion, for here there is an ongoing relationship between the *activities* of the advantaged and disadvantaged persons, not just a relationship between their *conditions*. Exploitation and domination are forms of structured inequality that require continual active cooperation between exploiters and exploited, dominators and dominated.

This contrast in the role of social relations within the three approaches to class analysis is summarized in Table 1.1. The individual-attributes approach is the least relational, since neither the economic conditions in which people live nor their activities are understood as directly reflecting social relations. The opportunity-hoarding approach sees the economic conditions of people as formed through relations of exclusion, but it does not specify class as embodying relations among activities. The exploitation/domination approach includes both forms of relations.

Approach to Class Analysis	Economic Conditions	Economic Activities
Individual attributes	Nonrelational	Nonrelational
Opportunity hoarding	Relational	Nonrelational
Domination/exploitation	Relational	Relational

Table 1.1. The Role of Social Relations in Different Approaches to Class Analysis

The domination and exploitation approach to class is represented in Figure 1.3. Like the opportunity-hoarding approach, power and legal rules that enforce social closure are important in defining the basic structure of social positions, particularly the potent form of social closure and exclusion we call "private ownership of the means of production." But here the critical effect of opportunity hoarding is domination and exploitation, not simply market advantage.

Figure 1.3. The Exploitation and Domination Approach to Class and Inequality

Within the domination/exploitation approach, the central class division in a capitalist society is between those who own and control the means of production in the economy—capitalists—and those who are hired to use those means of production—workers. Capitalists, within this framework, both exploit and dominate workers. Other kinds of positions within the class structure get their specific character from their relationship to this basic division. Managers, for example, exercise many of the powers of domination but are also subordinate to capitalists. CEOs and top managers of corporations often develop significant ownership stakes in their corporations and therefore become more like capitalists. Highly educated professionals and some categories of technical workers have sufficient control over knowledge (a critical resource in contemporary economies) and skills that they can maintain considerable autonomy from domination within work and significantly reduce, or even neutralize, the extent to which they are exploited.[13]

In both the opportunity-hoarding and exploitation/domination approaches to class, power plays an important role. In both of these approaches, inequalities in income and wealth connected to the class structure are sustained by the exercise of power, not simply by the actions of individuals. The inequalities generated by opportunity hoarding require the use of power to enforce exclusions, and the inequalities connected to exploitation require supervision, monitoring of labor effort, and sanctions to enforce labor discipline. In both cases, social struggles that challenge these forms of power potentially threaten the privileges of people in the advantaged class positions.

---

13   One way of capturing the complexity of these diverse, intersecting class mechanisms is to characterize class locations other than the polarized capitalist and working class locations as "contradictory locations within class locations." For an elaboration of this idea, see Wright, *Classes* and *Class Counts*.

INTEGRATING THE THREE CLUSTERS OF CLASS MECHANISMS

While sociologists have generally tended to base their research on one or another of these three approaches to class, there is no reason to see them as mutually exclusive. Instead, we can see the reality of class as being generated by the complex interactions of the different mechanisms identified within each approach. One way of combining the three approaches is to see each of them as identifying a key process that shapes a different aspect of the class structure:

1. The exploitation and domination mechanisms identify the fundamental class division connected to the capitalist character of the economy: the class division between capitalists and workers.

2. The opportunity-hoarding mechanisms identify the central mechanism that differentiates "middle class" jobs from the broader working class by creating barriers that in one way or another restrict the supply of people for desirable employment. The key issue here is not mainly *who* is excluded, but simply the fact that there are mechanisms of exclusion that sustain the privileges of those in middle class positions.

3. The individual attributes and life conditions mechanisms identify a key set of processes through which individuals are sorted into different positions in the class structure or marginalized from those positions altogether. Opportunity hoarding identifies exclusionary processes connected to middle class jobs. The individual attributes and life conditions approach helps specify what it is in the lives of people that explains who has access to those desirable middle class jobs and who is excluded from stable working class jobs.

These three processes operate in all capitalist societies. The differences in class structures across countries are produced by the details of how these mechanisms work and interact. The theoretical task is to think through the different ways these mechanisms are linked and combined. The empirical task is to figure out ways to study each and their interconnections.

One possible nested micro-macro model is illustrated schematically in Figure 1.5. In this model, the power relations and legal rules that give people effective control over economic resources (means of production, financial capital, and human capital) generate structures of social closure and opportunity hoarding connected to social positions. Opportunity hoarding, then, generates three streams of causal effects:

1. It shapes the micro-level processes through which individuals acquire class-relevant attributes.
2. It shapes the structure of locations within market relations (occupations and jobs) and the associated distributional conflicts.
3. It shapes the structure of relations within production, especially relations of domination and exploitation, and the associated conflicts within production.

The first of these causal streams, in turn, shapes the flows of people into class locations within the market and production. Jointly, the class attributes of individuals and their class locations (defined within the market and production) affect their levels of individual economic well-being.

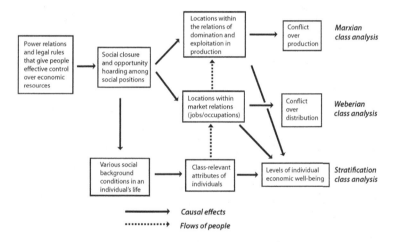

Figure 1.4. **Combined Class Analysis: Macro and Micro Processes**

One final element in the broad synthetic model is needed. Figure 1.4 treats power relations and legal rules as exogenous structures, whereas in fact these basic power relations are themselves shaped by class processes and class conflicts. This matters because structures of inequality are dynamic systems, and the fate of individuals within the system depends not just on the micro-level processes they encounter in their lives, or on the social structures within which those lives take place, but on the trajectory of the system as a whole within which those micro-processes occur. Treating the underlying power relations that support a given structure of class locations as fixed parameters is deeply misleading and contributes to the incorrect view that the fate of individuals is simply a function of their attributes and individual circumstances. What we need, therefore, is a recursive dynamic macro model in which the struggles generated by social relations contribute to the trajectory of change of the relations themselves. This suggests the macro model as pictured in a highly simplified form in Figure 1.5. A fully elaborated class analysis, then, combines this kind of dynamic macro model of conflict and transformation with the macro-micro multilevel model of class processes and individual lives. In such a model the key insights of stratification approaches, Weberian approaches, and Marxist approaches are combined.

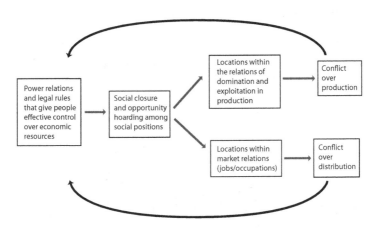

Figure 1.5. Dynamic Macro-Micro Model

THE AMERICAN CLASS STRUCTURE IN THE TWENTY-FIRST
CENTURY WITHIN AN INTEGRATED CLASS ANALYSIS

Economic systems differ in how unfettered are the rights and powers that accompany private ownership of the means of production, and thus in the nature of the class division between capitalists and workers. The United States has long been characterized as a capitalist economy with weak public regulation of capitalist property. This is reflected in a number of critical facts about the United

States: a very low minimum wage, which allows higher rates of exploitation than would otherwise exist; low taxation of high incomes, which allows the wealthiest segments of the capitalist class to live in extraordinarily extravagant ways; weak unions and other forms of worker organization that could act as a counterweight to domination within production. The result is that among developed capitalist countries the United States probably has the most polarized class division along the axis of exploitation and domination among the developed capitalist countries.

In terms of the formation of a middle class through mechanisms of opportunity hoarding, especially those linked to education, the United States has historically had one of the largest middle classes among developed capitalist countries. The United States was the first country to massively expand higher education, and for a long time access to higher education was very open and relatively inexpensive, allowing people with few resources to attend universities. The United States has also been characterized by a multi-tiered higher education system—with community colleges, junior colleges, liberal arts colleges, and universities—that made it possible for people to enter higher education later in life and to move from one tier to another. People could screw up as a young adult, but if they "got their act together" there was at least the possibility of going back to school, getting a credential, and gaining access to middle class employment. This large and diverse system of higher education helped support the creation of a large number of middle class jobs. This was complemented, in the decades after World War II, by a relatively strong labor movement that was able to mute competition for jobs in the core of the American economy that did not require higher education. The labor movement thus enabled unionized workers in those jobs to acquire income and security similar to the credentialed middle class.

Contrary to popular rhetoric, however, it was never the case that the United States was an overwhelmingly "middle class society." Most jobs in the US employment structure did not gain advantages from exclusionary credentials, and the labor movement never organized more than about 35 percent of the nonmanagerial labor force. Furthermore, in recent decades there has been an erosion of at least some of these processes of middle class exclusion: the labor movement has declined precipitously since the 1970s; many kinds of middle class jobs have become less secure and are less protected by the credentials associated with employment in such positions; and the economic crisis of the end of the first decade of the twenty-first century has intensified the sense of precariousness of many who still think of themselves as having middle class jobs. Thus, while it is still certainly the case that higher education and, increasingly, advanced academic degrees play a central role in providing access to many of the best jobs in the American economy, the future prospects for a large and stable middle class are much less clear.[14]

Finally, the US class structure has been characterized by a particularly brutal process through which individual attributes relevant to the fate of individuals in the class structure are formed. The educational system in the United States is organized in such a way that the quality of education available to children in poor families is generally vastly inferior to the quality of education of children of middle class and wealthy families. This deficit in publicly provided education for the poor is intensified by the extreme deprivations of poverty in the United States due to the absence of an adequate social safety net and supportive services for poor families. The rapid deindustrialization of the US economy and the absence of comprehensive job training programs for people displaced by deindustrialization means that a significant number of people find themselves without the kinds of skills needed for the current job structure. The result is that the US class structure is characterized by the highest rates of poverty and economic marginality of any comparable country. All of these processes are intensified by the enduring importance of racism, which makes African Americans and other racially oppressed groups especially vulnerable to marginalization.

Taking all of these processes together yields the following general picture of the US class structure at the beginning of the twenty-first century:

- An extremely rich capitalist class and corporate managerial class, living at extraordinarily high consumption standards, with relatively weak constraints on their exercise of economic power. The US class structure is the most polarized class structure at the top among developed capitalist countries.

- A historically large and relatively stable middle class, anchored in an expansive and flexible system of higher education and technical training connected to jobs requiring credentials of various sorts, but whose security and future prosperity is now uncertain.

---

14 For a discussion of the patterns of job polarization in recent decades, see Erik Olin Wright and Rachel Dwyer, "Patterns of Job Expansion and Contraction in the United States, 1960s–1990s," *Socio-Economic Review* 1: 3, 2003, 289–325

- A working class that once was characterized by a relatively large unionized segment with a standard of living and security similar to that of the middle class, but which now largely lacks these protections.

- A poor and precarious segment of the working class, characterized by low wages and relatively insecure employment, subjected to unconstrained job competition in the labor market with minimal protections by the state.

- A marginalized, impoverished sector of the population, without the skills and education needed for jobs above the poverty level, and living in conditions that make it extremely difficult to acquire those skills. The US class structure is the most polarized at the bottom among developed capitalist countries.

- A pattern of interaction of race and class in which the working poor and the marginalized population are disproportionately made up of racial minorities.

TOWARDS AN INTEGRATED CLASS ANALYSIS

Adopting the integrated framework of class analysis proposed here poses different kinds of challenges for analysts working in the Marxist tradition and those working within the stratification and Weberian traditions of sociology. For many Marxists the main challenge is recognizing that what is most powerful within Marxism is its theory of a specific array of causal mechanisms rather than its aspiration to be a comprehensive paradigm of social science. Historically, the relevance of these mechanisms has been defended with the rhetoric of incommensurable paradigms, including arguments for a distinctive Marxist epistemology and methodology that sharply differentiated Maxism from its rivals. I do not believe that this kind of defense of Marxist ideas is compelling. Marxism is a powerful tradition of social science because it provides powerful explanations for a range of important phenomena, not because it has some special method that differentiates it from all other currents of social science. Of course, it is always possible that this kind of paradigm aspiration could be realized in some future iteration of efforts to formulate Marxism as a distinctive comprehensive paradigm. But for now it seems better to see Marxism as a research program defined by attention to a specific set of problems, mechanisms, and provisional explanatory theories.

The challenge of an integrated class analysis may be even bigger for sociologists working in the stratification tradition. Marxist analysts of class, after all, have always in practice included discussions of individual attributes and the material conditions of life of people located within an economic structure, and opportunity hoarding is an integral part of the concept of social relations of production. Stratification theorists, on the other hand, have ignored the problem of exploitation, at most talking about "disadvantage," and even domination is absent from this approach to class. To recognize exploitation and domination as central axes of class analysis is to recognize the importance of a structure of social positions distinct from the persons who fill those positions, and this too is largely alien to stratification research.

In a way, Weberians may have the easiest task. On the one hand, most Weberian-inspired sociologists have not aspired to create a comprehensive paradigm and have been satisfied with a theoretical tradition that provided a rich menu of loosely connected concepts addressing specific empirical and historical problems. This has been one of the things that has made the Weberian tradition attractive—it is basically permissive about the incorporation of almost any concepts from other currents of social theory. On the other hand, Weberians have always emphasized the importance of power within social structures and have no difficulty in distinguishing persons and structured positions. While exploitation has not figured centrally within Weberian class analysis, there is no fundamental barrier within the logic of Weberian categories for including exploitation in the study of class.

It might seem from this assessment that in the end we should all simply declare ourselves Weberians. This was one of the accusations leveled against my work and the work of other Marxists thirty years ago by Frank Parkin when he wrote, "Inside every neo-Marxist there seems to be a Weberian struggling to get out."[15] I do not think, however, that this conclusion follows from the kind of pragmatist realism I am advocating here. Marxism remains a distinctive tradition of doing social science because of its distinctive set of problems, its normative foundations, and the distinctive inventory concepts and mechanisms it has developed.

---

15 Frank Parkin, *Marxism and Class Theory: A Bourgeois Critique*, New York: Columbia University Press, 1979, 25

PART I

Frameworks of Class Analysis

2

THE SHADOW OF EXPLOITATION
IN WEBER'S CLASS ANALYSIS

If theoretical frameworks are identified as loudly by their silences as by their proclamations, then one of the defining characteristics of class analysis in the Weberian tradition is the virtual absence of a systematic concept of exploitation. Nothing better captures the central contrast between the Marxist and Weberian traditions of class analysis than the difference between a concept of class centered on the problem of *life chances* in Weber and a concept rooted in the problem of *exploitation* in Marx. This is not to say that Weber completely ignores some of the substantive issues connected to the problem of exploitation. For example, Weber, like Marx, sees an intimate connection between the nature of property relations in capitalism and the problem employers face in eliciting high levels of effort from workers. But he does not theorize this issue in terms of a general concept of exploitation, nor does he see the problem of extracting labor effort as a pivotal feature of class relations and a central determinant of class conflict. Instead, Weber treats the problem of eliciting work performance within capitalism as an instance of technical inefficiencies reflecting a tension between formal rationality and substantive rationality within capitalist economic relations.

This chapter has two basic objectives: first, to understand as precisely as possible the inner structure of Weber's concept of class, its similarities to and differences from Marx's concept, and its relationship to the problem of exploitation; second, to use this interrogation of Weber's work to defend the importance of the concept of exploitation for sociological theory. The first two sections that follow set the context of the discussion by briefly situating the problem of class in Weber's larger theoretical project and then examining a number of striking similarities between Weber's and Marx's concepts of class. Although Marxist and Weberian traditions of sociology are often pitted against one another, within the narrower arena of class analysis there is

considerable overlap, particularly in their concept of class in capitalist society. The third section then characterizes the pivotal
difference in their concepts of class through the contrast between
"life chances" and "exploitation." A fourth section looks more
closely at exploitation, paying particular attention to the way
Weber deals with the problem of "extracting" labor effort under
conditions that Marxists would describe as "exploitation."
Finally, the last section examines the ramifications of Weber's
marginalization of the issue of exploitation for the broader
contours of a sociological analysis of class.

THE LOCATION OF CLASS ANALYSIS IN WEBER'S WORK

Unlike Marx, for whom class was a foundational concept in his
broad theoretical agenda, the problem of class plays a relatively
peripheral role in Weber's work.[1] It appears in his work in three principle ways. First, there are Weber's rare explicit theoretical discussions
of class, most notably in the chapter fragments assembled
posthumously in *Economy and Society*.[2] Second, early in his career

---

1   Because of the peripheral status of class in the Weberian oeuvre, it is surprising
that so much of the literature on class sees Weber as a central source. Aage Sørenson
suggests that Weber's prominence in class analysis comes from the accident that his
work on class was translated into English:

The importance of the Weberian class concept in the literature on class
analysis is a bit curious. In *Economy and Society* Weber deals with class in
two places but both are very short fragments. While Marx can be said to
never have given a single explicit development of the class concept, he
certainly has class as the central concern of analysis in all of his writings. For
Weber, there is neither a discussion nor an extensive analysis. Class simply
seems not to have been an important concept for Weber . . . Since only Marx
and Weber [among the German writers on class] have been translated into
English, Weber has become the main justification for developing class
concepts that are alternative to Marx's, despite the fragmentary nature of
Weber's writings about this and the lack of importance of class concepts in
his writings. (Sørenson, "Toward a Sounder Basis for Class Analysis,"
American Journal of Sociology 105: 6, May 2000, 1527 n3)

2   The chapter in *Economy and Society* in which Weber proposes to define the
concept of class (part 1, chapter 4, "Status Groups and Classes") is unfinished.
In a footnote to the first place in the text in which Weber refers to this chapter,
the editors of the English edition of the text comment: "This chapter is . . . a

Weber wrote a number of detailed empirical and historical studies in which the analysis of class figures prominently—most notably his studies of East Elbian agricultural workers (1894),[3] his research on the causes of the decline of the Roman Empire (1896),[4] and his more general work on the agrarian sociology of ancient civilizations, first published in the late 1890s and then revised in 1909.[5] Much of this work, especially the work on slavery in ancient civilizations, has a decidedly Marxian inflection and has had almost no impact on the analysis of class within what has come to be known as Weberian sociology.[6] Third, a great deal of Weber's work concerns the analysis of capitalism as a social order—its origins, its internal logic, its

---

mere fragment which Weber intended to develop on a scale comparable with the others. Hence most of the material to which this note refers was probably never written down." Weber, *Economy and Society*, ed. Guenther Roth and Claus Wittich, Berkeley: University of California Press, [1924] 1978, 210 n45.

3   Max Weber, "Developmental Tendencies in the Situation of East Elbian Rural Labourers," in Keith Tribe, ed., *Reading Weber*, New York: Routledge, 1989, 158–87.

4   Max Weber, "The Social Causes of the Decline of Ancient Civilization," in *The Agrarian Sociology of Ancient Civilizations*, trans. R. I. Frank, London: Verso, 1988, 387–411.

5   A detailed exegesis of Weber's work on agrarian class relations can be found in Dirk Käsler, *Max Weber: An Introduction to His Life and Work*, trans. Philippa Hurd, Chicago: University of Chicago Press, 1989.

6   The analysis in Weber's 1896 study of the causes of decline of ancient civilizations has a particularly Marxian flavor to it. His central argument is that the contradictions of slavery as a way of organizing production were the fundamental cause of the ultimate collapse of the Roman Empire. Although Weber's later concerns with issues of rationality and calculability in economic relations are already present in this early work, its main preoccupation is with the difficulty of extracting adequate surplus in a slave-based economy once slavery is no longer based on capturing slaves in slave hunts, and with the resulting transformations of the political conditions of reproduction of the Roman Empire. If one did not know that this piece was written by Weber, most people would assume it was a fairly sophisticated Marxist analysis of how the development of this particular kind of class system tended to erode the conditions of its own reproduction. For further discussion of this Marxian influence in Weber's early work, see Gerd Schroeter, "Dialogue, Debate, or Dissent: The Difficulties of Assessing Max Weber's Relationship to Marx," in Robert J. Antonio and Ronald M. Glassman, eds., *A Weber-Marx Dialogue*, Lawrence: University of Kansas Press, 1985, 6–7. For a contrary view, which denies that this work has a significant Marxian character, see Guenther Roth, "The Historical Relationship to Marxism," in Reinhard Bendix and Guenther Roth, eds., *Scholarship and Partisanship*, Berkeley: University of California Press, 1971.

dynamics of development, its ramifications, its contrasts with other social orders—and while the problem of class is rarely explicitly fore-grounded in these analyses, nevertheless much of what he says bears on the problem of understanding classes in capitalist societies. For example, Weber's *The Protestant Ethic and the Spirit of Capitalism* is not simply about the creation of the cultural-psychological condi-tions for modern capitalism to become a dynamic force in the world; it is also about the ways in which this "spirit" is embodied in the distinctive orientations of people located in different class positions within capitalism. Weber writes, "The treatment of labour as a call-ing became as characteristic of the modern worker as the corresponding attitude towards acquisition of the business man".[7]

Most discussions of Weber's work on class are based on the first of these clusters of writings, especially on his brief explicit conceptual analyses of class in *Economy and Society*.[8] What has become the

---

7 Weber, *The Protestant Ethic and the Spirit of Capitalism*, trans. Talcott Parsons, New York: Scribner's, [1904] 1958, 179. The details of Weber's argu-ment about the psychological ramifications of the ethic of ascetic Protestantism for the spirit of capitalism are familiar. Two more specific citations will suffice. For the Protestant bourgeoisie, wealth, Weber writes, "as a performance of duty in a calling . . . is not only morally permissible, but actually enjoined . . . the providential interpretation of profit-making justified the activities of the busi-nessman" (163). For the worker, on the other hand, "Labour must . . . be performed as if it were an absolute end in itself, a calling . . . The ability of mental concentration, as well as the absolutely essential feeling of obligation to one's job, are here most often combined with a strict economy which calculates the possibility of high earnings, and a cool self-control and frugality which enor-mously increase performance" (61, 63).

8 When Weber's work is excerpted in anthologies on stratification, the selec-tions concerning class are almost exclusively from the explicit definitional statement in chapter 11, section 6, of *Economy and Society*, "The Distribution of Power within the Political Community: Class, Status and Party" (e.g., see Reinhard Bendix and Seymour Martin Lipset, eds., *Class, Status, and Power: Social Stratification in Comparative Perspective*, New York: Free Press, 1966; Anthony Giddens and David Held, eds., *Classes, Power and Conflict: Classical and Contemporary Debates*, Berkeley: University of California Press, 1982; David Grusky, ed., *Social Stratification: Class, Race, and Gender in Sociological Perspective*, Boulder, CO: Westview, 2001). It should be noted that a second section of *Economy and Society* entitled "Status Groups and Classes" also contains definitional exposition of the concept of class (Weber, *Economy and Society*, 302–7). Although written later than the chapter, "Class, Status and Party," the discussion in "Status Groups and Classes" is much more fragmen-tary, consisting primarily of a series of unelaborated lists of items under general rubrics presented in the form of an outline. It has thus generally been given little

Weber-inspired tradition of class analysis is largely based on these fragmentary expositions (e.g., the work of Anthony Giddens, Frank Parkin, and John Scott).[9] Locating the concept of class within Weber's conceptual menu in these texts generates the familiar contrast of "class" and "status," the two most important terms in a threefold schema of stratification that also includes "party."[10] Two primary analytical dimensions demarcate these categories: first, the "sphere" or "order" within which social interaction occurs (economic, communal, or political),[11] and second, the degree to which the category intrinsically invokes subjective identity and collective forms of action. The combinations of these criteria differentiate class, status, and party, as illustrated in Table 2.1.

Sphere of Social Interaction*	Category that Locates Individuals within the Distribution of Power	Attributes Intrinsic to Categories of the Distribution of Power		
		Objective Properties	Subjective Identity	Collective Action
Economic	Class	Yes	No	No
Communal	Status Group	Yes	Yes	No
Political	Party	Yes	Yes	Yes

*Weber's terms for these spheres are "economic order," "social order" or "sphere of the distribution of honor," and "sphere of power" (Weber, *Economy and Society*, p. 938).

Table 2.1. Theoretical Location of the Concept of Class in Weber's Explicit Formulations in Economy and Society

attention by scholars interested in class. In any case, nothing in this later statement is at odds with the general interpretation of Weber's approach to class and his treatment of the problem of exploitation discussed here.

9 Anthony Giddens, *The Class Structure of the Advanced Societies*, New York: Harper and Row, 1973; Frank Parkin, *Class Inequality and Political Order*, New York: Praeger, 1971; John Scott, *Stratification and Power: Structures of Class, Status and Command*, Cambridge: Polity, 1996.

10 Nearly all of the chapter in *Economy and Society* that has most influenced subsequent discussions of Weber's approach to class—"The Distribution of Power within the Political Community: Class, Status and Party"—is devoted to class and status, with only one page at the end discussing "party."

11 The terms Weber uses in *Economy and Society* to differentiate these spheres of social interaction are "economic order," "social order" or "the sphere of the distribution of honor," and "the sphere of power" (938). This terminology is somewhat confusing because class, status, and party all concern questions of power (and thus power should not simply be identified with "party"), and all also involve social action (and thus the social should not simply be identified with status). It is for this reason that the terminological distinction between economic, communal, and political seems more useful in the present context.

Within this analytical schema, class is defined within the sphere of economic interaction and involves no necessary subjective identity or collective action. An individual can be in a specific kind of class situation without this generating a specific form of identity or participation in collective action: "In our terminology, 'classes' are not communities; they merely represent possible, and frequent, bases for social action."[12] Status groups are defined within the sphere of communal interaction (or what Weber calls the "social order") and always imply some level of identity in the sense of some recognized "positive or negative social estimation of *honor*."[13] A status group cannot exist without its members being in some way conscious of being members of the group: "In contrast to classes, *Stände (status groups)* are normally groups."[14] Status groups need not, however, imply any kind of collective action. Party, finally, always implies collective action: "As over against the actions of classes and status groups, for which this is not necessarily the case, party-oriented social action always involves association. For it is always directed toward a goal which is striven for in a planned manner."[15] In these terms, members of a class become a status group when they become conscious of sharing a common identity, and they become a party when they *organize* on the basis of that identity.[16]

The conceptual contrast between class and status for Weber is not primarily a question of the *motives* of actors: it is not that status groups are derived from purely symbolic motives and class categories are derived from material interests. Although people care about status categories in part because of their importance for symbolic ideal interests, class positions also entail such symbolic interests, and both status and class are implicated in the pursuit of material interests. As Weber writes, "Material monopolies provide the most effective motives for the exclusiveness of a status group."[17] Rather than motives, the central contrast between class and status is the

---

12   Weber, *Economy and Society*, 927.

13   Ibid., 932.

14   Ibid.

15   Ibid., 938.

16   Jones (1975) argues that because of the inherent qualities of collective action, members of class as defined by Weber could not even in principle act as a collective agent on the basis of their class interests because collective action requires forms of identification and rationality beyond mere instrumental interests. Bryn Jones, "Max Weber and the Concept of Social Class," *The Sociological Review*, Volume 23, Issue 4, pp 729–757, November 1975.

17   Op. cit., 935.

nature of the mechanisms through which class and status shape inequalities of the material and symbolic conditions of people's lives. Class affects material well-being directly through the kinds of economic assets people bring to market exchanges. Status affects material well-being indirectly, through the ways that categories of social honor underwrite various coercive mechanisms that, in Weber's words, "go hand in hand with the monopolization of ideal and material goods or opportunities."[18]

When the wider body of Weber's work is taken into consideration, especially his diverse writings on capitalism, the problem of class becomes embedded in a different conceptual space. Here the pivotal question is the relationship between the concept of class and the broad theoretical and historical problem of *rationalization* of social relations. Table 2.2 indicates how class is located with respect to this problem.[19] As in Table 2.1, this conceptual space is also defined by two dimensions: first, the *sources of social power* within social interactions; and second, the *degree of rationalization* of social relations. Running throughout Weber's work is a threefold distinction in the sources of power that individuals use to accomplish their goals: social honor, material resources, and authority. Each of these, in turn, can be organized within social interactions in highly rationalized forms or in relatively nonrationalized forms. Class, in these terms, designates highly rationalized social relations that govern the way people get access to and use material resources.[20] It thus contrasts, on the one hand, with nonrationalized ways of governing access to resources, especially ascriptively based consumption groups, and on the other hand, with rationalized forms of social relations involving other sources of social power.

---

18 Ibid.

19 Unlike Table 2.1, which is derived from the relatively explicit, if under-developed, theoretical statements by Weber about the properties of the concept of class and its contrast to other concepts, the typology in Table 2.2 is inferred from various arguments dispersed throughout Weber's work.

20 A number of commentators on differences between Weber and Marx have emphasized the centrality of the problem of rationalization in Weber's analysis of capitalism. (See Karl Lowith, *Max Weber and Karl Marx.* trans. Hans Fantel, London: Allen & Unwin, [1932] 1982; Bryn Jones, "Max Weber and the Concert of Social Class"; and Derek Sayer, *Capitalism and Modernity: An Excursus on Marx and Weber*, London: Routledge, 1991.) Jones and Sayer, in particular, link the problem of rationalization explicitly to Weber's analysis of classes.

Sources of Social Power	Degree of Rationalization of Social Relations	
	Rationalized Social Relations	*Nonrationalized Social Relations*
Social Honor	Meritocratic prestige	Ascriptive status groups
Material Conditions of Life	Class: capital, labor	Ascriptively based consumption groups
Authority	Rational-legal domination: bureaucracy	Patrimonial administration

Table 2.2. The Theoretical Location of "Class" in Weber's Analysis of Rationalization

Rationalization, of course, is perhaps the most complex multi-dimensional concept in Weber's arsenal. Following Levine's decomposition of Weber's conceptual array of rationalizations, the problem of class with Weber is primarily situated within one particular form of rationalization: the *objective instrumental* rationalization of social order.[21] In all societies the ways people gain access to and use material resources is governed by rules that are objectively embodied in the institutional settings within which they live. When the rules allocate resources to people on the basis of ascriptive characteristics, and when the use of those material resources is given by tradition rather than the result of a calculative weighing of alternatives, then economic interactions take place under nonrationalized conditions. When those rules enable people to make precise calculations about

---

21 Donald Levine differentiates eight different forms of rationality in Weber's work. To the standard distinction between *instrumental* rationality (the rationality of adopting the best means for given ends) and *value* rationality or *substantive* rationality (the rationality of choosing actions that are consistent with value commitments), he adds *conceptual* rationality (the formation of increasingly precise and abstract concepts) and *formal* rationality (the creation of methodical, rationally defendable rules). Within each of these four types of rationality, he then distinguishes between *objective* rationality (rationality inscribed in institutionalized norms) and *subjective* rationality (rationality in mental processes). After elaborating these forms of rationalization that occur in Weber's writing, Levine adds one distinction not found so explicitly in Weber's work: within each of the four forms of objective rationalization, Levine differentiates what he terms *symbolic* rationalization and *organizational* rationalization. The final result, then, is a typology of twelve forms of rationalization (Levine, *The Flight from Ambiguity: Essays in Social and Cultural Theory*, Chicago: University of Chicago Press, 1985, 210).

alternative uses of those resources and discipline people to use those resources in more rather than less efficient ways on the basis of those calculations, then those rules can be described as "rationalized." This occurs, in Weber's analysis, when market relations have the most pervasive influence on economic interactions (i.e., in fully developed capitalism). His definition of classes in terms of the economic opportunities people face in the market, then, is simultaneously a definition of classes in terms of rationalized economic interactions. Class, in these terms, assumes its central sociological meaning to Weber as a description of the way people are related to the material conditions of life under conditions in which their economic interactions are regulated in a maximally rationalized manner.

Two examples, one a discussion of rural class relations from early in Weber's career and the second a discussion of industrial class relations in *Economy and Society*, illustrate this close link in Weber's thinking between rationalization and class relations. Both Weber and Marx recognized the importance of the destruction of traditional peasant rights in the countryside as a central part of the development of capitalism in agriculture. In Weber's early writings on East Elbian rural labor, he describes the impact of this process on class relations in terms of rationalization. Prior to the infusion of market relations in the countryside, Weber writes, the rural laborer "found himself confronted not with an 'employer' but with a small-scale territorial lord. The low level of commercial ambition among estate owners was reinforced by the apathetic resignation of the labourer . . ."[22] The advance of capitalism destroyed these traditional labor relations. The resulting impact on class relations, Weber describes, as a process of rationalization:

> In place of the landed aristocracy there necessarily enters—with or without a change of person—a class of agricultural entrepreneurs who are in principle no different to commercial entrepreneurs in their social characteristics.
>
> This transformation in the general type of rural employer has significant consequences for the position of the labourer . . . [In the patriarchal estate economy,] labour relations were not arranged according to commercial principles and with the objective of profitability, but rather developed historically as a means of affording the landlords a suitable existence. Under these conditions as little deviation as possible was made from the natural and communal economic foundations of this order. Thus a rural working class with *common*

---

22 Weber, "Developmental Tendencies," 161.

economic interests could not and did not exist in the principal regions of the east.

Modern development seeks initially to introduce the principle of *economic rationality* into the wage forms within this natural economic order. Accordingly, the communal remnants (plots of land, threshing shares, grazing rates) are initially abolished . . .

With this transformation a necessary condition of the patriarchal relation collapses: the connection to *one particular* estate. The differentiation between various categories of labour are reduced and the employer becomes as "fungible" for the rural worker as he already is for the industrial labourer. In other words, this process of development brings the rural labourers steadily closer to the form of a *unified* class of a proletarian type in its material conditions of life, a state already attained by the industrial proletariat.[23]

The emergence of a rural proletariat thus represents the transformation of forms of access to material conditions of life governed by tradition to one governed by calculation and pure economic interests.

The same basic argument appears in Weber's analysis of the industrial working class. For Weber, as for Marx, a central defining characteristic of the "working class" is its complete separation (or "expropriation") from the means of production. For Marx, this is crucial because it enables capitalists to exploit workers; for Weber this expropriation is crucial because it allows for the full realization of economic rationality within production. In his extended discussion of this separation in *Economy and Society*, Weber stresses the relevance of expropriation for economic rationality:

The expropriation of workers *in general*, including clerical personnel and technically trained persons, from possession of the means of production has its *economic* reasons above all in the following factors: . . . The fact that, other things being equal, it is generally possible to achieve a higher level of economic rationality if the management has extensive control over the selection and the modes of use of workers, as compared with the situation created by the appropriation of jobs or the existence of rights to participate in management. These latter conditions produce technically irrational obstacles as well as economic irrationalities. In particular,

---

23   Ibid., 163, 172.

considerations appropriate to small-scale budgetary administration and the interests of workers in the maintenance of jobs ("livings") are often in conflict with the rationality of the organization.[24]

Similar discussions can be found in Weber's analysis of the relationship between rationalization and free wage labor in *The Protestant Ethic*,[25] and in his discussions of the inefficiencies in slavery.[26] In all of these cases, the central theoretical problem in which the analysis of class and the transformations of class relations are embedded is the problem of the rationalization of the economic order. While class per se may be a relatively secondary theme in Weber's sociology, it is, nevertheless, intimately linked to one of his most pervasive theoretical preoccupations—rationalization.

In the discussion that follows, I draw on both of these theoretical contexts of Weber's thinking about class—the contrast between class and status as two forms of stratification, and the salience of rationalization in defining the theoretical relevance of class. Weber's distilled contrast between class and status is particularly useful in clarifying the substantive criteria embodied in his definition of class relations in terms of market-based life chances; the broader analysis of rationalization will help to illuminate the ways in which Weber deals with the problem of exploitation in capitalist society.

WEBER AND MARX ON CLASS: CONVERGENCES

There is a long history of discussions of the relationship between Marx's and Weber's social theories, beginning with occasional comments by Weber himself, most famously in his discussion of the *Communist Manifesto* in a speech to Austrian officers towards the end of World War I.[27] Although Weber was appreciative of Marx's theoretical formulations, he was highly critical of its excessive

---

24 Weber, *Economy and Society*, 137–8.

25 "However, all these peculiarities of Western capitalism have derived their significance in the last analysis only from their association with the capitalistic organization of labour . . . Exact calculation—the basis of everything else—is only possible on a basis of free labour." Weber, *Protestant Ethic*, 22.

26 Weber, *Agrarian Sociology of Ancient Civilizations*, 53–6.

27 Max Weber, "Speech for the General Information of Austrian Officers in Vienna," trans. D. Hÿrch, in *Max Weber: The Interpretation of Social Reality*, ed. J.E.T. Eldridge, London: Michael Joseph, [1918] 1971.

materialism and dismissive of the utopianism of Marx's theory of history, with its optimistic deterministic prediction of the transcendence of capitalism and the disappearance of classes and the state. Much of the subsequent discussion of Marx and Weber has revolved around the sharp differences in the broad contours of their respective general theoretical frameworks for understanding the trajectory of historical change—in particular, the contrast between Marx's historical materialism as a quasi-teleological theory of history and Weber's multidimensional theory of historical development and contingency.[28] When the focus of comparison has centered on stratification issues, the central theme in most discussions has also been the contrast between Marx's preoccupation with a single aspect of stratification—class—and Weber's complex multidimensional view in which the relationship between class and other bases of stratification, especially status, is of central concern.[29] Relatively less attention has been given to the fact that, in spite of the different salience of class within the overall theoretical agendas of Marx and Weber, there are deep similarities between the concepts of class in these two traditions of social theory.[30] To give precision to the

28 Although much of the commentary on Weber and Marx's overall frameworks focuses on the differences in their approaches, some accounts emphasize significant convergences. For example, Löwith discusses the relationship between Weber's concept of rationalization and Marx's concept of alienation in their theories of modern capitalism, (Karl Löwith, *Max Weber and Karl Marx*, trans. Hans Fantel, London: Allen & Unwin, [1932] 1982); and Sayer analyzes their respective understandings of modernity (Sayer, *Capitalism and Modernity*). For anthologies of comparative analyses of Marx and Weber, see Robert J. Antonio and Ronald M. Glassman, eds., *A Weber–Marx Dialogue*, Lawrence: University of Kansas Press, 1985; and N. Wiley, ed., *The Marx–Weber Debate*, Beverly Hills, CA: Sage, 1987.

29 For a recent, analytically rigorous discussion of Marx's and Weber's approaches to class that stresses the contrast between the multidimensional character of Weber's approach and Marx's preoccupation with a single dimension, see Scott, *Stratification and Power*.

30 Some writers have noted similarities between Weber's and Marx's class concepts. Bendix sees Weber's analysis of class as departing from a "baseline that Marx had established" (Bendix, "Inequality and Social Structure," 152); Holton and Turner observe that "both Marx and Weber are concerned with market relations in the constitution of classes" (Robert J. Holton and Bryan S. Turner, *Max Weber on Economy and Society*, New York: Routledge, 1989, 181); Giddens sees Weber, like Marx, characterizing capitalism as a "class society"—a society within which class is the primary axis of stratification (Giddens, *Class Structure of Advanced Societies*). Still, in each of these cases the observation of similarity is given much less weight than are the

specific problem of the location of exploitation within class analysis, I first review these strong similarities.

Relational Rather Than Gradational Class Concepts

Both Marx and Weber adopt relational concepts of class. Neither defines classes simply as nominal levels on some gradational hierarchy. For both, classes are derived from an account of systematic interactions of social actors situated in relation to each other. Classes for both Weber and Marx are thus not primarily identified by quantitative names like upper, upper middle, middle, lower middle, and lower, but by qualitative names like capitalists and workers, debtors and creditors.[31]

The Centrality of Property Relations

Both Marx and Weber see property ownership as the fundamental source of class division in capitalism. For Marx, classes are defined by the "relation to the means of production," where "relation" here means ownership and control over resources used in production. Similarly, Weber writes, "'Property' and 'lack of property' are, therefore, the basic categories of all class situations."[32] What is more, Weber, like Marx, sees propertylessness as an essentially coercive condition: "[Those who are propertyless] have nothing to offer but their labor or the resulting products and . . . are compelled to get rid of these products in order to subsist at all."[33] He even

---

differences between Marx's and Weber's class concepts. Sayer is one of the few writers who regards the differences between Marx's and Weber's approach to both class and status as of secondary importance (Sayer, *Capitalism and Modernity*).

31   For more on relational and gradational concepts of class, see Stanislaw Ossowski, *Class Structure in the Social Consciousness*, London: Routledge, 1963; and Erik Olin Wright, *Class Counts*, Cambridge: Cambridge University Press, 1997, 5–8.

32   Weber, *Economy and Society*, 927.

33   Ibid. In an earlier statement in *Economy and Society*, while discussing economic motivations, Weber writes: "The motivation of economic activity under the conditions of a market economy . . . for those without substantial property [include] the fact that they run the risk of going entirely without provisions . . ." (110). Also see Weber's discussion of the "compulsion of the whip of hunger," Weber, *General Economic History,* trans. Frank H. Knight, New York, Collier, [1927] 1961, 209.

acknowledges, like Marx, that for the working class the apparently freely chosen, voluntary interactions of the market are simply a formal reality, masking an essentially coercive structure of social relations (which he refers to as "heteronomously determined action"):

> [Action that is motivated by self-interest can still be] substantively heteronomously determined . . . [in] a market economy, though in a formally voluntary way. This is true whenever the unequal distribution of wealth, and particularly of capital goods, forces the non-owning group to comply with the authority of others in order to obtain any return at all for the utilities they can offer on the market . . . In a purely capitalist organization of production this is the fate of the entire working class.[34]

Although this statement may lack the rhetorical force of Marx's account of the essential unfreedom of the worker, the point is fundamentally the same: Being separated from the means of production forces workers to subordinate themselves to capitalists.

Classes-as-Places versus Classes-as-Collective-Actors

Central to the conception of class in both Weber and in Marx is a distinction between classes as *objectively defined places* and as *collectively organized social actors*. Of course, the language they use to describe this contrast differs. Weber uses the expression "class situation" to designate the objectively defined places within social relations, whereas Marx uses the expression "class-in-itself," and contemporary Marxists have used the expressions "class location" or "class position" or "class structure" depending on the context.[35] Weber uses the expression "class-conscious organization" to designate class as a collectively organized social actor;[36] Marx uses the expression "class-for-itself," and contemporary Marxists use a variety of terms, such as "class formation" or "class organization." But regardless of terminology, the basic idea is similar: structurally defined classes may have a tendency to generate collectively organized forms of struggle, but the two must be conceptually distinguished.

---

34 Weber, *Economy and Society*, 110.
35 Ibid., 302, 927.
36 Ibid., 305.

Classes and Material Interests

Both Weber and Marx see objectively definable material interests as a central mechanism through which class locations influence social action. By objectively definable material interests I mean that an outside observer can, in principle, specify which courses of action that are available to an individual by virtue of their location in a social structure would improve that person's material conditions of life. Both Marx and Weber claim that (1) a person's class location, defined by their relation to property, systematically affects material interests in this sense; and (2) material interests so defined do influence actual behavior. These claims are relatively uncontroversial for Marx, even though much debate has been waged over whether "class interests" in Marxism are "objective." Weber, on the other hand, is often characterized as a theorist who emphasizes the subjective meanings of actors and who rejects the idea of a determinate relation between objectively specified conditions and subjective states of actors. Nevertheless, in his discussion of class, material interests rooted in individuals' objectively defined class situations are seen as a determinant—albeit a probabilistic determinant—of their behavior. Weber writes:

> According to our terminology, the factor that creates "class" is unambiguously economic interest, and indeed, only those interests involved in the existence of the market. Nevertheless the concept of class-interest is an ambiguous one: even as an empirical concept it is ambiguous as soon as one understands by it something other than the *factual direction of interests following with a certain probability from the class situation for a certain average of those people subjected to the class situation.*[37] (italics added)

Thus, Weber affirms that "for a certain average of those people subjected to the class situation" there is a "certain probability" that the "factual direction of interests" will coincide with class interests. Weber thus allows for deviations between individual behavior and the material interests associated with class situations, but he also argues that there is at least a tendency, on average, for behavior to be in line with those interests.

Of course, the expression "a certain probability" is rather vague and leaves open the possibility that this probability could be extremely low and thus the relationship between objectively defined

---

37 Ibid., 928–9.

class interests and the "factual direction of interests" could be very weak. Two earlier passages in *Economy and Society* suggest that Weber in fact believed that purely self-interested economic advantage had a high probability of giving "factual direction" to motivations of most people much of the time. The first passage comes in a discussion of economic motivations within the formation of organizations:

> Economic considerations have one very general kind of sociological importance for the formation of organizations if, as is almost always true, the directing authority and the administrative staff are remunerated. If this is the case, *an overwhelmingly strong set of economic interests* become bound up with the continuation of the organization, even though its primary ideological basis may in the meantime have ceased to exist.[38] (italics added)

Even more starkly, in a discussion of economic activity in a potential socialist society, Weber believes that motivations will be similar to those in a market society, and he thus expresses considerable skepticism about the possibility that ideological commitments will matter very much in socialism. In the long run, Weber argues, most people will be motivated by self-interested material advantage, just as in a market economy:

> What is decisive is that in socialism, too, the individual will under these conditions [in which individuals have some capacity to make economically relevant decisions] ask first whether to him, personally, the rations allotted and the work assigned, as compared with other possibilities, appear to conform with his own interests . . . It would be the interests of the individual, possibly organized in terms of the similar interests of many individuals as opposed to those of others, which would underlie all action. The *structure* of interests and the relevant situation would be different [from a market economy], and there would be other means of pursuing interests, but this fundamental factor would remain just as relevant as before. It is of course true that economic action which is oriented on purely ideological grounds to the interests of others does exist. But it is even more certain that the *mass of men do not act in this way and that it is an induction from experience that they cannot do so and never will.*[39] (italics added)

---

38   Ibid., 201–2.
39   Ibid., 203.

This is a powerful affirmation of the factual predominance of subjective orientations derived from objectively definable material interests: although it is theoretically possible that ideological motivations could be important, the mass of people do not act on purely ideological grounds and, furthermore, "they cannot do so and never will." For both Weber and Marx, therefore, the material interests structured by class locations have a strong tendency to shape the actual behavior of people within those locations.

The Conditions for Collective Class Action

If there is one aspect of class analysis where one might expect a sharp difference between Marx and Weber, it is in their understanding of the problem of class struggle. Although both may believe that class situations shape *individual* class behaviors via material interests, Marx believed that capitalism inherently generates *collectively* organized class struggles, eventually culminating in revolutionary challenges to capitalism, whereas Weber rejects this prediction. Yet even here there is more similarity in their views than one might initially expect.

In assessing arguments of this sort, it is important to distinguish (1) the *theoretical* analysis of the *conditions under which particular predictions hold*, in this case that class struggles are likely to emerge and intensify, from (2) *the empirical expectations about the likelihood of those conditions actually occurring*. In these terms, Weber shares much with Marx in terms of the first consideration, but disagrees sharply over the second.[40]

In *Economy and Society* in a section labeled "social action flowing from class interest", Weber lays out some of the conditions that he feels are conducive to collectively organized class struggles:

> The degree to which "social action" and possibly associations emerge from the mass behavior of members of a class is linked to general cultural conditions, especially to those of an intellectual sort. It is also

---

40 Bendix recognizes that Weber shares with Marx many elements of the theory of the conditions under which class mobilization is likely to succeed: "*Class organizations* occur only when an immediate economic opponent is involved, organization is technically easy (as in the factory), and clear goals are articulated by an intelligentsia . . . Weber accepted Marx's reasons for the success of such organizations." Reinhard Bendix, "Inequality and Social Structure: A Comparison of Marx and Weber," *American Sociological Review* 39: 2, 1974, 152.

linked to the extent of the contrasts that have already evolved, and is especially linked to the transparency of the connections between the causes and the consequences of the class situation. For however different life chances may be, this fact in itself according to all experience, by no means gives birth to "class action" (social action by members of a class). For that, the real conditions and the results of the class situation must be distinctly recognizable. For only then the contrast of life chances can be felt not as an absolutely given fact to be accepted, but as a resultant from either (1) the given distribution of property, or (2) the structure of the concrete economic order. It is only then that people may react against the class structure not only through acts of intermittent and irrational protest, but in the form of rational association . . . The most important historical example of the second category (2) is the class situation of the modern proletariat.[41]

This complex paragraph involves several very Marxian-like theses: First, the emergence of class associations depends on intellectual conditions; it is not simply the result of unmediated spontaneous consciousness of people in disadvantaged class situations. This is congruent with Marx's view of the role of ideological mystification in preventing class organization and the importance of class-conscious intellectual leadership in raising working class consciousness, a theme stressed in different ways by later Marxists such as Gramsci and Lenin.

Second, where class structures are experienced as natural and inevitable, as "absolutely given facts," class mobilization is impeded. Weber points here to the central issue that Marx, especially in his discussion of commodity fetishism and capital fetishism, also identifies as the most important intellectual obstacle to class consciousness: the belief in the naturalness and permanency of the existing conditions and thus the impossibility of any fundamental change. Much of Marx's work, in fact, can be viewed as an attempt at a scientific challenge to such apparent "naturalness" in the belief that such demystification would contribute to forging revolutionary consciousness.

Third, the transparency of class relations facilitates class mobilization. Marx also believed that class mobilization would be more difficult where there were lots of intermediary classes—petty bourgeois, peasants, professionals—than where class structures were highly polarized and the causal connection between the class structure and the conditions of people's lives were transparent. This is an

---

41   Ibid., 929–30.

important part of Marx's prediction that capitalism's destruction of all precapitalist economic relations and the immiseration of the proletariat would lead to intensified class conflict.

Last, because of the relative transparency of their class situation, the modern proletariat comes to understand that "the contrast of life chances . . . [is the result of] the structure of the concrete economic order." Modern capitalism therefore creates the required kind of transparency for class associations of workers to be likely.

Weber and Marx thus share many elements in the theoretical specification of the conditions for class associations to emerge, and Weber shares with Marx at least the limited expectation that these conditions will be minimally satisfied in the case of the modern proletariat in capitalist economies so that class associations and class struggles are likely to occur. Where they differ—and this is a difference that matters—is in the *empirical prediction* that the inner dynamics of capitalism are such that these conditions will be *progressively strengthened over time*, leading to a systematic tendency for long-term intensification of class struggles within capitalism. *If* Marx's empirical predictions about these conditions had been correct, then Weber would have shared with Marx the prediction that class conflicts would have a tendency to continually intensify in the course of capitalist development. Where they differ, therefore, is in their predictions about the long-term trajectory of capitalism more than in their views about the conditions within capitalism that are necessary for the emergence of a class-conscious organized working class.[42]

---

42 Another instance in which Weber shares Marx's theoretical analysis of conditions for effective, collective class mobilization is in their respective analyses of the peasantry. Marx is famous for arguing, in *The Eighteenth Brumaire of Louis Bonaparte*, that in spite of their common class interests, peasants had little capacity for collective action because they were so dispersed in the countryside and remained as separate entities with no interdependency—like a "sack of potatoes." Weber makes a similar point about East Elbian peasants: "For the [agricultural] labourer then the possibility of brutal personal domination that could be only escaped by flight gave way to commercial exploitation which, arising almost unnoticed, was actually much harder to evade and which as a smallholder he was not in a position to do. Formal equality then placed the labourers in a struggle of interests for which, dispersed far over the land as they were, they lacked the means of resistance" ("Developmental Tendencies," 171).

Class and Status

Finally, Marx and Weber even have some similar things to say theoretically in an area where sociologists generally think they are most divergent: in their treatment of the relationship between class and status. A central issue in Weberian sociology is the enduring importance of status groups as a source of identity and privilege. As such, status groups are seen as competing with class as bases of solidarity and collective action. Marx shared with Weber the views that (1) status groups impede the operation of capitalist markets; and further, that (2) they constitute an alternative basis of identity to class formation. And Weber shared with Marx the view that (3) capitalist markets tended to erode the strength of status groups and their effects on the system of stratification.[43] Weber writes:

> When the bases of the acquisition and distribution of goods are relatively stable, stratification by status is favored. Every technological repercussion and economic transformation threatens stratification by status and pushes the class situation into the foreground. Epochs and countries in which the naked class situation is of predominant significance are regularly the periods of technical and economic transformations.[44]

Using different rhetoric, Marx and Engels in the *Communist Manifesto* made parallel arguments:

> Constant revolutionizing of production, uninterrupted disturbances of all social conditions, everlasting uncertainty and agitation distinguish the bourgeois epoch from all earlier ones. All fixed, fast-frozen relations, with their train of ancient and venerable prejudices and opinions, are swept away.[45]

---

43 Mommsen makes the even stronger claim that, from early in his career, Weber believed that capitalism would not merely erode traditional status orders, but destroy them: "As early as 1893 Weber predicted that within a few generations, capitalism would destroy all tradition-bound social structures and that this process was irreversible" (Wolfgang J. Mommsen, "Capitalism and Socialism: Weber's Dialogue with Marx," trans. David Herr, in Antonio and Glassman, eds., *Weber-Marx Dialogue*, 234). Most sociologists drawing on Weber's work assume that status remains a salient dimension of stratification, even though capitalism significantly reduces its weight as a mechanism of identity and exclusion.

44 Weber, *Economy and Society*, 938.

45 Karl Marx and Friderich Engels, *The Communist Manifesto*, in

The reference to "all fixed, fast-frozen relations" taps the same kinds of categories that Weber theorized as "stratification by status," and Marx and Engels, like Weber, see these relations threatened by "revolutionizing of production . . . disturbances of all social conditions," or what Weber termed "periods of technical and economic transformations." Both Marx and Weber thus see capitalism as undermining status groups and fostering a predominance of what Weber called "naked class situation." They may have differed in their beliefs about the long-term consequences of this development for class mobilization and struggle—Marx believed it would reinforce tendencies towards polarized class struggle, whereas Weber believed that the development of capitalism was producing a much more complex class structure less vulnerable to polarized struggle[46]—but both saw capitalism as systematically eroding the salience of traditional status groups.

WEBER AND MARX ON CLASS: CENTRAL DIFFERENCES

If the above analysis is correct, both Weber and Marx deploy varieties of property-centered relational concepts of class in which, among other things, objectively definable material interests play a central role in explaining class action; class structure and class struggle are distinguished; collective class action is facilitated by class polarization; and the dynamic processes of capitalism create conditions favorable to class playing a pervasive role in systems of stratification. Where they differ most sharply is in their understanding of the causal mechanisms that are linked to such

---

Selected Works in One Volume, London: Lawrence and Wishart, [1848] 1968, 38.

46   In Weber's "Speech for the General Information of Austrian Officers in Vienna," in which he puts forth an extended discussion of Marxism and the prospects of socialism in Germany, Weber explains how changes in class structure tie the interests of large numbers of people to the bourgeoisie: "Parallel to these very complex processes, however, there appears a rapid rise in the number of clerks, i.e., in private *bureaucracy*—its growth rate is statistically much greater than that of the workers—and their interests certainly do not lie with one accord in the direction of a proletarian dictatorship. Then again, the advent of highly diverse and complicated ways of sharing interests means that at the present time it is quite impossible to maintain that the power and number of those directly or indirectly interested in the bourgeois order are on the wane." (207)

property-relational classes. For Weber, the pivotal issue is how classes determine the *life chances* of people within highly rationalized forms of economic interactions—markets. For Marx, the central issue is how class determines both life chances and *exploitation*.[47]

The basic idea of the determination of life chances by class is laid out in Weber's frequently cited passage from *Economy and Society*:

> We may speak of a "class" when (1) a number of people have in common a specific causal component of their life chances, insofar as (2) this component is represented exclusively by economic interests in the possession of goods and opportunities for income, and (3) is represented under the conditions of the commodity or labor markets. This is "class situation."
>
> It is the most elemental economic fact that the way in which the disposition over material property is distributed among a plurality of people, meeting competitively in the market for the purpose of exchange, in itself creates specific life chances . . .
>
> But always this is the generic connotation of the concept of class: that the kind of chance in the *market* is the decisive moment which presents a common condition for the individual's fate. Class situation is, in this sense, ultimately market situation.[48]

---

47 This is not the only way to characterize the core difference between Marx's and Weber's conceptualization of class. Other synoptic contrasts include production versus exchange (Val Burris, "The Neo-Marxist Synthesis of Marx and Weber on Class," in Wiley, ed., *Marx–Weber Debate*, 2:43–64; and Randall Collins, *Weberian Sociological Theory*, Cambridge: Cambridge University Press, 1986), unidimensional versus multidimensional (Burris, "Neo-Marxist Synthesis"; Scott, *Stratification and Power*); and dichotomous versus pluralistic class concepts (Giddens, *Class Structure of Advanced Societies*). Other authors who discuss the life chances/exploitation contrast include Rosemary Crompton and John Gubbay, *Economy and Class Structure*, London: Macmillan, 1977, 3–20. Derek Sayer also identifies the problem of exploitation as the central difference between Marx and Weber's approach to class, although he is skeptical that this matters very much: "On the question of exploitation there remains an unbridgeable gulf between Marx and Weber, which reflects the very different economic theories—respectively political economy and marginalism—upon which their sociologies of capitalism are predicated. How important this is, I would argue, is debatable . . . altogether too much ink has been wasted over their supposed differences." Sayer, *Capitalism and Modernity*, 104–5.

48 Weber, *Economy and Society*, 927–8.

"Opportunity" in this context is a description of the feasible set individuals face, the trade-offs they encounter in deciding what to do to improve their material conditions. The Weberian claim is that in a market society—a society in which people acquire the wherewithal to live by exchanging things with others in an instrumentally rational way—such opportunities are caused by the quality and quantity of what people have to exchange. When markets are fully and pervasively present, opportunities are not mainly caused by economically irrelevant ascriptive attributes or by individuals' control of violence, but by the resources a person can bring to the market for exchange. Owning the means of production gives a person different alternatives from owning credentials, and both of these differ from simply owning unskilled labor power. Furthermore, in a market economy, access to market-derived income affects a broad array of life experiences and opportunities for oneself and one's children. The study of the life chances of children based on their parents' market capacity—the problem of class mobility—is thus an integral part of the Weberian agenda of class analysis. Within a Weberian perspective, therefore, the salient consequence that flows from people's links to different kinds of economic resources deployed in markets is the way these links confer on them different kinds of economic opportunities and disadvantages, thereby shaping their material interests.

This understanding of class mechanisms is intimately connected to the problem of rationalization. When people meet to make an exchange in a market, they rationally calculate the costs and benefits of alternatives on the basis of the prices they face in the market. These prices provide the kind of information required for people to make rational calculations, and the constraints of market interactions force them to make decisions on the basis of these calculations in a more or less rational manner. Weber is, fundamentally, less interested in the problem of the material deprivations and advantages of different categories of people as such, or in the collective struggles that might spring from those advantages and disadvantages, than he is in the underlying normative order and cognitive practices—instrumental rationality—that are embodied in the social interactions that generate these life chances.

Marx would agree with Weber that the ownership of different resources used in market exchanges affects life chances. And like Weber, he recognizes that exchanges in the market constitute interactions based on calculation and instrumental rationality.[49]

---

49 In volume 1 of *Capital*, Marx describes exchange relations between labor and capital as taking place in a sphere in which "the only force that brings them

But in Marx's class analysis, the effect of exchange on life chances is only half the story. Of equal significance is how property relations shape the process of exploitation. Both "exploitation" and "life chances" identify inequalities in material well-being that are generated by inequalities in access to resources of various sorts. Thus, both of these concepts point to conflicts of interest over the distribution of the assets. What exploitation adds to this is a claim that conflicts of interest between classes are generated not simply by conflicts over the distribution and value of resources people bring to exchanges in the market, but also by the nature of the interactions and interdependencies generated by the use of those resources in productive activity.

Exploitation, for Marx, identifies the process by which labor effort performed by one group of economic actors is extracted and appropriated by another group. That appropriated labor is referred to as "surplus labor," meaning laboring activity above and beyond what is required to reproduce the laborers themselves. In capitalism, for Marx, this appropriation occurs because employers are able to force workers to work longer hours and perform more labor than is embodied in the products that they consume with their wages. Expressed in the classical language of the labor theory of value, the labor value of what they produce is greater than the labor value of what they consume. The difference—surplus value—is appropriated by the capitalist. This appropriation is exploitation.[50]

The concept of exploitation, defined in this way, is used by Marx in two general explanatory contexts. First, Marx sees exploitation as the source of profits in capitalism: capitalists appropriate surplus value from workers that, when capitalists sell the commodities embodying that surplus value, is turned into money profits. Profits, in turn, are essential for investment and capital accumulation. In

---

together and puts them in relation with each other, is the selfishness, the gain and the private interests of each" (*Capital*, New York: International, [1867] 1967, 1:176). Although he does not use the language of rational instrumental action, the description here is entirely in line with Weber's view of market exchange.

50   Although Marx elaborated the concept of exploitation in terms of the labor theory of value, as a sociological concept exploitation does not depend on this technical apparatus. See Wright, *Class Counts*, 4–17 and chapter 4 below for the elaboration of the concept of exploitation without the labor theory. For a trenchant philosophical discussion of why the concept of exploitation does not logically depend on the labor theory of value, see G. A. Cohen, "The Labour Theory of Value and the Concept of Exploitation," in G. A. Cohen, *History, Labour, and Freedom: Themes from Marx*, Oxford: Clarendon, 1988, 209–38.

this way, exploitation figures centrally in Marx's account of the dynamics of capitalism. Second, Marx sees exploitation as central to explaining the particular character of conflict between workers and capitalists. Exploitation constitutes a social relation that simultaneously pits the interests of one class against another, binds the two classes together in ongoing interactions, and confers upon the disadvantaged group a real form of power with which to challenge the interests of exploiters. This is an important point. Exploitation depends on the appropriation of labor effort in ongoing social interactions. Because human beings are conscious agents, they always retain significant levels of control over their expenditure of effort. The extraction of effort within exploitative relations is thus always to a greater or lesser extent problematic and precarious, requiring active institutional devices for its reproduction. Such devices can become costly to exploiters in the form of the costs of supervision, surveillance, sanctions, etc. The ability to impose such costs constitutes a form of power among the exploited.

The exchange relations that shape life chances also involve conflicts of interest. Yet, in an idealized competitive market in which direct coercion is absent from the exchange process itself, these conflicts are muted by the apparent voluntariness of the act of exchange. As Weber remarks, "'Exchange' is a compromise of interests on the part of the parties in the course of which goods or other advantages are passed as reciprocal compensation ... Every case of rationally oriented exchange is the resolution of a previously open or latent conflict of interests by means of a compromise."[51] Marx in a well-known passage in volume 1 of *Capital*, similarly sees the market exchanges between workers and capitalists as involving reciprocity and a degree of commonality of interests:

> [Exchange between labor and capital implies] equality, because each enters into relation with the other, as with a simple owner of commodities, and they exchange equivalent for equivalent ... The only force that brings them together and puts them in relation with each other, is the selfishness, the gain and the private interests of each. Each looks to himself only, and no one troubles himself about the rest, and just because they do so, do they all, in accordance with the pre-established harmony of things, or under the auspices of an all-shrewd providence, work together to their mutual advantage, for the common weal and in the interest of all.[52]

---

51 Weber, *Economy and Society*, 72.
52 Marx, *Capital*, 1:176.

Within production, on the other hand, the containment of the conflict of interests between the performers of labor effort and the appropriators of that effort requires the ongoing exercise of domination through complex forms of surveillance, discipline, and control of the labor process. The conflict over exploitation is not settled in the reciprocal compromise of a contractual moment; it is continually present in the ongoing interactions through which labor is performed.

The central difference between Marx's and Weber's concept of class, then, is that the Weberian account revolves exclusively around market transactions, whereas the Marxist account also emphasizes the importance of conflict over the performance and appropriation of labor effort that takes place after market exchanges are contracted. Weber's class analysis revolves around a single causal nexus that works through market exchange; Marxist class analysis includes the Weberian causal processes, but adds to them a causal structure within production itself. The Marxist concept of class directs our attention both theoretically and empirically towards the systematic interaction of exchange and production.[53]

One of the striking implications of this contrast between the Weberian and Marxist concepts of class is that Weber—at least in his most mature work when he is formalizing his concepts—rejects the idea that slaves are a class, whereas for Marxists slavery constitutes one form of precapitalist class relations.[54] Weber writes:

> Those men whose fate is not determined by the chance of using goods or services for themselves on the market, e.g. slaves, are not, however, a class in the technical sense of the term. They are, rather, a status group.[55]

---

53 See Figure 1.4 in chapter 1 for a schematic representation of this contrast.

54 For an alternative view of the relationship between class and status in Marx's and Weber's treatment of slavery and feudalism, see Sayer, who argues in *Capitalism and Modernity* that Marx used the word "class" in two quite different ways. In one sense, class is a generic term covering all systems of exploitation linked to production; in the other sense, it is specific to capitalism. This second usage of the word, Sayer argues, is the more fundamental to Marx's theory and thus, like Weber, Marx believed that only in capitalism were there fully developed classes.

55 Weber, *Economy and Society*, 928. In Weber's early work on agrarian economies of ancient civilizations, which is marked by a much more Marxian kind of analysis than is his later work in *Economy and Society*, slaves were treated as a class, and their relationship to slave-owners was treated as involving exploitation.

For Weber, slaves are a specific instance of a general theoretical category—*status groups*—that also includes ethnic groups, occupational groups, and other categories "that are stratified according to the principles of their *consumption* of goods as represented by special styles of life."[56] These groups differ by the meanings and criteria that accord differential social honor to different "styles of life," and "slavery" is just one way of organizing such status rankings. In contrast, Marxists would see slavery as, primarily, a special instance of a different general theoretical category—class—that includes capitalists and workers in capitalism, lords and serfs in feudalism, slaves and slave-owners in slavery. Although these categories differ in lifestyles and in the cultural criteria used to impart symbolic rankings, the crucial issue is their differences in mechanisms of exploitation—the ways in which labor effort is appropriated from one category by another. Marx, of course, like Weber, recognized that in precapitalist societies social division was organized around status orders involving personal dependence and extra-economic coercion. But for Marx the most salient feature of such status orders was how they underwrote distinctive forms of exploitation. It is this feature that justifies treating them as varieties of the abstract category "class relations" within a class concept centering on exploitation.

THE SHADOW OF EXPLOITATION IN WEBER

Although Weber's definition of the concept of class says nothing explicitly about exploitation, it is nevertheless the case that in various places in *Economy and Society* and elsewhere Weber touches on the substantive problems that, within Marxist coordinates, would be characterized as involving the exploitation of labor. How Weber deals with these problems reveals the inner logic of his general approach to class analysis.[57]

---

56 Ibid., 937.

57 The issue here is not the use of the *word* "exploitation." Even in English this term can mean simply taking advantage of some kind of opportunity, as in "exploiting natural resources," and thus the real meaning of the term must be derived from the context of its use. In any case, a variety of different German words can be translated into the English term "exploitation." The word does appear in a few places in the English translation of *Economy and Society* and even more frequently in Weber's earlier work on slavery. In *Economy and Society*, the words in the original German text that are translated as "exploitation" are never the German term used in Marxist technical discussions of

Weber engages the problem of the performance and appropriation of labor effort within the system of production primarily as an issue of work discipline, the "incentives to work," and economic efficiency. This identification of the problem of extraction of labor effort and technical efficiency is one of the themes in Weber's discussion in *The Protestant Ethic* of the problem of using piece-rates as a strategy for getting workers to work harder. Here is the relevant passage:

> One of the technical means which the modern employer uses in order to secure the greatest possible amount of work from his men is the device of piece-rates. In agriculture, for instance, the gathering of the harvest is a case where the greatest possible intensity of labour is called for, since, the weather being uncertain, the difference between high profit and heavy loss may depend on the speed with which the harvesting can be done. Hence a system of piece-rates is almost universal in this case. And since the interest of the employer in a speeding up of harvesting increases with the increase of the results and the intensity of work, their attempt has again and again been made, by increasing the piece-rates of the workmen, thereby giving them an opportunity to earn what for them is a very high wage, to interest them in increasing their own efficiency. But a peculiar difficulty has been met with surprising frequency: raising piece-rates has often had the result that not more but less has been accomplished in the same time, because the worker reacted to the increase not by increasing but by decreasing the amount of work . . . The opportunity of working more was less attractive than that of working less . . . This is an example of what is here meant by traditionalism. A man does not "by nature" wish to earn more and more money, but simply to live as he is accustomed to live and to earn as much as is necessary for that purpose. Whenever modern capitalism has begun its work of increasing the productivity of human labor by increasing its intensity, it has encountered the immensely stubborn resistance of this leading trait of pre-capitalistic labor.[58]

---

exploitation, *Ausbeutung*, or even the relatively morally charged term *Ausnutzung* (which suggests taking unfair advantage). Rather, Weber used the much more neutral terms *Benutzung* or *Verwertung*, which basically mean "to use." In his earlier work on slavery, on the other hand, Weber sometimes uses *Ausnutzung* and occasionally the more technical Marxist term *Ausbeutung*, again reflecting the greater Marxian character of that work. In one place, he uses the expression *exploitationsrate*, thus directly invoking the Marxist meaning of exploitation. In his later work, this Marxian usage is completely absent. I thank Phil Gorski for providing me with guidance on these linguistic issues.

58   Weber, *Protestant Ethic*, 59–60.

Weber concludes that this technical problem can be effectively solved only when the laborer adopts a set of attitudes towards work—the Protestant work ethic—that generates a moral imperative for him or her to expend a maximum of effort:

> Labour must, on the contrary, be performed as if it were an absolute end in itself, a calling. But such an attitude is by no means a product of nature. It cannot be evoked by low wages or high ones alone, but can only be a product of a long and arduous process of education."[59]

Weber discusses at greater length in *Economy and Society* the motivation of workers to expend effort in a discussion of the "conditions affecting the optimization of calculable performance by labor."[60] "Optimization of calculable performance" is a specific problem within the broader discussion of the conditions that foster or impede technical rationality in economic organization. Weber cites three primary conditions for this optimization to occur: "(a) the optimum of aptitude for the function; (b) the optimum of skill acquired through practice; (c) the optimum of inclination for the work."[61] The third of these concerns the performance of labor effort. Weber writes:

> In the specific sense of incentive to execute one's own plans or those of persons supervising one's work [the inclination to work] must be determined either by a strong self-interest in the outcome or by direct or indirect compulsion. The latter is particularly important in relation to work which executes the dispositions of others. This compulsion may consist in the immediate threat of physical force or

---

59 Ibid., 61. In *The Protestant Ethic* Weber also discusses the reasons why "low wages are by no means identical with cheap labor" as low wages may lead to a decline in effort and diligence: "Low wages fail even from a purely business point of view wherever it is a question of producing goods which require any sort of skilled labour, or the use of expensive machinery which is easily damaged, or in general wherever any great amount of sharp attention or of initiative is required. Here low wages do not pay, and their effect is the opposite of what was intended" (61). Here Weber is laying out the essential arguments of what is now tellingly referred to as "efficiency wage theory." Again, the extraction of labor effort is treated as a problem of instrumental rationality and efficiency rather than as a problem of antagonistic interests.

60 Weber, *Economy and Society*, 150.

61 Ibid.

of other undesirable consequences, or in the probability that unsatisfactory performance will have an adverse effect on earnings.

The second type, which is essential to a market economy, appeals immensely more strongly to the worker's self-interest.[62]

Weber then discusses a variety of conditions that need to be met for this "indirect compulsion" to be effective. He cites three factors:

(1) *That employers have a free hand in hiring and firing workers*: "It also necessitates freedom of selection according to performance, both qualitatively and quantitatively, though naturally from the point of view of its bearing on profit."

(2) *Workers lack both ownership and control over the means of production*: "It presupposes the expropriation of the workers from the means of production by owners is protected by force."

(3) *Workers bear the responsibility for their own reproduction*: "As compared with direct compulsion to work, this system involves the transferral [of] . . . the responsibility for reproduction (in the family) . . . to the workers themselves."[63]

Where these conditions are met, workers will expend the optimum amount of effort from the point of view of profits of the capitalist.

Where the above three conditions are not met, labor effort will tend to be restricted, resulting in a decline in technical rationality. In particular, Weber discusses situations in which the first condition is violated—conditions in which workers themselves retain some significant degree of control over the deployment of their labor:

Opportunities for disposal of labor services may be appropriated by an organization of workers, either without any appropriation by the individual worker or with important limitations on such appropriation. This may involve absolute or relative closure against outsiders and also prohibition of the dismissal of workers from employment by management without consent of the workers, or at least some kind of limitations on powers of dismissal . . .

Every form of appropriation of jobs in profit-making enterprises by workers . . . [results in] a limitation on the *formal* rationalization of economic activity.[64]

---

62 Ibid.
63 Ibid., 150, 151.
64 Ibid., 128

At the core of this limitation on formal rationalization is the problem of labor effort. If workers appropriate their jobs but owners still appropriate the products of labor, technical rationality is limited "through a tendency to restrict the work effort, either by tradition, or by convention, or by contract; also through the reduction or complete disappearance . . . of the worker's own interest in optimal effort."[65] Weber goes on to argue that the problem of getting a technically rational level of work effort from workers who control their jobs is similar to the problem of getting work effort from slaves:

> The very opposite forms of appropriation—that of jobs by workers and that of workers by owners—nevertheless have in practice very similar results. [When workers are slaves appropriated by owners] it is natural that exploitation of labor services should, to a large extent, be stereotyped; hence that worker effort should be restricted and that the workers have little self-interest in the output . . . Hence, almost universally the work effort of appropriated workers has shown a tendency to restriction . . . When jobs have been formally appropriated by workers, the same result has come about even more rapidly.[66]

If one wants the technically most efficient performance of labor effort by workers within production, therefore, workers must not only be expropriated from the means of production, but must also lose any real control over their jobs and the labor process.

One situation in which Weber sees that the appropriation of jobs by workers might not lead to restriction of work effort is where the workers are also owners of the means of production: "The appropriation of the means of production and personal control . . . over the process of workers constitute one of the strongest incentives to unlimited willingness to work."[67] But this situation creates other irrationalities, especially because "the interests of workers in the maintenance of jobs ('livings') is often in conflict with the rationality of the organization."[68] Thus, although it might be the case in a worker-owned cooperative that workers would work very hard, they would engage in technically irrational behavior in their allocation of labor and their unwillingness to hire and fire labor as the market required.

---

65 Ibid., 129.
66 Ibid., 129–30.
67 Ibid., 152.
68 Ibid., 138.

Weber's stance towards the problem of work effort in these passages is broadly in line with that of contemporary neoclassical micro-economics. Most neoclassical economists see any restriction by workers of managerial control of labor and the labor process as generating efficiency losses, both because of technically suboptimal allocations of resources and because of restrictions of labor effort by workers. Like Weber, these economists believe that control of the workplace by workers leads to worker opportunism—workers serving their own interests at the expense of efficiency. The only real solution to such opportunism is preventing workers from appropriating their jobs and making the alternative to conscientious performance of work especially unpleasant. Thus, they would endorse Weber's statement that "free labor and the complete appropriation of the means of production [by the owner] create the most favorable conditions for discipline."[69]

The problem of the performance and appropriation of work effort is thus, for Weber, above all a question of the degree and forms of rationality in economic organization. This does not mean that Weber was unaware that these forms of rationality may impose harms on workers: "The fact that the maximum of *formal* rationality in capital accounting is possible only where the workers are subjected to domination by entrepreneurs is a further specific element of *substantive* irrationality in the modern economic order."[70] Indeed, as Mommsen, Löwith, Schroeter,[71] and others have noted, running throughout Weber's work is the view that rationalization has perverse effects that systematically threaten human dignity and welfare, particularly because of the ways in which it intensifies bureaucratic domination.[72] Weber thus hardly

---

69   Ibid.

70   Ibid.

71   In Mommsen, "Capitalism and Socialism"; Löwith, *Max Weber and Karl Marx*; and Schroeter, "Dialogue, Debate, or Dissent."

72   Mommsen describes Weber's stance towards capitalism this way: "Although he vigorously defended the capitalist system against its critics from the Left . . . he did not hesitate to criticize the system's inhuman consequences . . . His concern for the preservation of human dignity under the societal conditions created by and typical for mature capitalism (particularly the severe discipline of work and exclusion of all principles of personal ethical responsibility from industrial labor) is entirely consistent with Marx's effort to find a way of overcoming the social alienation of the proletariat under industrial capitalism" ("Capitalism and Socialism," 235). Where Weber most deeply differed from Marx is in Weber's belief that socialism, in whatever form, would only intensify this oppression, and thus no viable

held a benign view of capitalism and the work organization it entailed. Nevertheless, he did not treat this problem of extracting work effort as central to the class relations of capitalism and the conflicts of interests that those relations engendered.

RAMIFICATIONS

All in all, the formal characteristics of the concept of class in capitalist societies are rather similar in Weber and Marx. They differ primarily in the broader theoretical context in which these definitions are embedded and in their accounts of the central causal mechanisms that are linked to class relations. For Weber, these mechanisms are primarily centered in the ways in which ownership of property affects life chances via instrumentally rational exchanges in the market; for Marx, they concern the ways in which ownership of property affects life chances and exploitation through the interplay of markets and production. Although Weber also, if only in passing, touches on issues closely related to exploitation, particularly the problem of labor discipline and domination, he does not integrate these concerns into the general concept of class but treats them primarily as issues in the technical efficiency of systems of production.

One might still ask, so what? Does this really matter? Even if Weber underplayed the importance of extraction of labor effort, there is nothing in his framework that actively blocks attention to this issue. And indeed, class analysts in the Weberian tradition have paid varying degrees of attention to the problem of work discipline, labor effort, and related matters.

Nevertheless, there are consequences of elaborating the concept of class strictly in terms of market relations and life chances without a systematic connection to the problem of exploitation. Conceptual frameworks matter, because, among other things, they direct thinking and research in particular ways. Here I would emphasize two issues: first, the ways in which explicitly linking exploitation to the concept of class changes the way class conflict is understood; and second, the ways exploitation infuses class analysis with a specific kind of normative concern.

The concept of exploitation draws attention to the ways in which class conflicts do not simply reflect conflicting interests over the

---

alternative to capitalism would be possible (unless one were willing to accept a dramatic decline in technical rationality).

distribution of a pie. Rather, to characterize class relations as exploitative emphasizes the ways in which exploiting classes are *dependent upon* the exploited class for their own economic well-being, and because of this dependency, the ways in which exploited classes have *capacities for resistance* that are organic to the class relation. Because workers always retain some control over the expenditure of effort and diligence, they have a capacity to resist their exploitation; and because capitalists need workers, there are constraints on the strategies available to capitalists to counter this resistance. This dependence of the exploiter on the exploited thus means that exploiters must seek ways of responding to resistance of the exploited that reproduce, rather than destroy, their interactions with the exploited.[73]

Exploitation thus entails a specific kind of duality: conflicting material interests plus a real capacity for resistance. This duality has implications for the way we think about both the individual and collective power of workers. As individuals, the power of workers depends both on the scarcity of the kind of labor power they have to offer in the labor market (and thus their ability to extract individual "skill rents" through the sale of their labor power) and on their ability to control the expenditure of their individual effort within the labor process. As a collectivity, workers' power depends on their ability to collectively regulate the terms of exchange on the labor market (typically through unions) and their ability to control the organization of work, surveillance, and sanctions within production. The concept of exploitation, therefore, suggests a research agenda in which class conflict and the balance of class power must be understood in terms of the systematic interplay of interests and capacities within both exchange and production.

When the appropriation of labor effort is treated, not in terms of the basic social relations that bind together workers and capitalists, but in terms of the formal rationality of the "conditions affecting the optimization of calculable performance by labor,"[74] the issue of the performance of labor effort becomes analyzed primarily as a technical problem of overcoming the traditionalism or opportunism of workers as individuals. Capitalists face a wide range of problems in enhancing rational calculability in economic action. One problem revolves around the work performance of employees.

---

73 The logic of this interdependence is discussed in greater detail in chapter 4 below.

74 Weber, *Economy and Society*, 150.

The most fundamental solution to this problem is for workers to develop the right kinds of attitudes, as described in *The Protestant Ethic and the Spirit of Capitalism*. When workers see the performance of labor effort as a calling—when they have the proper work ethic—then the problem of optimizing the calculable performance of labor is greatly reduced, perhaps even eliminated. In the absence of this ethic, then, even with close supervision, the actual extraction of optimal levels of effort is an enduring problem. Instead of understanding the capacity of workers to control their own effort as a fundamental source of class-based power available to workers in their class struggles with capitalists, Weber sees this control as one of the obstacles to forming a fully rationalized economic order.

Beyond the issue of the conceptual mapping of research agendas, Marx's and Weber's conceptual frameworks direct class analysis towards different sets of normative concerns linked to the material interests of different classes. Both theorists ask questions and pursue agendas rooted in their values, although Weber is undoubtedly more self-conscious than Marx about trying to keep his values from shaping his conclusions.[75] The issue here is that the specific way the concept of class is built directs attention towards different kinds of normative agendas.

Weber's treatment of work effort as primarily a problem of economic rationality directs class analysis towards a set of normative concerns centered above all on the interests of capitalists: efficiency and rationalization. Although Weber is not blindly uncritical of capitalism and recognizes that, from the point of view of workers, the organization of work may be "substantively irrational," nevertheless, throughout his discussion of work effort the emphasis is on how arrangements that enhance worker control and autonomy are technically irrational. Whether or not Weber was sympathetic to the conditions of workers, this preoccupation is very much in line with the interests of owners and managers. In contrast, the Marxist tradition of linking the problem of work effort to exploitation directs class analysis towards normative concerns centered on the interests of workers. The issue becomes not simply a

---

75 Weber is, of course, famous for arguing that social science should attempt to be "objective" in the sense of trying to restrict its moral concerns to the posing of questions rather than to the substance of research and the selection of answers. Marx also believed in scientific objectivity, but was skeptical that in social analysis the analyst could in practice keep the substance of ideas from being influenced by the analyst's own relationship to social forces—especially class interests—in the society.

question of which arrangements are the most technically efficient from the point of view of profit maximization, but how particular ways of organizing exchange and production impose harms on workers. Marxists recognize that increasing exploitation is "efficient" from the point of view of capitalist economic organization, but the conceptual framework constantly brings to the foreground the ways in which this imposes harms on workers and poses the question "under what conditions can such harms be challenged and eliminated?"

3

METATHEORETICAL FOUNDATIONS OF CHARLES TILLY'S *DURABLE INEQUALITY*

One of the great virtues of Charles Tilly's *Durable Inequality* is that it might be wrong. So often attempts at constructing grand theories in sociology turn out, on close inspection, to consist largely of tautologies and vacuous propositions—conceptual frameworks that are so flexible and indeterminate that no empirical observations of the world would ever count as surprising. That is not the case for the central arguments in this book. Consider, for example, a claim that Tilly makes early in the book about the relatively limited significance of beliefs in the explanation of durable inequality:

> Mistaken beliefs reinforce exploitation, opportunity hoarding, emulation and adaptation but exercise little independent influence on their initiation . . . It follows that the reduction or intensification of racist, sexist, or xenophobic attitudes will have relatively little impact on durable inequality, whereas the introduction of new organizational forms . . . will have great impact.[1]

This is a forthright statement about the relative explanatory importance of different sorts of causes: beliefs, attitudes, and other discursive elements of culture may contribute to stabilizing inequalities, but they are of less causal importance in explaining inequality than are the organizational structures in which inequality becomes embedded. Many people will object to such claims, either because they believe that culture in general should be accorded greater weight in the explanation of inequality than such processes as the organizational bases for exploitation, or because they object in principle to any broad, transhistorical claims about the relative importance of different sorts of causes. Of course, it may be very

---

1   Charles Tilly, *Durable Inequality*, Berkeley: University of California Press, 1999, 15.

difficult to give empirical precision to claims about one cluster of causes being more important than another cluster of causes in a complex, multicausal system. Nevertheless, it is a strength of Tilly's book that he does not pull his punches in advancing such bold and provocative claims.

If the strength of the book lies in the boldness of the substantive propositions that map out a positive research agenda, its weakness, in my judgment, occurs in many of the more abstract discussions of concepts and methods, particularly when these involve criticisms of alternative views and approaches, where many of the arguments seem quite imprecise, confusing, or even inaccurate. The result, I think, is that, because of dissatisfaction with his treatment of some of these more abstract conceptual issues, many people will reject the arguments of the book without really engaging Tilly's positive proposals for what he calls "an organizational perspective of inequality."

In these remarks I will try to clarify both parts of this general assessment of *Durable Inequality*. In section 1, I lay out the core arguments of Tilly's theory of inequality by examining some of the metatheoretical foundations for his arguments and then elaborating what I see to be a series of nested functional explanations at the core of his theory. I argue that the basic underlying structure of these functional explanations brings Tilly's overall argument much closer to the core logic of classical Marxism than he seems prepared to acknowledge. I then take one element of this theory—the argument about how categorical inequality works within organizations—and try to represent this as a set of specific empirical hypotheses. In section 2, I examine some of the conceptual problems I see in his treatment of a number of theoretical debates and ideas.

I. THE ARGUMENT

1. The Explanandum

The title of Tilly's book announces its explanandum: *durable inequalities*, "those that last from one social interaction to the next, . . . [especially] those that persist over whole careers, lifetimes and organizational histories."[2] The central, overarching thesis of the book is that such durable inequalities almost always are built around categorical distinctions among people rather than around gradient attributes of individuals: "Large, significant inequalities in

---

2 Ibid., 6.

advantages among human beings correspond mainly to categorical differences such as black/white, male/female, citizen/foreigner, or Muslim/Jew rather than to individual differences in attributes, propensities or performances."[3]

The theoretical task, then, is to explain why this should be the case. I will first elaborate some of the central metatheoretical foundations that underpin Tilly's approach to this problem, then show that his theory of such categorical inequalities is built around a series of functional explanations, and finally explore in more detail one central piece of his argument in order to develop somewhat more formal hypotheses.

2. Metatheoretical Foundations

Tilly's approach is built on two metatheoretical foundations: *anti-individualism* and what might be termed *combinatory structuralism*. Throughout the book Tilly continually emphasizes the differences between his approach to social inequality and what he characterizes as individualist approaches. In individualist approaches, he argues, the central causes of social inequality are seen as operating through the attributes of individuals. Poverty is explained by the attributes of poor people, not by the relations of exploitation within which poor people live; gender inequality is explained by sexist attitudes, not by organizational structures that underwrite the hoarding of various kinds of opportunities by men. Tilly relentlessly attacks such views, seeing them as the main intellectual obstacle to a proper understanding of social inequality not only within mainstream social science but in many strands of radical social theory as well. Many feminist analyses of gender inequality, he argues, are grounded in essentially individualist accounts of sexist discrimination. In contrast, Tilly insists that explanations of inequality must be at their core *social relational*: to the extent that individual attributes explain inequalities, they are explanatory by virtue of the nature of the social relations within which those individual attributes operate. The starting point of the analysis, therefore, must be the investigation of the relations themselves.

How, then, should one approach the investigation of social relations? While Tilly does not himself lay out methodological principles for relational analysis, his style of theory building can be described as "combinatorial structuralism." The basic idea is this: for whatever problem one is considering, begin by mapping out what might

---

3 Ibid., 7.

be termed a menu of elementary forms. All more complex structural configurations, then, are analyzed as specific forms of combination of these elementary forms. This menu is basically the equivalent of the periodic table of elements in chemistry, which provides the building blocks for the investigation of compounds.

In *Durable Inequality*, Tilly elaborates two such basic menus: one is a menu of *types of social relations*, and the second is a menu of *inequality-generating mechanisms*. The menu of relations he refers to as "building blocks" that define "basic social configurations." Five of these are highlighted: chain, hierarchy, triad, organization, and categorical pair.[4] Of these five elementary forms of social relations, the most pivotal for the study of durable inequality, Tilly argues, is organization. The centerpiece of the analysis of durable inequalities, then, is the claim that these are, above all, constructed within and through organizations. It is for this reason that he dubs his approach an "organizational view of inequality-generating mechanisms."[5]

The second menu is an inventory of causal mechanisms through which categorical inequality is generated and sustained by organizations. These Tilly labels *exploitation, opportunity hoarding, emulation,* and *adaptation.* He advances the singularly bold claim that these four mechanisms account for virtually all durable inequality in all times and places:

> Categorical inequality in general results from varying intersections of exploitation, opportunity hoarding, emulation and adaptation . . . Although historical accumulations of institutions, social relations and shared understandings produce differences in the day-to-day operation of various sorts of categories (gender, race, citizenship, and so on) as well as differences in various sorts of outcomes (e.g., landed wealth versus cash income), ultimately interactions of exploitation, opportunity hoarding, emulation and adaptation explain them all.[6]

Let us now turn to the substance of the explanatory argument within which these causal mechanisms are deployed.

---

4 Tilly also argues that in an even more stripped-down sense, there are only three elementary forms since hierarchy is really a special kind of chain and an organization is what he calls "an overgrown categorical pair." All social structures, then, can be viewed as complex forms of combination and development of three elementary forms: chain, triad, and categorical pair.

5 Ibid., 9.

6 Ibid., 13–14.

3. The Explanatory Strategy

The basic explanatory strategy Tilly adopts is a variety of *functional explanation*. That is, throughout the book Tilly argues that certain kinds of social structural relations are *solutions to problems* generated within social systems. This does not mean that he argues for a smooth, homeostatic kind of functionalism in which all social relations organically fit together in fully integrated social systems. The functional explanations in Tilly's arguments allow for struggles and contradictions and extended periods of disruptions. Nor does he argue that functional solutions are spontaneously secreted by social dynamics entirely behind the backs of actors; intentional strategies of collective actors are part of the explanation for how solutions are found and institutionalized. Nevertheless, his arguments rely on functional explanations insofar as at crucial steps of the analysis he poses a problem generated by a set of social relations and then treats the demonstration that a particular social form is a solution to the problem as the core of the explanation of that social form.[7]

The theory is built up through a sequence of three nested problems-to-be-solved and their associated solutions.

Problem 1: How to secure and enhance rewards from the resources to which one has access. Resources are essential for production and acquisition of all sorts of values, especially, but not merely, material goods. But resources are scarce and competition to control them pervasive. The problem people then face, both individually and collectively, is how to secure their stable access to such resources and how to enhance the advantages they have by virtue of such access.

Solution to problem 1: Opportunity hoarding and exploitation. Two mechanisms are particularly important in stabilizing and enhancing the advantages people derive from access to value-generating resources: *opportunity hoarding* and *exploitation*. The first of these implies that those in control of the resource are able to systematically exclude other people from having access to the

---

7 There is a large literature on the nature of functional explanations and their role in explanations of social phenomena. The discussion here has been especially influenced by Arthur Stinchcombe, *Constructing Social Theories*, New York: Harcourt, Brace & World, 1968; G. A. Cohen, *Karl Marx's Theory of History: A Defense*, Oxford: Oxford University Press, 1978; and Jon Elster, "Marxism, Functionalism and Game Theory," *Theory and Society*, 11:4, July, 1982, pp. 453–82

resources in question; exploitation additionally implies that the returns on the use of the resources are enhanced by the ways in which those resources enable exploiters to control the effort of others in ways that prevent the exploited from receiving the "full value added by that effort." Of these two mechanisms, Tilly generally accords exploitation a more fundamental role in the overall social production of durable inequality because of its centrality in underwriting the power and privileges of elites. Opportunity hoarding, he argues "complements exploitation" by creating sustainable advantages for various nonelite categories. Broadly, he claims that

> a correlation, but not an equation, exists between elite positions and exploitation, between nonelite position and opportunity hoarding. Elites typically become elites and maintain themselves as elites by controlling valuable resources and engaging the effort of less favored others in generating returns from those resources, whereas nonelites commonly have to settle for the identification of niches not already fully exploited by elites.[8]

Like Marxists, Tilly argues that at the most fundamental level of analysis, exploitation is the pivotal mechanism for the generation of durable forms of deep inequality.

Problem 2: How to sustain and deepen exploitation and opportunity hoarding. It is all very well to say that exploitation and opportunity hoarding confer advantages on those who control resources. But since both of these mechanisms impose harms on others, they immediately pose a range of problems for would-be exploiters and opportunity hoarders. Above all they face what Tilly calls "organizational problems" of creating solidarity, trust, interlocking expectations, and reliable forms of enforcement *among those with stakes in hoarding and exploitation.*

Solution to problem 2: Categorical inequality. The creation of categorical forms of inequality helps solve this organizational problem. Tilly writes:

> Durable inequality among categories *arises* because people who control access to value producing resources solve organizational problems by means of categorical distinctions. Inadvertently or otherwise, those people set up systems of social closure, exclusion and

---

8   Tilly, *Durable Inequality*, 94.

control. Multiple parties—not all of them powerful, some of them even victims of exploitation—then acquire stakes in these solutions.[9]

In the absence of durable, categorical distinctions, exploiters and opportunity hoarders face constant difficulty in identifying their allies, in knowing whom to trust and whom to exclude, in being able to reliably protect their monopolies and enforce subordination. Durable, categorical distinctions make all of this easier. As Tilly puts it, "Organizational improvisations lead to durable categorical inequality. In all these cases, but with variable weight, exploitation and opportunity hoarding favor the installation of categorical inequality . . ."

This explanation has a distinctly functionalist structure, although Tilly does not characterize the explanation in these terms, and indeed explicitly rejects what he calls "teleological reasoning" (which is often identified with functional explanations). In summarizing the basic argument, he distills the core explanation of categorical inequality to three propositions:

1. "Organizationally installed categorical inequality facilitates exploitation." This is a claim about the effects of categorical inequality on exploitation: the former facilitates the latter.

2. "Organizations whose survival depends on exploitation therefore tend to adopt categorical inequality." This is a selection argument: the functional trait—categorical inequality—is adopted, through an unspecified process, because it is functional.

3. "Because organizations adopting categorical inequality deliver greater returns to their dominant members and because a portion of those returns goes to organizational maintenance, such organizations tend to crowd out other types of organizations." This is, in effect, a quasi-Darwinian selection explanation that explains why the functional traits generalize.[10]

This sequence of claims constitutes a classic functional explanation. What is more, as in standard functional explanations, Tilly explicitly argues that the functional arrangements need not be created by design when he states that "inadvertently or otherwise, those people set up systems of social closure, exclusion and control." What matters is that certain traits—categorical inequalities in this

---

9 Ibid., 8.
10 Ibid., 85.

case—become stable features of organization because they enhance the survival of organizations that have such traits, and that as a result over time organizations with such traits predominate. The adoption of the organizational trait in question may be a conscious strategy intentionally designed to enhance exploitation and opportunity hoarding, but equally it may result from quite haphazard trial and error.

Problem 3. How to stabilize and reproduce categorical inequalities? While categorical inequalities may facilitate exploitation and opportunity hoarding, they also pose new challenges to organizations since they potentially constitute the bases for solidarities and networks *opposed* to the dominant categories. On the one hand, they reduce the transaction costs for sustaining exploitation and opportunity hoarding by solving a variety of information and trust problems for elites; on the other hand, they also potentially reduce transaction costs for collective struggles by subordinates. Categorical inequality, in short, sets in motion a pattern of contradictory effects.

Solution to problem 3: Emulation and adaptation. To the extent that a given form of categorical inequality can be diffused throughout a society ("emulation") so that it appears ubiquitous and thus inevitable, and to the extent that people living within these relations of categorical inequality elaborate daily routines ("adaptation") that enable them to adapt to the conditions they face, the categorical inequalities themselves will be stabilized. This is what emulation and adaptation accomplish: "Emulation and adaptation lock such distinctions into place, making them habitual and sometimes even essential to exploiters and exploited alike."[11] The result is that the exploited and excluded groups along the axes of categorical inequality are less likely to form the kinds of oppositional solidarities that pose a serious threat to the beneficiaries of exploitation and opportunity hoarding.

Taken together, therefore, categorical inequality is explained by a complex of mechanisms clustered into three intersecting functional explanations: exploitation and opportunity hoarding are functionally explained by the problem of sustaining and augmenting advantages from control over resources; categorical inequalities are functionally explained by the problem of stabilizing exploitation and opportunity hoarding, and emulation and adaptation are functionally explained by the problem of stabilizing categorical inequality.

---

11 Ibid., 11.

This interconnected explanatory structure can be clarified using a diagrammatic representation of functional explanation elaborated by Arthur Stinchcombe.[12] The basic structure of Stinchcombe's representation of functional explanation is given in Figure 3.1. The pivot of the explanation is a problem-in-need-of-a-solution. This problem is itself generated by a causal process referred to by Stinchcombe as a "tension" in the system. Through some kind of selection mechanism—the "black box" of functional explanations—the problem stimulates the production of a solution, which in turn dampens the problem. At some point an equilibrium may be reached in which the negative effects of the solution on the problem counterbalance the positive effects of the tension which originally generated the problem-in-need-of-a-solution. This "feedback loop" constitutes the core of the functional explanation.

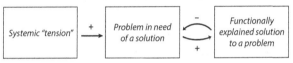

Figure 3.1. Basic Form of a Functional Explanation
Source: Based on models in Arthur Stinchcombe, *Constructing Social Theories*, New York: Harcourt, Brace & World, 1968.

Tilly's model of durable inequality consists of a series of interlocking functional explanations of this type, as illustrated in Figure 3.2. The distinctive feature of this model is the way in which the functional solution to one problem becomes, in turn, a source of systemic tension that generates a new system-problem and corresponding functional solution.

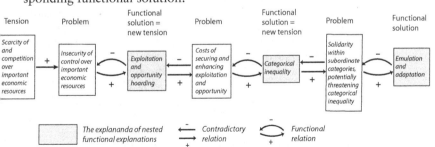

Figure 3.2. The Underlying Functional Logic of *Durable Inequality*

12 Arthur Stinchcombe, *Constructing Social Theories* (New York: Harcourt Brace & World, 1968)

4. The Underlying Marxist Logic

Figure 3.2 is obviously a stripped-down version of Tilly's theory of categorical inequality, but it does, I believe, capture the essential explanatory structure of the argument. The theoretical tradition in social science that comes closest to this general framework is Marxism, although except in passing Tilly makes almost no reference to Marxist theory in the book. In one of the few explicit discussions of the theoretical pedigree of his approach, Tilly characterizes it as a kind of synthesis of Marxist and Weberian ideas: the analysis, he writes "builds a bridge from Max Weber on social closure to Karl Marx on exploitation and back."[13] In fact, if the representation of the argument in Figure 3.2 is roughly correct, Tilly's analysis is much closer to the logical core of Marx's theory than of Weber's.[14] Rather than treating Tilly's theoretical framework as a *fusion* of Marx and Weber, therefore, I think it is more appropriate to see Tilly as importing some Weberian ideas and insights into the Marxist tradition. The result is an enrichment of an essentially Marxist form of class analysis by extending that analysis to include forms of categorical inequality that are not systematically discussed by Marx.

There are a number of reasons for affirming this close conceptual affinity between Tilly's approach and classical Marxism:

1. Exploitation is the centerpiece of Marx's theory of class as it is of Tilly's theory of categorical inequality. Class relations in Marxism are social relations within which exploiters appropriate the labor effort of the exploited by virtue of their control over pivotal economic resources. This is virtually the same as Tilly's formulation. And both Marx and Tilly accord exploitation central importance for basically the same reason: exploitation not only creates advantages for exploiters by excluding others from access to resources—this much is true of opportunity hoarding more generally—but also because it involves appropriation of value-producing effort, exploitation allows elites to accumulate resources that they can use to buttress their power in all sorts of ways.

2. Forms of categorical inequality emerge and are sustained in Tilly's analysis above all because of the ways they help stabilize exploitation and secondarily because of the ways they facilitate

---

13   Ibid., 7.
14   See the discussion of Weber's work in chapter 2.

opportunity hoarding. Marx certainly believed that class categories emerge for this same reason: they make possible a stable reproduction of exploitation to a far greater extent than would be possible if exploitation existed simply on the basis of fluid relations between individuals.

3. Tilly treats the relevance of culture and beliefs for inequality almost entirely in terms of the ways they help reproduce categorical inequality, but not as autonomous, powerful causal forces in their own right. This is much closer to Marx's materialism, specifically his functionalist theory of the relationship between the economic base and ideological superstructure, than to Weber's view of the relationship between culture and social structure.

4. As G. A. Cohen has pointed out, the use of functional explanations plays a central role in classical historical materialism.[15] They play at most a marginal role in Weber's social theory. In Marxism, class relations are functionally explained by the level of development of the forces of production, and superstructures are functionally explained by the necessary conditions for stabilizing and reproducing class relations. While Tilly's analysis does not directly contain an analysis of forces and relations of production, the functional relation between categorical inequality on the one hand and emulation and adaptation on the other is quite parallel to the functional explanation of ideological superstructures in Marxism.

5. In classical historical materialism, class relations are thought to endure and remain stable so long as the forces of production continue to develop, and those class relations become vulnerable once the forces of production are fettered. The underlying rationale for this claim is that the costs of sustaining class relations rise precipitously when the forces of production stagnate. Again, there is nothing in Tilly's analysis that directly concerns the specific argument about forces of production, but he does argue that the central condition for the erosion of systems of categorical inequality is the rising transaction costs for maintaining existing relations and the lowered costs of an alternative:

Existing social arrangements have enduring advantages because their theoretical alternatives always entail the costs of movement away

---

15 Cohen, *Karl Marx's Theory of History: A Defense.*

from the present situation; change therefore occurs under conditions that reduce the returns from existing arrangements, raise their current operating costs, lower the costs of transition to alternative arrangements or (much more rarely) increase expected returns from alternative arrangements sufficiently to overcome transition costs.[16]

In broadest terms, they [conditions for successful challenge to categorical inequality] occur when the benefits from exploitation and opportunity hoarding decline and/or costs of exploitation, opportunity hoarding, emulation and adaptation increase. In those circumstances, the beneficiaries of categorical inequality tend to split, with some of them becoming available as the underdogs' allies against other exploiters and hoarders ... When the altered structural position of a subordinated population increases its leverage or internal connectedness ... eventually the costs of controlling that population expand, along with the capacity to resist control.[17]

This closely parallels classical Marxist views of the conditions for qualitative transformations in the relations of production: the old relations of production become very costly to maintain; new alternative relations become historically feasible; and agents capable of executing the transformation become sufficiently strong to overcome transition costs. Nothing remotely like this formulation occurs in Weber's account of social change and inequality.

These deep parallels with the Marxist tradition of class analysis do not imply that Tilly's arguments are simply recapitulations of Marxist themes in a new language. Tilly's attempt to subsume gender, race, nationality, and every other form of inequality under a unitary conceptual framework goes well beyond Marx; his differentiation of opportunity hoarding from exploitation is largely absent from most varieties of Marxist class analysis;[18] and his elaboration of emulation and adaptation as mechanisms for stabilizing categorical inequality introduces concepts that are not explicitly present in Marxist discussions of similar themes. Nevertheless, if

---

16 Tilly, *Durable Inequality*, 192.

17 Ibid., 225.

18 Although different terms are used, the distinction between opportunity hoarding and exploitation is almost identical to the distinction between "nonexploitative economic oppression" and "exploitation" in my elaboration of the conceptual foundations of class analysis. See especially Wright, *Interrogating Inequality*, London: Verso, 1994, 39–46; and *Class Counts: Comparative Studies in Class Analysis*, Cambridge: Cambridge University Press, 1997, chapter 1.

my characterization of Tilly's argument is on track, the work should be regarded as much more deeply linked to the Marxist tradition of social theory than any other.

So far we have examined and reconstructed in more formal terms the broad contours of Tilly's argument. In the next section I want to look in more detail at one piece of this argument and try to formulate a set of more formalized hypotheses about the formation and reproduction of categorical inequality.

5. Generating Categorical Inequality
Through Organizations: Hypotheses

In order to develop a more fine-grained account of the ways in which categories are used by organizations to enhance exploitation and opportunity hoarding, Tilly proposes a fourfold typology of the different ways categorical distinctions *within* organizations (e.g., between managers and workers) can be linked to categorical distinctions *external* to organizations (e.g., black and white, male and female, etc.):

1. *Gradients*: a situation in which there exist internal inequalities across individuals but without any categorical divisions.

2. *Local frontiers*: internal categorical divisions alone, unlinked to any exterior categories.

3. *Imported frontiers*: externally based categorical divisions alone, not matched to any internal organizational divisions.

4. *Reinforced inequality*: a situation in which there are "matching interior and exterior categories."

While all four of these may exist, Tilly argues that there will be a general tendency for inequalities to move to the fourth of these types except under the special condition that "surplus extraction is already operating efficiently by means of gradients or local frontiers." If exploitation occurs efficiently without categorical inequality, then in Tilly's words, "those who control the crucial resources rarely incorporate exterior categories" since there would be little incentive for them to do so. Since, however, exploitation is rarely efficient and sustainable in the absence of categorical inequality, organizations will tend to move towards a system in which exterior categories are matched with interior ones.

The argument hinges on claims about the relative transaction costs required to maintain a given level of stability of inequality

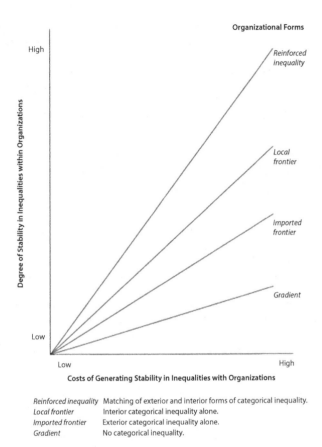

Reinforced inequality   Matching of exterior and interior forms of categorical inequality.
Local frontier   Interior categorical inequality alone.
Imported frontier   Exterior categorical inequality alone.
Gradient   No categorical inequality.

Figure 3.3. Definitions of Alternative Organizational Forms of Inequality

within the organization across these four configurations. Organizations will tend to move towards "reinforced inequality" because in general, Tilly argues, this is the cheapest way of sustaining a given level of inequality within organizations: "matching interior and exterior categories lowers transaction costs and increases stability."[19] A system of inequality based exclusively on gradients would in

19 Ibid., 80.

general be the least stable and the most costly to maintain because, he writes, "Without strong incentives to endure short-term injustice in the expectation of long-term mobility or other rewards, turnover and small-scale conflict make gradients unstable arrangements." Inequality based on local frontiers, in Tilly's judgment, would be the second most stable: "For the same difference in rewards, inequality that depends on organizationally defined categorical differences alone (local frontiers) is more stable than gradients or imported frontiers . . ." Taking these observations together generates a rather complex general hypothesis for what might be called the "production functions for stabilizing inequalities within organizations." This hypothesis is pictured in Figure 3.3.

Like many of Tilly's claims in this book, this is a bold hypothesis. There are, undoubtedly, many empirical contexts in which these claims are plausible. It is less clear, however, why we should believe that this specific rank-ordering of the costs required to produce stability associated with different configurations of categorical inequalities should be a universal tendency. Why, for example, should we believe that as a broad generalization across societies with different cultures, different technologies, different political systems, it will be the case that "for the same difference in rewards, inequality that depends on organizationally defined categories alone . . . is more stable than either gradients or imported frontiers"? What are the general mechanisms that imply that, for any given level of inequality, the stability-effects of categorical inequalities imported from the society at large will have a transhistorical tendency to be weaker than the stability-effects of internally generated categorical inequality? Similarly, while it is certainly plausible that in many situations tightly matching internal and external categories might be the cheapest way of stabilizing a system of exploitation, it is much less clear why this should be a transhistorical universal.

In spite of these questions and the need for a more sustained argument for the universality of the tendencies in these propositions, Figure 3.3 represents a challenging and suggestive agenda for research.

II. CONCEPTUAL IMPRECISION

When *Durable Inequality* is elaborating its positive agenda it is on its firmest and most interesting ground. When it engages in debates with other perspectives or tries to clarify a range of abstract conceptual and methodological issues, it frequently becomes much less satisfactory. In what follows I will review some of these problems.

1. Problematic Anti-essentialism

In his effort to demarcate the distinctiveness of his approach to inequality, Tilly draws a sharp contrast between views that assume *essences* of various social entities and views that assume *bonds*. "Most people seeking to explain any sort of social process," he writes, "presume the existence and centrality of self-propelling essences (individuals, groups, or societies)."[20] In contrast, Tilly advocates "a possibility of assuming not essences but bonds: *relational* models of social life beginning with interpersonal transactions or ties."[21] The contrast between "essences" and "bonds" or "relations" seems to me quite misleading. A "bond" is not the opposite of an "essence." A theorist can just as easily be an "essentialist" *about* bonds or interpersonal transactions or ties as about the entities bonded together, the persons interacting, or the things that are tied together. Indeed, I think it reasonable to say that Tilly himself is a committed essentialist about social relations. He sees exploitation, opportunity hoarding, emulation, and adaptation as having certain "essential" features that are sufficiently invariant across contexts that he is prepared to make very general transhistorical propositions using these relational terms.

The central issue in essentialism versus anti-essentialism is the issue of whether or not there are any salient properties of the elements that figure in our social theories that are stable and invariant across radically different contexts. One can thus be an essentialist or an anti-essentialist both about social relations and about the relata within those relations. Many scholars who in Tilly's terms focus on individuals and their mental states can well be nonessentialists about those individual attributes: they could see those attributes as entirely contingent upon specific cultural constructions rather than inherent in the human individual.

I have no objections at all to Tilly's insistence on the general importance of relations in social theory, or about the centrality of relations in the explanation of the specific phenomena he is studying. And I have no objection to his claim that many social scientists tend to pay less systematic attention to relations than to nonrelational attributes of individuals or groups (although I am skeptical

20   Ibid., 17.
21   Ibid., 18.

that this sin characterizes "most people seeking to explain social processes," as he claims). But it confuses rather than clarifies this issue to couch these metatheoretical commitments in terms of a generic critique of essentialism.

2. Conflating Methodological Individualism with Atomism

Throughout the book the main theoretical target for Tilly's critiques is what he terms "individualist" explanations in social science. For Tilly,

> *Methodological individualism* presumes that social life results chiefly or exclusively from the actions of self-motivated, interest-seeking persons.

> Methodological individualists who seek to explain social inequality have so far faced an insurmountable obstacle. Their causal mechanisms consist of mental events: decisions.

> These analyses fail . . . to the extent that essential causal business takes place not inside individual heads but within social relations among persons and sets of persons.[22]

This characterization of methodological individualism collapses the distinction between individualistic and atomistic social theories.[23] Methodological *atomism*, to be sure, completely marginalizes relational properties, but this is generally not the case for methodological individualists. One of the most articulate spokesmen for methodological individualism, Jon Elster, insists that methodological individualism includes an account of all sorts of relational properties of individuals, especially power.[24] And those relational properties are certainly treated as causal and explanatory. What Elster rejects is methodological *collectivism*, not relational analysis. Methodological collectivism posits collective entities like classes as actors. Elster vehemently objects to statements of the form "the working class had no choice but to fight," since "classes" are not the sorts of entities that "make choices."

---

22   Ibid., 17, 20, 33.

23   For an extended discussion of this distinction between methodological individualism and methodological atomism, see Wright, Levine, and Sober, *Reconstructing Marxism: Essays on Explanation and the Theory of History*, London: Verso, 1992.

24   Jon Elster, *Making Sense of Marx* (Cambridge: Cambridge University Press, 1985), 5–6.

Even the methodological individualists of neoclassical economics and game theory do not universally fit the description of atomized methodological individualism offered by Tilly. Tilly insists that methodological individualists see causes as operating "inside of individual heads" with causal mechanisms consisting only of "mental events." But the actors in neoclassical economics face budget constraints (dependent upon access to resources); they have endowments, including endowments in external assets; they produce with production functions determined by technologies; and they interact in markets governed by specific rules. Neoclassical economists, for example, recognize that when firms have monopoly power markets behave differently, not because anyone's preferences or mental states are different, but because monopolies have the power to extract rents through exchange relations. None of these are "mental events." In game theory actors face payoffs from alternative strategies, and, depending upon the nature of the game, the outcome is determined not just by the choices of a given actor but by the iterated unintended effects of the combined interacting choices of many actors. Payoffs and joint outcomes depend upon the "rules of the game," which define the nature of the interactions of players. These are also not "mental events," but, at their core, "relations." To be sure, neither game theorists nor most neoclassical economists characteristically use a language of "social relations," and some neoclassical economists like to play with models in which they can pretend that actors act entirely atomistically (the purely competitive market with perfect information, etc.). Nevertheless, as a general matter social relations are implicit in both of these intellectual traditions.

What distinguishes methodological individualism, then, is not a rejection of relations as relevant to social explanations nor a stipulation that all causes are reducible to mental events, but an insistence on the primacy of micro-level analyses over macro-level analysis. Methodological individualism is committed to *microfoundationalism*, and perhaps even, as Jon Elster argues, to micro-reductionism, but not atomism. Relations are therefore explanatory for methodological individualists, but these are restricted to relations among individual persons.

Tilly's work therefore does constitute a potential criticism of methodological individualism, but not because of their rejection of relations or (as stated earlier) their essentialism. Rather, at the core of Tilly's analysis are a set of claims about the effects of macro-structures and relations. While micro-relations among individuals in the form of interpersonal networks of various sorts are certainly important in Tilly's analysis, at least part of the explanatory work is done by relations-among-relations, not simply relations-among-individuals.[25]

3. Misplaced Metatheoretical Criticism

One of the examples Tilly uses throughout the book to highlight the difference between his approach to inequality and the approach of most other social scientists is "discrimination" against women and racial minorities. He characterizes conventional analyses as individualistic in the following way:

> Despite disagreements in other regards, analysts of wage inequality generally accept the conventional definition of discrimination as the remainder after taking account of human capital and effort ... Neoclassical economists commonly give strong weight to the interaction of human capital and effort, whereas radical feminists often assign the fundamental causal role to discrimination in one form or another. All sides invoke an essentially individualist explanation of inequality.[26]

> We should reverse the conventional procedure for analyzing discrimination: instead of treating it as the residual difference between categories once all possible sources of individual variation are taken into account, treat it as the portion of inequality that corresponds to locally relevant categories, and then see how much of the residual can be explained by variation in human capital, effort, and similar individual-level factors.[27]

I believe this criticism is largely misplaced. The specification of discrimination as the "residual" difference between categories after

---

25 One way to distinguish macro-analysis from micro-analysis in social science is to see micro-analysis as focusing on relations among individual persons and macro-analysis as focusing on relations-among-relations. This suggests that there is a continuous movement from the micro-level to ever-more macro-levels that is relational all the way down: the most micro social level consists of relations-among-individuals; the next level is relations among the relations-among-individuals; the next level is relations among the relations among the relations-among-individuals; etc. For a discussion of this understanding of micro-to-macro analysis, see Wright, *Class, Crisis and the State*, chapter 10.

26 Tilly, *Durable Inequality*, 133.

27 Ibid., 239–40.

individual attributes have been accounted for is the result of pragmatic methodological considerations, not the result of any
substantive priority given to individual attributes over structural
causes of inequality. The idea is basically this: the total empirically
observed differences in earnings between two categories—say, men
and women—can in principle be partitioned into two main components: (1) a component that is the direct result of systematic,
structural discrimination of various sorts, ranging from job exclusions to glass ceilings in promotion to unequal treatment within
given jobs; (2) a component that is a direct result of human capital,
effort, and other variables under the immediate control of the individual.[28] This is not to reject the claim that these individual attributes
might themselves also be caused by structural discrimination of
various sorts, but simply to argue that at the time of employment
itself a decomposition of intergroup differences can be made
between a component tied to individual attributes and a component
tied to categorical discrimination. The pragmatic question thus
becomes: what is the best way to make estimates of these two
components? One could try to get direct measures of each component, or one could try to measure one quite accurately and then
attribute the remainder of the variance to the other. For pragmatic
reasons, the latter strategy is generally adopted because obtaining
good measures directly about the effects of discrimination is difficult. Discrimination is not inherently treated as a *substantive*
residual in such a study, but simply a *methodological* residual.

Beyond this pragmatic point, I think Tilly misdescribes a great
deal of work on gender inequality by both feminists and mainstream
sociologists when he characterizes the logic of their inquiries as
strongly individualist, claiming that they reduce gender inequality to
the attributes of individuals and the causal processes to the mental
events of actors. Much analysis of gender inequality has placed
considerable emphasis on such things as social networks, especially
the "old boys network," struggles over the family wage and the male
breadwinner model, union rules of exclusion, marriage bars, and so
forth. In the more Marxian currents of gender analysis, gender
inequality in labor markets is seen as a mechanism of superexploita-
tion, of securing a stable supply of cheap labor, and of divide and
conquer strategies to undermine class solidarity. None of these
processes is properly characterized as "essentially individualist."

---

28 There is a third component that enters empirical investigations of these
issues that is the result of the interaction between structural effects and individual attributes.

Tilly's great concern to denounce individualistic explanation sometimes leads him to reject certain kinds of causal claims simply on the grounds that they smack of individualism, thus turning what is rightfully a substantive debate about causes in the world into a metatheoretical debate about what sorts of explanations are legitimate. One of the standard explanations for discrimination among economists is what is termed "statistical discrimination." Statistical discrimination occurs when an employer makes a hiring decision not on the basis of inter-individual differences in attributes, but on the basis of the (perceived) average attributes of members of some category. The idea here is that the employer in question would like to hire people on the basis strictly of individual attributes, but that it is too costly to get accurate information on those individual attributes, so as a rough proxy the employer imputes group average attributes to individuals. Tilly rejects such explanations as *in principle* illegitimate. He writes:

> The ideas of "statistical discrimination" individualizes a collective process radically: it portrays an employer who avoids hiring members of a whole category on the basis of beliefs or information—however well founded—that on average workers belonging to the category contribute less to productivity than their counterparts from outside the category.[29]

While Tilly may be correct that statistical discrimination is an unsatisfactory explanation for discriminatory hiring decisions, this is fundamentally an empirical matter subject to empirical adjudication. If statistical discrimination were the main operative process, this would imply that if the costs of acquiring high-quality information about individual-level attributes declined, then the apparent discrimination would also decline. In the limiting case of a system of pure statistical discrimination, state policies that fully subsidized information costs would eliminate the associated categorical inequality. I personally would predict that solving the information problem would only have a modest effect on the relevant kinds of categorical inequalities, but this is an empirical prediction, not one derived from an a priori rejection of hypotheses simply because they place individual decision-making at the center of a causal process. Tilly, in contrast, rejects the hypothesis on metatheoretical grounds.

---

29 Tilly, *Durable Inequality*, 31.

Durable Inequality is an incredibly ambitious book. Whether or not one agrees with its arguments, its core substantive ideas are distinctive and provocative. Particularly if one works within the broadly defined Marxist tradition of social theory, Tilly's reconfiguration of the concept of exploitation as part of a general theory of categorical inequality could provide interesting ways of framing a wide range of empirical projects. These ideas are more likely to play such a provocative and constructive role, I feel, if they are disengaged from many of the more abstract methodological and metatheoretical themes in which the arguments are currently embedded.

4

CLASS, EXPLOITATION, AND ECONOMIC RENTS: REFLECTIONS ON SØRENSEN'S "TOWARD A SOUNDER BASIS FOR CLASS ANALYSIS"

The concept of exploitation has been at the core of the Marxist tradition of class analysis, but to many people this concept now seems like esoteric and irrelevant radical jargon. Particularly since the abandonment by most Marxists of the labor theory of value as a coherent framework for economic analysis, the concept of exploitation has come to seem more like a heavy-handed piece of antiquated rhetoric than a rigorous tool for understanding the inner workings of class relations in capitalist society.

In his essay "Toward a Sounder Basis for Class Analysis," Aage Sørensen argues that Marxists are correct in placing exploitation at the center of class analysis, since an exploitation-centered concept of class has a much greater potential for explaining the structural foundations of social conflicts over inequality than does its principle rival, the material "life-conditions" conception of class.[1] But he

---

1 Aage Sørensen, "Toward a Sounder Basis for Class Analysis," *American Journal of Sociology* 105: 6, May 2000, 1523–58. Sørensen proposes a three-fold classification of concepts of class: purely *nominal* class concepts define classes in terms of arbitrary demarcations in systems of stratification; *life conditions* concepts "make claims about the empirical existence of observable groupings with identifiable boundaries" sharing common material conditions of existence (1526); *exploitation* concepts define classes as conflict groups with inherently antagonistic interests. To this typology I would make two further subdistinctions: within the life conditions concept of class I would distinguish between class concepts that are built around common material conditions of life as such, and those that are built around common *opportunity for achieving* material conditions of life (or what is sometimes called "life chances"). Within the exploitation concept of class I would distinguish between class concepts that are built around antagonistic interests over material advantages as such and concepts that emphasize the *interactive interdependency* of classes. This chapter is primarily about this distinction within the family of exploitation-centered concepts of class.

also believes that existing concepts of exploitation are seriously compromised due to an absence of rigorous theoretical foundations. To solve this problem he proposes rehabilitating the concept of exploitation by closely identifying it with the economic concept of rent. This, he believes, retains the fundamental sociological meaning of exploitation while giving the concept much more theoretical precision and analytical power.

I share with Sørensen the commitment to reconstructing an exploitation-centered concept of class.[2] And, like Sørensen, I believe that a rigorous concept of exploitation can be elaborated without the use of the labor theory of value. I have also argued that there is a close link between the concept of economic rent and various forms of exploitation. I disagree, however, that exploitation can be fruitfully defined simply in terms of rent-generating processes, or that a class analysis built on such foundations will be satisfactory. The objective of this chapter is to explain why I believe that rent alone does not provide a "sounder basis" for class analysis.

In the next section I briefly summarize the central ideas of Sørensen's proposal. This summary is followed by an explication of an alternative conceptualization of exploitation that sees exploitation as not simply rent-generated advantages, but advantages that involve the appropriation of labor effort of the exploited by exploiters. The chapter concludes with a discussion of the complex relationship between rent and exploitation.

SØRENSEN'S MODEL OF RENT-BASED EXPLOITATION

Sørensen begins by endorsing what might be called the root meaning of exploitation in Marx: "Exploitation, for Marx and here, means that there is a causal connection between the advantage and disadvantage of two classes. This causal connection creates latent antagonistic interests which, when acted upon as a result of the development of class consciousness, creates class conflict."[3] The pivot of this definition is the idea of *antagonistic interests*: "Interests may be said to be antagonistic when the gain of one actor, or a set

---

2 Erik Olin Wright, *Class, Crisis and the State*, London: Verso, 1978; *Classes*, London: Verso, 1985; *The Debate on Classes*, London: Verso, 1989; *Class Counts: Comparative Studies in Class Analysis*, Cambridge: Cambridge University Press, 1997.

3 Sørensen, "Toward a Sounder Basis," 1524.

of actors, excludes others from gaining the same advantage."[4] An exploitation-centered concept of class, therefore, sees class relations as structured by processes of exploitation which causally generate antagonistic interests.

The central problem, then, is figuring out what properties of social relations in fact generate such antagonistic interests. Sørensen argues, correctly I believe, that the traditional Marxist strategy of basing such an account in the labor theory of value is unsatisfactory. He proposes a simple and straightforward alternative by identifying exploitation with economic rents. Owning assets of various sorts gives people a stream of income—call this returns on owning the asset—when those assets are deployed in production or exchanged in a market. The "value" of the asset to an individual is defined by the total returns one obtains from that asset during the period in which one owns it. We can then define a special counterfactual: the returns to the asset under conditions of "perfect competition." Any return to the asset above this counterfactual is a rent: "The difference between the actual price and the competitive price is what is called an *economic rent* ... Rents are payments to assets that exceed the competitive price or the price sufficient to cover costs and therefore exceeding what is sufficient to bring about the employment of the asset."[5]

Perfect competition is a quite demanding condition. It implies *perfect information* and a complete *absence of any power relations* between actors within a market. Economists are used to including the power condition in discussions of competitive markets. This is where the contrast between competitive and monopolistic markets comes from. Much less attention is generally paid to the information conditions. If actors in a system of exchange and production have incomplete information, then contracts are not costlessly enforceable (since resources must be devoted to monitoring compliance with contracts). In general in such situations, the empirical prices in exchange relations will deviate from the prices that would pertain under conditions of perfect information, thus generating rents associated with transaction costs.

With this standard economic definition of rents in hand, Sørensen then proposes to define exploitation in terms of rents: "I propose ... to restrict exploitation to inequality generated by ownership or possession of *rent-producing assets*. Rent-producing assets or resources create inequalities where the advantage to the owner is obtained at the expense of nonowners. These nonowners would be

---

4 Ibid.
5 Ibid., 1536.

better off if the rent-producing asset was redistributed or eliminated."[6] *Exploitation class* is thus defined as "structural locations that provide rights to rent-producing assets."[7]

This definition of exploitation class produces some startling conclusions that run quite counter to the conventional intuitions of most class analysts:

1. Capitalist property relations by themselves do not generate classes. "In perfectly competitive markets, with no transaction costs, there are no permanent advantages or above-market returns, to be obtained at the expense of somebody else. Thus class location would be irrelevant."[8] Strictly speaking, within Sørensen's framework the claim here should be even stronger: it is not simply that class location would be irrelevant; there would be no class locations at all. A capitalist market economy with perfect competition would be a classless society.

2. When labor unions negotiate "solidarity wages" in which wage differentials are reduced by raising the wages of unskilled workers, unskilled workers become an exploiting class: "The main effect of unions is to reduce wage inequality. Unions are especially effective at decreasing the wage spread between more or less productive workers. Unions may create substantial rents to low skilled or otherwise less productive workers."[9]

3. The existence of a high minimum wage increases exploitation in a society and renders workers at or near the minimum wage an exploiting class. A strong welfare state also increases exploitation; welfare recipients are an exploiting class.

4. While some of the increase in inequality in the last two decades in many capitalist societies may reflect a redistribution of rents from one category of actors to another (particularly when capitalists are able to capture a higher proportion of what Sørensen calls "composite rents"), mostly this increasing inequality reflects a reduction in rents: "The increase in inequality is very much driven by an increase in wages and earnings of the highest paid and stagnation or decline for others. The stagnation and

---

6   Ibid., 1532.
7   Ibid., 1525.
8   Ibid., 1527–8.
9   Ibid., 1550.

decline follow from rent destruction."[10] This implies less exploitation in the system under neoliberal, deregulated labor markets and thus a move towards a classless society.

Sørensen recognizes that these conclusions are deeply counterintuitive. He responds by arguing that in capitalist societies reducing exploitation may in fact be a bad thing for many ordinary people. "Nothing," he writes, "guarantees that efficient labor markets create good lives. Rents are required in modern society to provide decent standards of living for the poorest part of the population. These rents are provided from the state in the form of income support and other welfare goods."[11] Ironically, then, the elimination of class and exploitation increases human misery, and thus a humane capitalist society is one that fosters certain kinds of antagonistic class interests, particularly by strengthening state-sanctioned forms of exploitation.

There is nothing intrinsically wrong with bold, provocative, counterintuitive claims. Indeed, the hallmark of the best sociology is discovering properties of social relations that go against conventional wisdom and thus counteract the definition of sociology as "the painful elaboration of the obvious." Nevertheless, when such striking counterintuitive claims are made they may suggest that there are problems and missing elements in a theoretical proposal. This, I will argue, is the case in the simple equation of exploitation and rents.

AN ALTERNATIVE DEFINITION OF EXPLOITATION

The definition of exploitation I will elaborate shares much with that proposed by Sørensen. Like Sørensen, I argue that exploitation generates antagonistic interests in which the material welfare of exploiters is causally dependent upon harms to the material interests of the exploited. I also believe that this causal dependence is rooted in the ways in which productive assets of various sorts are owned and controlled. And, like Sørensen, I argue that defining class in terms of exploitation rather than simply material conditions of life provides the richest conceptual foundations for linking an account of material inequality with an account of social conflict. We differ, however, in two respects: first, I do not think that rents provide a full account of the explanatory mechanisms of exploitation; and second, I think that capitalism generates antagonistic class

10 Ibid., 1552.
11 Ibid., 1553.

interests even under the imaginary conditions of perfect competition. The first of these points involves examining the ways in which exploitation requires the appropriation of "labor effort" rather than simply "advantage"; the second involves showing how capitalist property relations generate antagonisms even with perfectly competitive markets.

Exploitation and the Appropriation of Labor Effort

Exploitation, as I define the concept, exists when three criteria are satisfied:[12]

(1) *The inverse interdependent welfare principle.* The material welfare of exploiters causally depends upon the reductions of material welfare of the exploited.[13]

(2) *The exclusion principle.* This inverse interdependence of welfares of exploiters and exploited depends upon the exclusion of the exploited from access to certain productive resources.

(3) *The appropriation principle.* Exclusion generates material advantage to exploiters because it enables them to appropriate the labor effort of the exploited.

Exploitation is thus a diagnosis of the process through which certain inequalities in incomes are generated by inequalities in rights and powers over productive resources: the inequalities occur, in part at least, through the ways in which exploiters, by virtue of their exclusionary rights and powers over resources, are able to appropriate

12 See Wright, *Class Counts*, 9–19, for details.

13 It is often noted that in a market economy both parties to an exchange gain relative to their condition before making the exchange. This applies to ordinary market exchanges of commodities and also to the employment exchange: both workers and capitalists gain when an exchange of labor power for a wage occurs. Such mutual gains from trade can occur, and it can still be the case that the magnitude of the gains from trade accruing to one party comes at the expense of another party. As has often been noted (paraphrasing the British economist Joan Robinson), "The only thing worse than being exploited by capitalists is not being exploited by capitalists." This general point applies to Sørensen's conception of exploitation-as-rents as well to the conception being proposed here: in situations in which capitalists obtain monopoly rents in the market it is still the case that there are mutual gains from trade by the people who purchase the products at monopolistic prices.

labor effort of the exploited.[14] If the first two of these principles are present, but not the third, what might be termed *nonexploitative economic oppression* may exist, but not exploitation. The crucial difference is that in nonexploitative economic oppression, the advantaged social category *does not itself need* the excluded category. While the welfare of the advantaged does depend upon the exclusion principle, there is no ongoing interdependence of their activities with those of the disadvantaged. In the case of exploitation, the exploiters actively need the exploited: exploiters depend upon the effort of the exploited for their own welfare.

Sørensen explicitly rejects this third criterion and thus rejects the proposed distinction between exploitative and nonexploitative oppression. He writes:

> Wright (1997) proposes a related definition of exploitation though it is not formulated in terms of the concept of rent. In addition to the causal link between advantages and disadvantages of classes, Wright requires that the advantaged class depend on the fruits of labor of the disadvantaged class for exploitation to exist. Thus when the European settlers displaced Native Americans they did not exploit by obtaining an advantage at the expense of Native Americans; they engaged in "nonexploitative economic oppression" (Wright, 1997: 11). The European settlers clearly created antagonistic interests that brought about conflict so it is not clear what is added by the requirement of transfer of the fruits of labor power.[15]

One way of seeing "what is added by the requirement of transfer of the fruits of labor" is to contrast historical situations in which exploitation occurs with those characterized by nonexploitative oppression. Consider the difference in the treatment of indigenous people in North America and Southern Africa by European settlers. In both places the first two criteria above are satisfied: in both there is a causal relationship between the material advantages of settlers and the material

---

14   "Appropriation of labor effort" can take many forms. Typically this involves appropriating the products of that labor effort, but it may involve a direct appropriation of labor services. The claim that labor effort is appropriated does not depend upon the thesis of the labor theory of value that the value of the products appropriated by capitalists is determined by the amount of labor those products embody. All that is claimed is that when capitalists appropriate products they appropriate the laboring effort of the people who make those products.

15   Sørensen, "Toward a Sounder Basis," 1541, n21

disadvantages of indigenous people; and in both this causal relation is rooted in the exclusion of indigenous people from a crucial productive resource, land. In Southern Africa, however, the third principle was also present: the settler population appropriated the fruits of labor of the indigenous population, first as agricultural labor working the land and later as mineworkers, whereas in North America the labor effort of indigenous people was generally not appropriated.

Does this matter? It doesn't matter, perhaps, if all we are concerned with is the sheer presence or absence of "antagonistic interests," for in both instances there surely was deep antagonism. But the dynamics of the antagonism are fundamentally different in the two cases: in North America, because the settler population didn't need Native Americans, they could adopt a strategy of genocide as a way of responding to the conflicts generated by the exclusion of indigenous people from the land. There is a morally abhorrent folk expression in US culture that reflects this quality of antagonism: "The only good Indian is a dead Indian." No comparable expression exists for workers, slaves, or other exploited classes. One might say "the only good slave is a docile slave" or "the only good worker is an obedient worker," but it would make no sense to say "the only good worker is a dead worker" or "the only good slave is a dead slave." Why? Because the prosperity of slave-owners and capitalists depend upon the expenditure of effort of those whom they exploit. Sørensen's definition of exploitation does not distinguish between what I call exploitative and nonexploitative oppression and thus does not capture this strong sense in which *exploiters depend upon and need the exploited.*

This deep interdependence makes exploitation a particularly explosive form of social relation for two reasons: first, exploitation constitutes a social relation that simultaneously pits the interests of one group against another and that requires their ongoing interactions; and second, it confers upon the exploited group a real form of power with which to challenge the interests of exploiters. This is an important point. Exploitation depends upon the appropriation of labor effort. Because human beings are conscious agents, not robots, they always retain significant levels of real control over their expenditure of effort. The extraction of effort within exploitative relations is thus always to a greater or lesser extent problematic and precarious, requiring active institutional devices for its reproduction.[16] Such devices can become quite costly to exploiters in the

---

16 The claim that, because of the antagonistic interdependency of material interests generated by exploitation, class relations *require* active institutional

form of the costs of supervision, surveillance, sanctions, and so forth. The ability to impose such costs constitutes a form of power among the exploited.

Our first conclusion, then, is that a concept of exploitation based solely on the notion of rent misses the ways in which exploiters are not merely advantaged because of the disadvantages of the exploited, but are dependent upon the exploited. This dependency is a central feature of class relations.

Class, Exploitation, and "Perfect Competition"

In Sørensen's rent-centered concept of class and exploitation, a capitalist market economy with perfect competition (which would also require perfect information) would be a classless society, since all returns to assets would be exactly equal to their costs of production.[17] There would therefore be no rents and thus no exploitation or class.

Traditional Marxist conceptions of class and exploitation are sharply at odds with this diagnosis. In the framework of the labor theory of value it was easy to demonstrate that workers were exploited even under conditions of perfect competition. What happens when we abandon the labor metric of value?

Let us examine the three criteria for exploitation specified above in a capitalist economy with perfect competition in which there are only two categories of economic actors: capitalists, who own means of production—and thus have the effective power to exclude others from access those assets—and workers, who own only their labor power. We will not call these "classes" yet because we first need to see if the three criteria for exploitation are satisfied. For simplicity, let us assume

---

devices for their reproduction is at the core of the Marxist tradition of class analysis. This claim provides the basis for the attempt to build an endogenous theory of ideology and the state, either in the strong form of the base/superstructure theory of classical historical materialism or weaker forms of contemporary neo-Marxism. The theory predicts that if class relations are to be stably reproduced, forms of ideology will tend to emerge that mask that exploitation and forms of the state will tend to emerge that obstruct challenges to those class relations.

17   The concept of "costs of production" in this context includes such things as the "costs of deferring present consumption for greater future consumption." Thus, in a perfectly competitive market with perfect information, the interest rate on loans and the profit rate on investments are both simply the necessary returns on the relevant assets needed to exactly compensate the owners of those assets for the "costs" of foregone consumption. (There are further complications introduced by issues of risk, but the basic idea is the same.)

that capitalists are pure *rentiers*: they invest their capital in production and receive a rate of return on those capital assets, but they do not work themselves (managers are thus a type of worker in this simple case). Are the inverse interdependent welfare principle and the exclusion principle satisfied in this case? Is the material welfare of capitalists causally dependent upon the exclusion of workers from access to capital assets? The test here is whether or not it is the case that workers would be better off and capitalists worse off if property rights were redistributed so that workers would no longer be "excluded" from capital.[18] It seems hard to argue that this is not the case: in the initial condition capitalists have a choice of either consuming their capital or investing it, as well as the choice of whether or not they will work for earnings. Workers have only the latter choice. To be sure, they can borrow capital (and in a world of perfect information they would not need collateral to do so since there would be no transaction costs, no monitoring costs, no possibility of opportunism), but workers would still be better off owning capital outright than having to borrow it.

In his analysis of rent-based exploitation Sørensen argues that where rent-producing assets exist "nonowners would be better off if the rent-producing asset was redistributed or eliminated."[19] What we have just noted is that where capital assets are privately owned and unequally distributed—in particular, where one group of agents have no capital assets and another group have capital assets sufficient to not need to work—even if those assets do not generate rents it is still true that "nonowners would be better off if the income-producing asset was redistributed."[20]

18 This is the test John Roemer (*A General Theory of Exploitation and Class*, Cambridge: Cambridge University Press, 1982) proposes for assessing the existence of what he terms capitalist exploitation: would workers be better off and would capitalists be worse off if workers left the "game" of capitalism with their per capita share of capital? His answer is that in general they would be better off, and this demonstrates that within capitalism itself capitalists' welfare occurs at the expense of workers.

19 Sørensen, "Toward a Sounder Basis," 1532.

20 It should be noted that if we have a competitive market in all respects except for the perfect information condition, the ownership of capital will also generate rents in Sørensen's sense. That is, as Stiglitz and Weiss and Bowles and Gintis have shown, under conditions of imperfect information, interest rates in credit markets will be below the "market clearing rate" (implying that credit is rationed rather than allocated strictly on the basis of price). Joseph E. Stiglitz, and Andrew Weiss. "Credit Rationing in Markets with Imperfect Information," *American Economic Review* 71, 1981, 393–410; Samuel Bowles and Herbert Gintis, "Contested Exchange: New Microfoundations for the Political Economy

What about the third criterion for exploitation: the appropriation principle? Does it make sense to say that in a system of perfect competition with perfect information and equilibrium prices, rentier capitalists appropriate the "labor effort" of workers? As Sørensen correctly points out, in such an imaginary system, in equilibrium workers who expended more effort would be paid more, workers who shirked would be paid less, and (according to standard marginalist reasoning) the amount they were paid for their effort level would exactly reflect the price of the product they produced with that effort. This is the kind of reasoning that has always led neoclassical economists to deny the existence of exploitation in capitalism.

Nevertheless, even under these conditions the following is true: (1) the only labor effort performed in the system is by workers; (2) capitalists appropriate that product and thus appropriate the "fruits of labor effort" of workers;[21] (3) for any given wage level capitalists have an interest in getting workers to expend more labor effort than workers would spontaneously want to expend; (4) if workers owned their own means of production, capitalists would find it more difficult to get workers to work as hard for a given level of wages. In a purely competitive capitalist economy, therefore, antagonistic interests over the expenditure and appropriation of labor effort continue to exist.

CLASS, EXPLOITATION, AND RENTS

If one accepts the arguments above, the simple equation of exploitation with economic rents is an unsatisfactory basis for class analysis. This does not mean, however, that the concept of economic rent is irrelevant to class analysis, but simply that it has a more complex

---

of Capitalism," *Politics & Society*, 18:2, June 1990, 165–222. This implies that profits generated through the use of that credit will contain a rent component, functionally equivalent to the employment rent in nonclearing labor markets. Capitalists who deploy their own capital in production receive this rent as well. Imperfect information is the universal condition in credit markets, and thus profits will always have a rent component. Even in Sørensen's framework, therefore, the sheer ownership of capital should generate rent-based antagonisms of interests.

21 This claim does not depend upon the strong claim that the entire value of what capitalists appropriate is a function of the amount of labor embodied in that production. Cohen provides a careful defense of the view that the appropriation of the fruits of labor effort as such constitutes exploitation. G. A. Cohen, "The Labour Theory of Value and the Concept of Exploitation," in Cohen, *History, Labour and Freedom*, Oxford: Clarendon Press, 1988, 209–38.

relationship to the problem of exploitation. Let us examine two specific examples: employment rents derived from transaction costs in the employment contract, and solidarity rents generated by union power.

In Sørensen's analysis, the employment rents workers receive because of transaction costs in the employment relation count as a form of exploitation, rendering such workers an exploiting class. In the analysis proposed here, in general employment rents constitute one of the ways workers are able to mitigate their own exploitation.

Here is the basic argument: Where imperfect information exists—which is the usual condition of labor contracts—capitalists are generally prepared to pay employment rents to workers in order to extract adequate labor effort from them. The mechanism in play here has been carefully elaborated by Bowles and Gintis, following earlier work on efficiency wages by Ackerloff and Yellen and others.[22] Because of imperfect information in the labor market and labor process, capitalists are forced to spend resources on enforcing the labor contract (through supervision, monitoring, etc.) in order to detect shirking. Catching workers shirking is only useful for capitalists if workers care about being punished, especially about losing their jobs. The salience of the threat of being fired for shirking increases as the cost of job loss to workers increases. Paying workers an employment rent—a wage significantly above their reservation wage—increases the cost of job loss and thus the potency of employer threats. The costs to employers of extracting labor effort thus consist of two components: the costs of catching workers shirking (monitoring costs) and the costs of making job loss hurt (employment rents).[23] The "employment rent" is thus a wage premium that workers are able to get because of their ability to resist capitalist attempts at extracting labor effort. In conditions of perfect (and thus costlessly acquired) information, the capitalist capacity to appropriate effort is enhanced since workers lose this ability to resist. Rather than seeing employment rents as a form of

---

22   George Ackerloff and Janet Yellen, *Efficiency Wage Models of the Labor Market*, New York: Cambridge University Press, 1986.

23   As Bowles and Gintis stress in their analysis of "contested exchange," the relationship between these two costs can be viewed as a "labor extraction function" within the production process. Employers can increase labor extraction by allocating more resources to monitoring (thus increasing the probability of detecting shirking) or by increasing employment rents. Employers in general thus face a strategic trade-off between these two costs.

exploitation by workers, it is thus more appropriate to see such rents as the outcome of resistance to exploitation by workers.

As a second example of the relationship of rents and exploitation to class, consider the role of unions in reducing wage differentials among nonmanagerial employees. In Sørensen's provocative characterization of this phenomenon, low-skilled workers—the principal beneficiaries of the solidarity wage—are an exploiting class. In terms of the labor-effort appropriation formulation of the concept of exploitation one would want to ask: "Who is exploited by these low-skilled workers"?[24] There are three principle candidates: unemployed low-skilled workers, skilled workers, and capitalists.

An argument can certainly be made that unemployed workers are potentially harmed by solidarity wages. By raising the wages of low-paid workers, employers are likely to hire fewer low-skilled workers than they would do in unregulated labor markets. Solidarity wages—like minimum wages, job security protections, and other such institutional arrangements—create labor market rigidities that advantage insiders at the expense of outsiders. But does this warrant the claim that employed low-skilled workers who get solidarity wages "exploit" the unemployed? In terms of the proposed definition of exploitation adopted here, they do not. The key question is this: If the unemployed simply disappeared—if they emigrated to another country, for example—would the material welfare of the employed low-skilled workers rise or fall? If anything, the welfare of employed low-skilled workers would go up if the "reserve army of the unemployed" were to decrease. Unemployed workers in this situation may be subjected to a form of nonexploitative oppression by being denied access to jobs, but they are not exploited.

What about skilled workers? It is certainly the case that in conditions of solidarity wages the wages of skilled workers are, at least statically, lower than they would be in the absence of union-generated reductions of wage differentials. There are two reasons why it still does not make sense to say that the unskilled exploit the skilled in this context. First, one of the reasons for the solidarity wage is the belief that it enhances overall class solidarity and thus shifts the balance of power between organized workers and capitalists in favor of workers. In the long run such solidarity advances the material interests of both skilled and unskilled workers. Second, if

---

24 It should be noted that throughout Sørensen's paper there is very little explicit discussion of *who* is exploited. The general idea is that for any given category of agents who receive rents of one sort or another, the complement of the category is exploited.

in the absence of the solidarity wage skilled workers would themselves be recipients of union-generated rents, then what the
solidarity wage really does is simply reduce the rents acquired by
skilled workers and redistributes some of these rents to unskilled
workers. Even if one regards rents per se as a form of exploitation,
this would not constitute a form of exploitation *of* skilled workers
by the unskilled, but of the economic agents who pay the rents to
the skilled workers in the first place.

If solidarity wages are viewed simply as a redistribution of rents
from the skilled to the unskilled, perhaps the unskilled are exploiting the capitalists since, after all, capitalists are paying the wages
and thus the rents. But capitalists—under the definition of exploitation being used here—are themselves exploiters of workers by
virtue of appropriating the fruits of labor of workers. The rent
component of the solidarity wage—like the more general wage
premium of employment rents—should therefore in general be
thought of as a mitigation of capitalist exploitation rather than a
form of exploitation in its own right.

Both of these examples show that once the appropriation of
labor effort is added as a criterion for the concept of exploitation,
the relationships between class, exploitation, and rents become
much more complex. In some cases rents might still be directly a
form of exploitation. The rents that a landowner charges a tenant
farmer constitute a direct appropriation of the labor effort of the
farmer, for example. In other cases, rent acquisition is better
thought of as a way of mitigating exploitation. It is for this reason
that in general I have argued that employees who are the recipients
of various forms of rents within their earnings should be regarded
as occupying "privileged appropriation locations within exploitation relations."[25] The concept of economic rent therefore can play a
useful role in the theory of class and exploitation by clarifying the
range of mechanisms by which exploitation is enhanced or counter-
acted, but not by reducing the concept of exploitation simply to
advantages obtained by asset-owners under conditions of imperfect
competition and imperfect information.

---

25 Wright, *Class Counts*, 22. This formulation represents a change from my
earlier work in *Classes* on class and exploitation, in which I regarded both skill
rents and loyalty rents (rents appropriated especially by managers because of
their control over organizational apparatuses) as distinctive forms of exploitation. For a discussion of the reasoning behind this shift, see Wright, *The Debate
on Classes*, 331–40.

MICHAEL MANN'S TWO
FRAMEWORKS OF CLASS ANALYSIS

This chapter elaborates the central principles that underlie the concept of class in Michael Mann's extraordinary work *The Sources of Social Power*.[1] My central thesis is that there is a disjuncture between the general programmatic discussions of class in which Mann lays out the logic of his theoretical framework and at least some of the empirical analyses in which he concretely explores specific problems in class analysis. In his general programmatic exposition Mann adopts a quite restrictive understanding of the explanatory relevance of class, seeing class almost exclusively in terms of the ways in which *organized collective actors* are formed around economic power resources. Class, in this formulation, is only of sociological interest to the extent that classes are constituted as collective actors. In the concrete empirical analyses, on the other hand, he often develops the concept of class in terms of the ways in which the location of individuals within market and work organizations shapes their individual interests, experiences, and capacities. Class, in this formulation, looks much more like a structural concept identifying a set of causal forces that operate on the lives of individuals. While these two conceptualizations of the explanatory relevance of class are not inherently incompatible, Mann does not provide a theoretical argument for their integration.

In what follows I first briefly chart what might be called the raw materials of alternative approaches to class analysis.[2] This will

---

1 *The Sources of Social Power*, vol. 1, *A History of Power from the Beginning to A.D. 1760*, Cambridge: Cambridge University Press, 1986; *The Rise of Classes and Nation States*, vol. 2, Cambridge: Cambridge University Press, 1993; *Global Empires and Revolution, 1890–1945*, vol. 3, Cambridge: Cambridge University Press, 2012.

2 I use the term "class analysis" in an encompassing way to include both the

provide some specificity to the distinctive strategies in Mann's work. In section two I discuss Mann's overall framework of sociological analysis, which he terms "organizational materialism." Section three then outlines Mann's general programmatic claims about class, while part four looks at his detailed discussion of the middle class in the nineteenth century. Part five concludes with some general comments on the multiple levels of class analysis.

I. THE RAW MATERIALS OF ALTERNATIVE
APPROACHES TO CLASS ANALYSIS

In one way or another, most theoretical approaches to class analysis embody three clusters of interconnected concepts: *class relations, class location, and class structure*; *class structuration and class formation*; and *collective class actors*.[3] All three of these clusters constitute "realist" concepts insofar as they attempt to identify real causal processes and their effects. While in principle there is no inherent need to choose among them, in practice, class analysts tend to center their work on one or another of them.

Class Relations, Class Locations, Class Structures

Among social theorists who stress the importance of a structural concept of class, there is a considerable amount of debate about how best to define class relations. Some of these have been reviewed in chapter 1. Weberians emphasize the social relations of exchange in markets: locations within class relations—or what Weber called "class situations"—are defined by the nature of the assets that people bring to exchange relations. Marxists generally define class relations in terms of a more encompassing idea of social relations of production, which include the relations of exchange in the labor market, but also relations within production itself. John Goldthorpe argues that in defining class locations one must be attentive not merely to the assets actors bring to labor market exchanges, but

---

study of class phenomena as such—class relations, class structure, class formation, class struggle, etc.—and the study of the effects of class phenomena.

3   There is no consensus among class analysts over precisely what labels to use for these three conceptual clusters. Sometimes the term "class formation" is used to cover both the formation of structurally cohesive aggregate groups and the formation of collective actors. Sometimes "class position" or "class situation" is used instead of "class location."

also to the nature of the employment contract that results from this exchange.[4] All of these conceptualizations share one basic idea in common: locations-within-class-relations generate systematic effects of one sort or another on the lives of the people occupying those locations.

Class *location* is a micro-level concept: it enables us to identify a set of causal processes impinging on the lives of individuals. Class *structure* is a more macro-level concept. It is defined by the set of class relations within any relevant unit of analysis. One can thus speak of the class structure of a firm, of a city, of an economic sector, of a society, perhaps even of the world. *Class relations* is the common term to both the micro- and macro-level concept: class locations are defined within class relations; class structures are composed of sets of class relations.

Class Formation and Structuration

Class relations and the locations they determine do not, by themselves, define a social *group* with any real identity or cohesion. The set of people occupying a common location within class relations do indeed share something important in common—they are subjected to a common "causal component of their life chances," to use Weber's famous expression—and this justifies treating them as a socially relevant *category*, but they do not necessarily share a real *collective* existence, they are not necessarily a *real social group* with real social boundaries.[5] Class relations and locations can still have

---

4 Goldthorpe distinguishes between what he calls a "labor contract," in which workers exchange a specific amount of labor for a wage, and a "service contract," in which employees exchange an open-ended service for a salary. The best statement of this argument is in John Goldthorpe, "Social Class and the Differentiation of Employment Contracts," in John Goldthorpe, *On Sociology*, vol. 2, *Illustration and Retrospect*, 1st edn., Oxford: Oxford University Press, 2000, 206–29.

5 The word "group"—like many words in social theory—is fraught with ambiguities. The key idea here is the existence of some social process that forms a real boundary around the people within the group and which accordingly demarcates insiders from outsiders. It is this boundary-forming process that justifies using words like "membership" to describe belonging to the group. A collection of individuals subjected to a common causal process is by virtue of that experience a *category* of people, but not necessarily a group in this stronger sense. A "category" still designates real processes insofar as the causal processes that define the commonality of the collection of people within the category are

real and systematic effects on the lives of people even if such well-bounded social groups are not formed, but clearly the ramifications of class are greater when classes become social groups in this stronger sense.

The central causal processes that affect the degree of such social formation of classes-as-groups—or what Anthony Giddens refers to as the process of class *structuration*—include inter- and intragenerational class mobility, class patterns of marriage and friendship formation, the degree of class homogeneity of neighborhoods, the class stratification of schooling in ways that reinforce class boundaries, and many other processes that render the commonalities of common class situations/locations salient to the people in those locations.

For some class analysts, the decisive problem in class analysis is the formation of classes-as-groups in this sense. Pierre Bourdieu regards "classes" that are not constituted as real groups as merely "classes on paper," suggesting by this metaphor that they are just nominal categories invented by the analyst. We need to break, he argues, "with the intellectualist illusion that leads one to consider the theoretical class, constructed by the sociologist, as a real class, an effectively mobilized group."[6] Paul Kingston goes even further, insisting that if classes are not formed into such bounded groups with high levels of internal homogeneity, then classes don't exist. He thus refers to the United States today as a "classless society."[7] Jan Pakulski and Malcom Waters refers to such situations as "classless inequality."[8] The central idea here is that one can identify an indeterminate number of attributes as characterizing the social "location" of a person, and there is no reason to give special importance to any of them unless they are crystallized into "real social groups"; it is only this that establishes the realism of the hypothesized "real causal processes" identified with class relations.

real, but the category is still just a collection of separate, individual people with a common property until some boundary-forming process is added.

6 Pierre Bourdieu, "The Social Space and the Genesis of Groups," *Theory and Society* 14: 6, November 1985, 723.

7 Paul Kingston, *The Classless Society*, Stanford, CA: Stanford University Press, 2000.

8 Jan Pakulski and Malcom Waters' views are discussed in depth in chapter 7.

Class Actors

Classes can be formed into relatively coherent social groups without there being any collective organizations acting strategically on behalf of those groups. In some historical contexts, such organized collective actors don't exist because of repression; in others, a variety of countervailing processes—ethnic, racial, linguistic, national, and religious divisions, for example—obstruct the formation of organizations of collective class action. And in all situations a myriad of sectional and segmental forces—to use Michael Mann's formulation—tend to erode the formation of coherent, extensive class-wide organizations. Nevertheless, the explanatory relevance of class, some theorists argue, hinges on the extent to which class-based "power actors" emerge and confront each other in the various sites in which social structures are produced and transformed. Marx's famous assertion that "History is the history of class struggle" is the most extreme form of this argument. In this formulation, a fundamental part of the explanation of the overall trajectory of human history is the formation of classes-as-collective-actors whose struggles have the effect of transforming social structures. But even if one rejects this very strong proposition about the transhistorical importance of collective class actors, it is still possible to see the formation of class actors contesting for power as the central axis of class analysis.

2. MICHAEL MANN'S GENERAL APPROACH TO CLASS ANALYSIS: ORGANIZATIONAL MATERIALISM

In terms of these three clusters of concepts, Mann takes a fairly extreme position within the spectrum of possible approaches to class analysis: class analysis, in his view, should be almost entirely concerned with the formation of classes as collective power actors. To understand this view we need to first briefly outline Mann's general approach to the study of social structure and social change, what he terms "organizational materialism."[9] Organizational materialism consists of a conceptual menu for the study of power and what I will term Mann's foundational proposition about power and society.

---

9 Mann, *Sources of Social Power*, 1:36.

The Conceptual Menu

Mann's framework for the study of power involves two clusters of concepts: the first is a typology of *substantive sources of social power*, and the second is an inventory of *forms of variation of the organizations* that deploy these sources of power. The four sources of social power are ideological power, economic power, military power, and political power (thus the designation the IEMP model). While these are four distinct sources of power, Mann insists that their effects are always the result of complex forms of interaction— or what he terms "entwining": "The four power sources are not like billiard balls, which follow their own trajectory, changing direction as they hit each other. They 'entwine,' that is, their interactions change one another's inner shapes as well as their outward trajectories."[10] The forms of variation of the organizations linked to these sources of power are expressed as dichotomies: collective versus distributional power, extensive versus intensive power, authoritative versus diffused power.[11] Taken together, these concepts allow for fine-grained descriptions of power organizations and their interactions in concrete historical settings.

The Foundational Thesis of Mann's Organizational Materialism: Power Organizations Determine the Structure and Transformation of Society

Early in the second volume of *The Sources of Social Power*, Mann writes: "In pursuit of our goals, we enter into power organizations . . . that determine the overall structure of society."[12] This statement can be considered, perhaps, the foundational claim of Mann's general approach to sociological theory: the structure of society is at its core determined not by culture or values, nor by the rational choices of individuals acting as individuals, nor by the property relations within which people work, but by *power organizations*.[13] Of course, such power organizations exercise power

---

10   Mann, *Sources of Social Power*, 2:2.

11   For definitions of these conceptual elements, see Mann, *Sources of Social Power*, 2: 6-10.

12   Ibid., 6.

13   In volume 1 of *The Sources of Social Power* there is a slightly different formulation. Instead of saying that the overall structure of society is *determined* by power organizations, Mann writes, "Societies are *constituted of* multiple overlapping and intersecting sociospatial networks of power" (*Sources of*

through their ability to shape and control values and beliefs, to create the parameters within which individuals make choices, and to enforce specific patterns of property relations; but it is power organizations as such that are the fundamental determinants of social structure in society.

Mann does not provide an extended metatheoretical defense of this view. I think it is fair to say that he believes that the empirical insights of his historical research provide the best defense of this model. Nevertheless, rudiments of such a defense are implicit in his analysis. Mann's approach is a variety of what might be termed an agency-centered framework of social analysis. The central idea is this: people act to achieve goals by deploying various kinds of capabilities. They can do so as individuals interacting strategically with other individuals or through their involvement in collective organizations. The creation, reproduction, and transformation of social structure is the result of such strategies. Mann's foundational proposition, then, asserts that it is the collective organizational form of pursuing goals through the use of power, rather than simply the interactions of individuals within social relations, that is decisive for explaining social structure and social change. Why should we believe this? Mann's answer is, basically, that organizations are able much more effectively to mobilize resources of all sorts in pursuit of goals than are individuals, and that they therefore have a much greater potential impact on the reproduction and transformation of all social institutions. The explanatory primacy of the four sources of power as deployed by organizations, Mann writes,

> comes not from the strength of human desires for ideological, economic, military, or political satisfaction, but from the particular *organizational means* each possesses to attain human goals, whatever these may be ... The four sources of social power offer

---

Social Power, 1:1). There are three rhetorical shifts from the earlier to the later formulation: first, the earlier formulation refers to "societies," whereas the second refers to "the structure of society"; second, the earlier formulation invokes the general idea of networks of power, whereas the later formulation focuses on power organizations; and third, the earlier formulation talks of societies as "constituted of" power networks, whereas the later formulation talks about power organizations "determining" social structure. It is not clear whether these different formulations are meant to signal some change in meaning. In any case, I will assume that saying that the structure of society is "determined" by power organizations means roughly the same thing as saying that societies are "constituted" by such organizations (or, more broadly by "networks of power").

alternative organizational means of social control. In various times and places each has offered enhanced capacity for organization that has enabled the form of its organization to dictate for a time the form of societies at large.[14]

Because of this logistical efficacy,

> The struggle to control ideological, economic, military, and political power organizations provides the central drama of social development. Societies are structured primarily by entwined ideological, economic, military, and political power . . . The four power sources offer distinct, potentially powerful organizational means to humans pursuing their goals."[15]

The general, abstract claim that "power organizations determine the overall structure of society," then, is a synoptic statement of the idea that social structures are the result of goal-directed actions, and that organizational devices for such action will have the most pervasive, long-term effects.

Mann's general framework of sociological analysis thus starts from a root idea that is quite similar to that of rational choice theory: people have goals and deploy resources strategically to accomplish them. But he rejects the individualistic way of elaborating this idea by insisting that the core actors that matter in shaping the structured properties of societies are not individuals as such, but individuals combined into power organizations. These power organizations, deploying the four sources of power and varying along the three dichotomies of organizational variation, explain both the principle structural features within which individuals live their lives, and the dynamic processes of large-scale trajectories of social change.

3. CLASSES AS ECONOMIC POWER ORGANIZATIONS

Within Mann's general framework of organizational materialism, classes are not sets of locations-within-social-relations, nor are they demographically closed, economically hierarchical groups; rather, they are a particular kind of collective actor formed into organizations that deploy economic power resources. Nowhere, however, does he provide a compact definition of class organizations so that

---

14   Mann, *Sources of Social Power*, 1: 2–3.
15   Ibid., 122:9.

one would know for sure that a particular economic power organization was an instance of a "class" organization as opposed to some other kind of economic power organization. The closest thing to this is a brief discussion in which Mann differentiates classes from two other kinds of collective actors based on economic power: sections and segments. It is worth quoting this passage in full:

> All complex societies have unequally distributed control over economic resources. Thus classes have been ubiquitous. Marx distinguished most basically between those who own or control the means of production, distribution, and exchange and those who control only their own labor—and we can obviously go into more detail distinguishing further classes with more particular rights over economic resources. Such classes can also be broken down into smaller, sectional actors, like a skilled trade or a profession. Classes relate to each other vertically—class A is above class B, exploiting it. Yet other groups conflict horizontally with one another. Following anthropological usage I term such groups "segments." The members of a segmental group are drawn from various classes—as in a tribe, lineage, patron-client network, locality, industrial enterprise, or the like. Segments compete horizontally with each other. Classes, sections, and segments all cross-cut and weaken one another in human societies.[16]

In this formulation, classes are economic power organizations whose economic power is derived from "rights over economic resources." "Sections" are subdivisions of classes: they acquire their conceptual status as a "section" by virtue of being nested within a class organization. The only reason why sections are not themselves an instance of a class organization is because they are subdivisions of a more encompassing class organization. If that more encompassing power organization were to disappear as a collective actor while the sectional organizations remained intact, they would—presumably—become "classes."[17] Segments, on the

---

16   Ibid., 2:7–8.

17   If this interpretation of the contrast between sectional power organization and class power organization is correct, then it is not entirely clear what Mann means when he writes: "We can obviously go into more detail distinguishing further classes with more particular rights over economic resources" (*Sources of Social Power*, 2:8) It would seem that "more particular rights" would be nested within "more general rights," and thus these more "detailed" classes would have the equivalent status as sections.

other hand, are economic power organizations that combine heterogeneous sets of rights over economic resources. This is what it
means to say that segments cross-cut classes.

Understood in this way, the core agenda of class analysis is
understanding the patterns of formation of classes as power organizations and how these have developed historically. In most of
human history, Mann argues, classes were not the main form of
economic power organization. Until the modern era

> segments and sections . . . usually predominated over classes. Classes
> were generally only "latent": owners, laborers, and others struggled,
> but usually semicovertly, intensively, confined to an everyday local
> level. Most extensive struggle was between segments.[18]

The main story about classes in the course of the development of
capitalism is the gradual emergence of class as the predominant
form of economic power organization, first among capitalists and
then later among laborers. While no capitalist society reached the
point predicted by Marx of fully polarized, symmetrical, extensive
class organizations engaged in "a head-on dialectical struggle with
one another"—sectional divisions and segmental rivals always
played an important role in power struggles—capitalist development did generate a predominance of class organization and at least
some tendencies towards extensive forms of class conflict.[19]

Mann's class analysis is thus firmly anchored in the third conceptual cluster of class analysis discussed earlier. But he goes further,
rejecting the usefulness of any systematic analysis of the objective
relational aspects of class structures. In commenting on Marx's
discussion of capitalists and proletarians as economically defined
classes, Mann writes:

> Such classes might be considered "objective," but we might choose
> to define classes by other "objective" criteria. So-called industrial
> society theorists distinguish classes according to their specialized role
> in the division of labor, which method yields numerous occupational
> classes. Weberians identify classes according to market capacities,
> producing many classes based on ownership of property, scarce job
> skills, professional powers, and educational levels. How do we
> choose among these equally "objective" schemes?

---

18 Mann, *Sources of Social Power*, 2:8.
19 Ibid., 2:26.

. . . The economic without the organizational criterion gives only what I term "latent class"—corresponding roughly to the term "objective class" or "class in itself." *Such a latent class is of little sociological interest.* Theorists may develop what analytical categories they like, as ideal types, but only some of these help explain the real world. If classes are significant power actors in the real world they must be organized, extensively or politically. (italics added)[20]

This is a telling passage. In effect Mann argues that much of what class and stratification analysts study is of little sociological interest because they focus on the effects of objective properties of the locations of people within social structures rather than the effects of collectively organized power actors. Such research is, at best, a sideshow; all of the real causal action lies with collectively organized power actors.

Mann's dismissal of the analysis of objective properties of class relations would be compelling if it were the case that there were no systematic causal connections between these properties and the formation the collective power actors that are Mann's central concern. If there was a more or less random relationship between the structure of social relations and the formation of collective actors—i.e., that the probabilities of the latter were unaffected by the configurations of the former—then the study of "latent" classes would have little relevance for the broad problems Mann addresses. But if the objective properties of the "social relations of production" make certain kinds of power organizations more likely and sustainable than others, class analysis should pay attention to both of these conceptual clusters. This, in fact, is precisely what Mann does when he gets down to the business of explaining the formation of the middle class as a collective actor in the nineteenth century.

---

20 Ibid. Mann's position here is similar in some ways to Adam Przeworski's view that "[c]lasses are not prior to political and ideological practice. Any definition of people as workers—or individuals, Catholics, French-speakers, Southerners, and the like—is necessarily immanent to the practice of political forces engaged in struggles to maintain or in various ways alter the existing social relations. Classes are organized and disorganized as outcomes of continuous struggles . . . The ideological struggle is a struggle *about* class before it is a struggle *among* classes." Adam Przeworski, *Capitalism and Social Democracy*, New York: Cambridge University Press, 1985, 70.

4. THE MIDDLE CLASS

Mann sums up his analysis of the middle class in nineteenth-century capitalism by stating:

> A middle class emerged with a distinctive relation to power resources with its own organizations and collective consciousness—a relation summed up by the "impure" dual formula: segmental middling participation in organizations generated by the diffused circuits of capital and more independent, varied participation in the authoritative nation-state.[21]

As dictated by his programmatic formulation, the pivotal criterion here is "participation in organizations." The resulting class is "impure" because it contains heterogeneous "internal fractions each with distinct power organizations,"[22] and because the power organizations of the middle class are themselves deeply entwined with power organizations of the capitalist class and with the state (a nonclass, political power organization). Impure or not, the middle class formed power organizations that played an increasingly crucial role in a wide range of political struggles in the course of the nineteenth century.

True to his explanatory program, Mann's analysis of the middle class is thus anchored in the problem of its formation as a collective actor. But, unlike his programmatic declarations, he does not treat the investigation of the "objective" properties of the economic location of these fractions of the middle class as being "of little sociological interest." Indeed, it is the careful investigation of the location of the middle class within the relational aspects of production and exchange that constitutes the core of Mann's *explanation* of the formation of these disparate social categories into a single, collectively organized class.

Mann distinguishes three fractions of the middle class: "1. The *petite bourgeoisie*: proprietors of small, familial business. 2. *Careerists*: wage or salaried employees moving up corporate and bureaucratic hierarchies. 3. *Professionals*: 'learned,' collectively organized occupations licensed by the state."[23] The problem, then, is to explain why people in these three categories are formed into

---

21 Mann, *Sources of Social Power*, 2:590.

22 Ibid., 2:547.

23 Ibid., 2:549ff.

a single class, albeit a class with internal fractions. On the face of it, this might seem implausible: the petite bourgeoisie are the self-employed and small owners; careerists are salaried employees, typically in corporations; and professionals are highly credentialed occupations with considerable autonomy. Mann argues that two processes forge these categories into a single class: (1) the objective properties of the economic situation of people in all three of these categories deeply tie their life chances to "circuits of capital"; (2) the relationship of these three categories to the state forges them into a particular kind of ideological and political citizenship that further integrates the categories into a single middle class. Here I focus mainly on the first of these causal processes.

Mann identifies three economic processes that integrate all three of these fractions into a single class:

1. *Links to economic hierarchy.* "The three fractions participate in economic hierarchy."[24] This is most obvious for careerists: "the careerist's loyalty is rational and sincere. Capitalism works, especially for himself . . . As individuals some careerists succeed and others fail, but collectively they have staffed the organizations responsible for most of the sustained economic development of the twentieth century."[25] It is less obvious for the petite bourgeoisie, since many small employers are hurt by competition from capitalist corporations and squeezed by capitalist financial institutions. Yet, Mann argues, "Among the petite bourgeoisie growth aspirations also integrate. Most small business gets bigger upgrading its clientele, developing symbiosis with bigger business and wealthier consumers."[26] As for professionals, for most professions "client demand has come from capitalist and middle class families and businesses." This is especially true for lawyers who "participate diffusely in the circuits of capital," but even in the case of professions less directly serving the needs of capital "professional powers are partly expressed through quasi-capitalist enterprises or quasi-state departments."[27] In short, for all three fractions, Mann argues, the life chances of individuals are shaped by their connection to capitalist hierarchy.

24 Ibid., 2:570.
25 Ibid., 2:563.
26 Ibid., 2:570.
27 Ibid., 2:569.

2. *Consumption patterns.* "The middle class consumes distinctively (as neo-Weberians note)."[28] The common life chances derived from participation in hierarchy generate relatively high incomes, which underwrite distinctive, comfortable standards of living. Common consumption standards in turn help forge a sense of common position and also underwrite intermarriage and other forms of demographic class formation.

3. *Capital investments.* "The three fractions can convert income into small investment capital." This potential clearly differentiated the economic situation of the middle class in the nineteenth century from the working class, since workers rarely were able to accumulate stable savings.

Taken together, "whatever their peculiarities and internal diversity, the three fractions of the middle class have shared diffused capitalist participation in segmental hierarchies, class consumption badges, and conversion of surplus income into supplementary investment capital."[29] Or, to put it in more standard language paraphrasing Weber, in spite of apparent differences, these three fractions share common causal components of their life chances based on their location within capitalist markets and employment relations.

What Michael Mann has done here, then, is argue against theorists who see the material interests of these categories as sufficiently different as to generate distinct locations within a class structure. His arguments may or may not be persuasive,[30] but the form of the argument is precisely the sort of argument about "latent" classes that he regards as being of "little sociological interest." He proposes objective criteria for deciding whether or not two apparently dissimilar social locations should be treated as subcategories of a larger, conceptually coherent aggregation, and then defends a specific account of such classification. Virtually all of this part of his

---

28   Ibid., 2:570.

29   Ibid., 2:571.

30   It is not my purpose here to evaluate the details of these arguments. The least persuasive, I think, is the claim that in the nineteenth century the petite bourgeoisie—defined as small businesses and self-employed manual workers—was, as a whole, part of the same class as corporate managers and liberal professions. The largest segment of the petite bourgeoisie were farmers, and it seems fairly strained to regard the economically conditioned life chances of small farmers as basically similar to these other categories, even if many farmers might have had "growth aspirations" linked to market performance.

discussion of the middle class is concerned with identifying the pivotal causal forces that shape the life chances of people within capitalist economies, and on this basis he argues that the petite bourgeoisie, careerists, and professionals are three components of a middle class. None of this discussion directly concerns their formation into a common, distinctively middle class collective actor as such.

One could respond that I have misrepresented this part of Mann's analysis, since from the outset he argues that the formation of the middle class as an integrated, class-based collective actor cannot be explained simply by these economic factors, but also involves the construction of a specific kind of middle class ideological and political citizenship. These political and ideological elements are indeed central to his narrative. But, I would argue, the claim that the resulting collective actors are indeed *classes* is based not on the political and ideological processes as such, but on the prior establishment of the claim that these categories share roughly common life chances forged within the economic conditions of work and consumption. It is not an accident that in his elaboration of the problem of the middle class Mann spends the first half of the chapter discussing these objective material conditions and their effects, and only after he has established this commonality of class conditions does he shift to the discussion of political and ideological factors that forge a stronger form of collective organization and action.

5. MULTIPLE LEVELS OF CLASS ANALYSIS

My central criticism of Michael Mann's *announced* strategy of class analysis is his dismissal of the relevance of studying what he calls "latent" classes. Rather than insisting that classes should be understood exclusively as organized power actors, I believe that our deeper theoretical understanding of these historical processes is advanced by trying to systematically bring together the three conceptual clusters of class analysis: classes as social structure, classes as social groups, and classes as organized social actors. This is, in fact, closer to what Mann actually does in his specific historical investigations than one would expect given his abstract prescriptions. His arguments about latent classes, however, are less carefully developed and the conceptual foundations less clear because, I think, Mann regards debate over the objective properties of latent classes to be largely a waste of time.

Mann's objections to the study of latent classes comes, at least in part, from his rejection of the classical *class-in-itself/class-for-itself* conceptualization of class. In that understanding of class, there is a one-to-one mapping of classes formed as collective actors and the categories within objectively defined class structures, combined with a teleological theory of the process by which the structurally defined classes are transformed into classes as collective actors. Mann correctly rejects all such teleological views and the simple class correspondence principles that accompany them.

To reject Mann's programmatic position, however, does not mean reverting to the teleology of class-in-itself/class-for-itself. One can believe that class relations and class structures are real and generate real effects without also believing in any one-to-one mapping between the complex structure of class relations and the formation of collective actors. Adam Przeworski, who, like Mann, anchors his class analysis in the problem of collective class actors and categorically rejects the class-in-itself/class-for-itself framework, states the problem well: "Positions within social relations constitute limits upon the success of political practice, but within these historically concrete limits the formation of classes-in-struggle is determined by struggles that have class formation as their effect."[31] If this claim is correct—if the structure of class relations imposes limits on possible formations of collective class actors—it is worthwhile to try to understand the general properties of these sets of class relations (class structures) that generate these limits.

My work on contradictory class locations is one strategy of doing this. I have argued that individuals are located in complex ways within the social relations of production. There are a variety of dimensions of this complexity:

• Complexity in the way *jobs* are located within the social relations of production: in particular, jobs are relationally defined with respect to both capitalist property relations and authority relations.

• Complexity in the way market relations are linked to employment relations: this is especially relevant for the problem of skills and expertise.

---

31 Przeworski, *Capitalism and Social Democracy*, 67.

- Complexity in the temporal aspects of class locations: this corresponds closely to Mann's discussion of careerist positions and Goldthorpe's notion of the service class.

- Complexity in the way individuals are linked to class relations through family and kinship: this is especially salient in households in which both husband and wife are in the labor force.

- Complexity generated by the way people within what I term "privileged locations within the process of exploitation" are able to capitalize their surplus income in the form of capital investments.

An individual's objective location-within-class-relations is determined by the totality of these complexities. These locations are not "classes"; they are locations within complexly structured class relations. A class structure is defined by the set of such locations within some appropriate unit of analysis.

A central goal of class analysis, then, is to understand the causal connections between the objectively defined properties of class relations on the one hand, and class formation and organized class struggle, on the other. There is no necessary reason, of course, that in pursuing this task one should focus one's energy on the elaboration of the structural class concepts. It may well be that most of the interesting action lies in all of the contingent political and ideological processes that mediate the effects of class relations rather than in the class relations themselves. But equally, there is no reason to reject the task of refining the class structural concepts.

PART 2

Class in the Twenty-First Century

6

OCCUPATIONS AS MICRO-CLASSES: DAVID GRUSKY AND KIM WEEDEN'S RECONFIGURATION OF CLASS ANALYSIS

Beginning in the late 1990s, David Grusky and Kim Weeden, in collaboration with a number of their colleagues, have developed a strikingly original framework for class analysis.[1] At its core, their proposal is to build class analysis on the basis of highly disaggregated occupational categories. They call these categories "micro-classes" in contrast to the typical "big classes" constructed by sociologists working in the Marxist and Weberian traditions. Grusky has referred to this conceptualization of class as a neo-Durkheimian approach to class analysis in recognition of Durkheim's understanding of occupations as the fundamental unit of economic activity, solidarity, and interests in developed capitalist economies.[2]

---

1   The main publications in this stream of work are David B. Grusky and Jesper B. Sørensen, "Can Class Analysis Be Salvaged?" *American Journal of Sociology* 103: 5, March 1998, 1187–234; David B. Grusky, Kim A. Weeden, and Jesper B. Sørensen, "The Case for Realism in Class Analysis," *Political Power and Social Theory* 14, 2000, 291–305; David B.Grusky and Jesper B. Sørensen, "Are There Big Social Classes?" in *Social Stratification: Class, Race, and Gender in Sociological Perspective*, 2nd edn., ed. David B. Grusky, Boulder: Westview Press, 2001, 183–94; David B. Grusky and Kim A. Weeden, "Decomposition without Death: A Research Agenda for a New Class Analysis," *Acta Sociologica* 44: 3, 2001, 203–18; David Grusky, "Foundations of a Neo-Durkheimian Class Analysis," in *Approaches to Class Analysis*, ed. Erik Olin Wright, Cambridge: Cambridge University Press, 2005, 51–81; Kim A. Weeden and David B. Grusky, "Are There Any Social Classes at All?" *Research in Social Stratification and Mobility* 22, 2005, 3–56; Kim A. Weeden and David B. Grusky, "The Case for a New Class Map," *American Journal of Sociology* 111: 1, July 2005, 141–212; Kim A. Weeden and David B. Grusky, "The Three Worlds of Inequality," *American Journal of Sociology* 117: 6, May 2012, 1723-1785.

2   Grusky's characterization of his approach as neo-Durkheimian is most clearly developed in "Foundations of a Neo-Durkheimian Class Analysis." His treatment of occupations as the core basis for solidarities in the division of

The Grusky-Weeden approach does not fit neatly into the general framework of an integrated class analysis proposed in chapter 1 of this book, so in this chapter I propose a different way of connecting their conceptualization of class to Marxist and Weberian class analysis. As in chapter 1, I argue that, rather than seeing these as rival schools of class analysis, they tap different kinds of causal mechanisms that are appropriate for different contexts of analysis. Section 1 lays out the central arguments of the Grusky-Weeden model. Section 2 elaborates a strategy for understanding different contexts of power and interest conflicts that are relevant to class analysis. Section 3 then connects this model to Marxist, Weberian, and the Grusky-Weeden neo-Durkheimian class analysis.

I. THE GRUSKY-WEEDEN MICRO-CLASS MODEL

Before discussing the theoretical foundations of the Grusky-Weeden model, a brief comment is needed about their use of the word "class." The heart of the Grusky-Weeden model is the exploration of the importance of disaggregated occupations for explaining a wide range of phenomena that are also often studied using conventional class categories. One possible criticism of their work is their use of the term "class"—albeit with the prefix "micro." Why not just stick to the more transparent term "occupation" and frame the discussion as occupational analysis versus class analysis? While I personally think it would have been better to use the term "occupational analysis" for their framework, I don't think that the main issues in play here are about words and I will not quibble with their terminology. The critical issue is whether they have identified real causal processes in the world that matter and how these processes are related to more conventionally understood classes. In my exploration of their approach to class analysis I therefore adopt their convention of referring to their categories as micro-classes in contrast to the "big classes" of most sociologists.

Grusky and Weeden's model of class is animated by a very general question: What is it about a person's location within a

---

labor differs from Durkheim's analysis by dropping the idea of the functional interdependence among occupations, collective consciousness, and other elements of Durkheim's theory of organic solidarity. It retains an affiliation with Durkheim in its focus on occupations within the division of labor as the central units of coherent social organization in modern society, but largely disengages from Durkheim's broader agenda of social theory.

system of production that best explains the sorts of things theorists of class have always wanted to explain: life chances, income, political attitudes and behavior, cultural tastes, etc.? There must be, they reason, something about the homogeneity of interests, experiences, and other conditions connected to a location that generates homogeneity of these outcomes. This intuition closely follows Pierre Bourdieu's well-known formulation that "homogeneous conditions of existence impose homogeneous conditionings and produce homogeneous systems of dispositions capable of generating similar practices."[3] Most sociologists see this homogeneity as generated within "big classes." Grusky and Weeden argue that this homogenization of conditions operates much more intensively at the level of detailed occupations.

The pivotal concept within this approach to class is "occupation." Grusky writes:

> The starting point for a modern Durkheimian analysis is . . . the "unit occupation," which may be defined as a grouping of technically similar jobs that is institutionalized in the labor market through such means as (a) an association or union, (b) licensing or certification requirements, or (c) widely diffused understandings (among employers, workers, and others) regarding efficient or otherwise preferred ways of organizing production and dividing labor. The unit occupations so defined are often generated through jurisdictional struggles between competing groups over functional niches in the division of labor.[4]

Occupation, defined in this way, is for Grusky and Weeden a *realist* category that defines a person's location within a system of production. The realism of this category is crucial here: the categories are institutionalized in the actual practices of employers and associations; they are not simply analytical categories produced by academics: "The homogeneity of big classes arises because sociologists attempt analytically to combine jobs or occupations into coherent groups, whereas the homogeneity of occupations arises because employers (and, to some extent, workers) fashion jobs that correspond with ideal-typical occupational templates."[5]

---

3   Pierre Bourdieu, *Distinction: A Social Critique of the Judgment of Taste*, Cambridge, MA: Harvard University Press: 1984, 104, quoted in Weeden and Grusky, "The Three Worlds of Inequality," 1728.
4   Grusky, "Foundations of a Neo-Durkheimian Class Analysis," 66.
5   Weeden and Grusky, "Case for a New Class Map," 153.

They see the reliance on invented analytical categories by most sociologists as one of the failings of class analysis that focuses exclusively on "big classes":

> Class analysis has become disconnected from the institutional realities of contemporary labor markets, with scholars positing class mappings that are represented as analytically meaningful even though they have no legal or institutional standing and are not salient to employers, workers, or anyone else (save a small cadre of academics).[6]

Employers advertise jobs in terms of occupations. Workers and their organizations fight over the jurisdictional boundaries of occupations. People answer the question "what do you do?" by naming an occupation. None of this is true for "big classes." Whether the big classes are themselves defined as aggregations of occupations—such as professionals or skilled manual workers—or are defined in terms of domination and exploitation, they remain analytical abstractions created by the theoretical reasoning of analysts rather than categories that are formally institutionalized in the protocols of organizations and the everyday practices and understanding of real people.[7]

The Grusky-Weeden model of micro-class analysis, then, argues that disaggregated occupations constitute the real boundaries of locations within production that have sufficient internal homogeneity to generate the outcomes of interest to class analysis: "Occupations act collectively on behalf of their members, extract rent and exploit non-members, shape life chances and lifestyles, and otherwise behave precisely as class theorists have long thought aggregate classes should."[8]

With this definition, there are hundreds, perhaps even thousands, of micro-classes in a large, complex society such as the United States. In their empirical work, Grusky and Weeden differentiate

---

6 Grusky, "Foundations of a Neo-Durkheimian Class Analysis," 65.

7 A case can be made that at least some theorists of "big classes" are as realist in their construction of categories as are Grusky and Weeden, but that they are just realists about different phenomena. Such things as ownership of the means of production, or being able to hire and fire an employee, or selling labor power on a labor market and following orders from a boss identify real mechanisms embedded in social relations. The fact that occupations may be combined into larger aggregate categories as a way of grouping people with respect to these mechanisms is a strategy of operationalization, but does not imply that the underlying concept isn't realist.

8 David Grusky, "Foundations of a Neo-Durkheimian Class Analysis," 67.

126 occupations, but it is largely data constraints that limit them to this number. At one point in their analysis they even suggest that academic sociologists and economists constitute two different micro-classes.[9] The critical point is that the number of micro-classes is a consequence of the number of institutionally grounded, internally homogeneous occupational categories that exist in a society.

The next step in the argument is to specify the actual causal mechanisms through which these effects are generated. In different papers, Grusky and Weeden identify different clusters of mechanisms or processes that are closely tied to disaggregated occupations, but mostly they discuss three clusters of such mechanisms:

1. *Allocation*, both selection into an occupation by employers and self-selection by job-seekers.

2. *Social conditioning*, including education and training; interactional closure (higher density of repeated social interactions among people within an occupation than across the occupational boundary); interest formation; and what can be broadly called the occupational environment, which generates occupation-specific lifestyles and social attitudes.

3. *Institutionalization of conditions*, especially through formal licensing, employer protocols in defining jobs, and practices of occupational associations.[10]

These are all the sorts of processes that many writers on class often invoke to explain how class generates effects. Once again, the claim by Grusky and Weeden is that these processes operate more coherently and powerfully within occupationally defined micro-classes than within the more aggregated categories of conventional class analysis: "selection, socialization, and other homogeneity-inducing mechanisms operate with special force at the occupation level, implying that conventional big-class models will conceal a substantial portion of the structure at the site of production."[11]

---

9 The argument is basically that the sharply different political attitudes of academic sociologists and economists reflect three specific mechanisms connected to micro-classes: self-selection, training, and interactional closure. See Weeden and Grusky, "Case for a New Class Map," 191–2.

10 Ibid., 149–53; and Weeden and Grusky, "Three Worlds of Inequality," 1728–30.

11 Weeden and Grusky, "Case for a New Class Map," 149.

With these arguments in hand, Grusky and Weeden and their collaborators have set out to empirically compare the explanatory power of big classes and micro-classes and to see how the relative strength of their effects has changed over time. While I will not review the details of these complex empirical investigations here, there are two general results of importance. First, micro-classes generally have greater explanatory power than any of the models of big classes for a very wide range of individual level outcomes. The only variables for which big-class models do reasonably well relative to micro-class are those most closely connected to life chances: education, income, and wealth. Second, over the past several decades there has been a general trend in the weakening of the effects of big classes, except for the association of big classes with life chances, whereas in general there have been no such trends of diminishing effects for micro-classes. The final conclusion of their investigations, then, is that sociologists interested in the consequences of how people are located within a system of production should devote their primary attention to occupationally defined micro-classes rather than the traditional big classes.

2. THE STRATEGIC CONTEXTS OF INTEREST-CONFLICTS FOR CLASS ANALYSIS

I do not challenge the central thrust of Grusky and Weeden's empirical analyses. While it is always possible to raise objections to specific measures and strategies of analysis, I think their basic claims are probably robust: for purposes of explaining variations across individuals in lifestyles, tastes, and political and social attitudes, micro-classes have a more systematic effect than do more aggregated categories. Even for explaining income and wealth, which Grusky and Weeden call "the structural backbone to big classes," micro-classes have substantial effects after controlling for the effects of big classes. What I want to explore is a way of connecting these results and arguments about micro-classes to the central theoretical agenda in Marxist and Weberian currents of class analysis. To do so, it will be useful to elaborate a way of thinking about the strategic contexts of political conflicts introduced by Robert Alford and Roger Friedland.[12]

---

12 See Robert Alford and Roger Friedland, *The Powers of Theory: Capitalism, the State, and Democracy*, Cambridge Unviersity Press, 1985, 6–11.

Alford and Friedland develop a typology of political struggles in capitalist societies over three different forms of power: systemic power, institutional power, and situational power.[13] They use the metaphor of a game to illuminate the distinction across these three kinds of conflicts. Struggles involving systemic power can be thought of as struggles over *what game should be played*; struggles over institutional power are over the *rules of a given game*; and struggles involving situational power concern *moves within a fixed set of rules*. Think about this in terms of a sport: different games give athletes with different physical characteristics different advantages and disadvantages, and thus they have interests in playing one kind of game over another. Consider two athletes, one 1.7 meters tall who has great strength and weighs 150 kilos, the other 2.1 meters tall with great agility and stamina. They live in a world where they can play one sport of the only two that are allowed: American football or basketball. Clearly, if basketball becomes hegemonic, the heavy athlete becomes marginalized. Once playing a particular game, occasionally the rules themselves are called into question, and changes in the rules can also favor athletes with different attributes. For example, the change in the rules of basketball that allowed players to touch the rim of the hoop, which in turn made dunking possible, added to the advantages of height. And finally, given a set of fixed rules, the players of the game adopt specific training regimes and strategies in their plays within the game. Dynamically, what can then happen is that players invent all sorts of new strategies and ways of training designed to exploit specific opportunities within the existing rules of the game. In time these altered moves in the game begin to change the feel of the game in various ways. Sometimes these changes are seen as eroding the spirit or integrity of the game by spectators, players, or "the powers that be" that govern the rules of the game. This perception can trigger changes in the rules. Changes in the height of the pitching mound or strike zone in baseball to alter the balance of power between pitcher and batter, or changes in the rules about defenses against the pass in American football are familiar examples. Rules are altered to address what are seen as problems in the balance of power between players in the moves of the game.

Politics, then, can be analogously understood as directed at

---

13 Alford and Friedland use the term "structural power" instead of "institutional power" for the second of these forms of power, but since they are concerned with the kind of power that operates especially in state institutions, institutional power seems a clearer label.

different levels of the game we call a social system. *Revolutionary* versus *counterrevolutionary* politics constitute struggles over what game should be played. In some times and places this was seen by political forces as capitalism versus socialism. *Reformist* versus *reactionary* politics within capitalist societies constitute struggles over the rules of the game of capitalism: What kinds of regulations of markets and sectors are permissible? How organized and coordinated should be the principal collective actors in capitalism? What kind of insurance against risks should be provided by the state? The game of capitalism can be played under a wide variety of rules, whose terms matter a lot insofar as they give advantages and disadvantages to different kinds of players who play the game; but these all constitute varieties of capitalism. Finally, *interest group* politics constitute struggles between social forces engaged in moves within a fixed set of rules over immediate interests.[14] Classic examples would be conflicts over spending priorities, tax rates, levels of state subsidies and specific provisions in a tax code. The logic of this game metaphor for mapping politics is presented in Table 6.1.

Level of System at which Conflict Is Focused	Game Metaphor	Political Form of Conflict	Stakes in the Conflict	Form of Class Analysis
System level	What game to play	Revolutionary versus counter-revolutionary	Capitalism versus socialism	Marxist
Institutional level	Rules of the game	Reformist versus reactionary	Varieties of capitalism	Weberian
Situational level	Moves in the game	Interest group politics	Immediate economic interests	Durkheimian

Table 6.1. The Game Metaphor for Mapping Politics and Class Analysis

14 Alford and Friedland refer to political conflicts at the level of moves in the game as *liberal* versus *conservative* politics, in traditional American usage of these terms in which both liberals and conservatives accept the basic parameters of the American variety of capitalism and mostly engage in struggles over marginal changes. In the present context it is simpler to refer to conflict within fixed rules as "interest group politics" in which there are no clearly defined ideological differences.

Real societies are, of course, much more complex than represented in this model. The social system that constitutes a society is not a single, integrated totality in which everything fits together under a unified set of rules. A society is not a system in the same way that an organism is a system. It is more like the loosely coupled system of an ecosystem in which a variety of processes interact in relatively contingent ways. Multiple "games" are being played simultaneously, often with inconsistent rules. Furthermore, it is not always so clear how to draw the distinction between a change in the "rules of the game" and a change from one game to another. It is always possible that the cumulative effect of small changes in rules can alter the nature of the game to such an extent that eventually a new game is being played. The idea of "evolutionary socialism" can be interpreted as a transformation of the inner nature of the game of capitalism by gradual changes in its rules. Nevertheless, for many purposes it is possible to talk about a dominant game with its internal rules and moves, and this can help to clarify the conceptual status of different currents of class analysis.

3. THE CLASS ANALYSIS OF GAMES, RULES, AND MOVES

The final column of Table 6.1 proposes a connection between Marxist, Weberian, and Durkheimian currents of class analysis and the society-as-game metaphor.[15]

Marxist class analysis is anchored in the problem of what game to play. At the very heart of Marxism as a social theory is the idea of emancipatory alternatives to capitalism. The fundamental point in analyzing class relations and both the individual practices and collective struggles that are linked to those class relations is to understand the nature of oppression within capitalism and the possibility of an emancipatory systemic alternative. The critique of capitalism in terms of exploitation, domination, and alienation is intimately connected to the Marxian concept of class, and the normative vision of a democratic and egalitarian alternative to capitalism is grounded in an account of the transformation of those class relations. Sometimes Marxist class analysis is elaborated in

---

15 In this discussion I do not distinguish between a tradition of class analysis and its "neo-" incarnation, even though in each case one can distinguish the kind of analysis directly present in the founding thinkers' own work from the subsequent, contemporary forms of analysis with a particular theoretical pedigree.

terms of a "grand narrative" about how the internal contradictions of the game of capitalism set in motion a dynamic that both makes the rules unstable and creates a collective agent capable of challenging the game itself; at other times the idea of an alternative is framed more modestly as an immanent possibility with a much more open-ended understanding of the collective agents that might strive to realize the alternative. But in any case it is the connections among class, the critique of capitalism, and emancipatory alternatives that animates Marxist class analysis.

Weberian class analysis is situated especially at the level of the rules of the game. Weber, indeed, only used the term "class" to describe inequalities generated through market interactions. For Weberians, capitalism is the only viable game in town, but its institutional rules can vary a lot. At stake in the variation of rules are the ways markets are organized and regulated and the ways in which players with different market capacities enter into exchange. The "big classes" of Weberian class analysis consist of people who are situated in different ways with respect to the possible capitalist rules of the game: rules governing labor organizing; rules governing the autonomy of capitalists in determining working conditions and employment rights; rules governing monopolies and competitive practices; rules governing access to education and job training; and so on. Some of these rules are created by states, others by firms, and still others by associations of various sorts. The purpose of class analysis, then, is to define the relevant categories of people similarly situated with respect to this variability in the rules of the game.

Durkheimian class analysis takes both capitalism and its specified institutional rules as given and focuses on the moves of players within the game. This is the world of micro-classes and fine-grained occupational differentiation. The interests of professors in research universities are different from those in community colleges, given the rules of the game in academic labor markets and the rules that govern working conditions, pay, and autonomy in these different kinds of institutions. Thus, people in these different micro-classes will develop different identities and make different moves for realizing their interests. Autoworkers, coal miners, truck drivers, and oil rig workers all operate under different labor market conditions, work in industries facing different kinds of sectoral competition and challenges, and have different collective capacities, and thus also face a different set of possible moves to realize their interests. So long as there is no real prospect of challenging the general rules of the game, their interests remain largely distinct and fragmented most of the time.

While each of these traditions of class analysis is anchored at a different level of the game, scholars working within each tradition to a greater or lesser extent venture out of their home territory for various purposes. Take Marxist class analysis: the rationale for Marxist class analysis is understanding the conditions for challenging and transcending capitalism, but Marxists are also deeply engaged in understanding struggles within capitalism that don't call the game into question. When Marxists analyze class struggles over rules of the game and moves in the game they often invoke differentiations in market position, employment relations, skills, and other characteristics that have a distinctively Weberian provenance, as well as occupational and sectoral specificities and solidarities that might even have a more Durkheimian character.

One way of interpreting the history of the past half-century is that there has been a gradual shift in the levels of the game at which, for many analysts, class analysis seems most relevant. In the 1960s and 1970s, class analysis was carried out at all three levels. In particular, the idea of Marxist class analysis anchored in the possibility of an alternative game seemed compelling to many people. Social and political movements embodied visions of an alternative, and the ideological battle between capitalism and various conceptions of socialism was an important dimension of political life, even in places like the United States where socialism was never a real political threat.

The rise of what came to be known as neoliberalism in the 1980s and then the end of the command-and-control systems that went under the banner of Communism largely removed the idea of an alternative to capitalism from the popular imagination. Thatcher proclaimed, "There is No Alternative" (TINA), and most academic sociologists seemed to agree. The idea of engaging in a class analysis at the level of the game itself seemed largely irrelevant outside of Marxist circles.

The decline in class analysis anchored in the problem of capitalism versus socialism coincided with the rise of the "varieties of capitalism" discussion within political economy and economic sociology. Class analysis continued to play an important explanatory role in understanding such variation in the rules of the game: neocorporatism in Northern Europe constituted a class compromise between organized labor and organized capital mediated by the state; disorganized capitalism of the English-speaking world reflected the relative weakness of trade unions. Many other varieties and permutations of these themes were discussed and interpreted as the result of the specific ways in which path-dependent processes of state formation, class formation, and other factors interacted. All these variations presupposed capitalism, but the variations still mattered a great deal and were reproduced over time. Class analysis thus continued at the level of the rules of the game.

In the second decade of the twenty-first century, in the face of the globalization and financialization of capitalist economies and the general triumph of neoliberal views of the optimal rules for managing the capitalist economy, there is much less emphasis on such variation. While these processes remain uneven internationally—Sweden and the United States are still different—many analysts believe that institutional configurations across capitalist economies are converging. TINA has spread from capitalism versus socialism to variation in the rules within capitalism itself. The death—or at least the decline—of class analysis embedded in the rules of the game is proclaimed; all that is left is class oriented to moves within the system.

In these terms, then, the Grusky-Weeden neo-Durkheimian model of micro-class analysis is firmly anchored in the arena of immediate economic interests within a single game with a stable set of largely uncontested rules. It is a class analysis for the era of triumphant neoliberalism.

Still, even in the current era, it is a mistake to treat the relevance of different levels of class analysis as simply a question of which type of class concept is "most important" in empirically explaining variations in some outcome across individuals. After all, even in this period of apparent dissolution of "big classes" there are times in which the rules of the game do become hotly contested and "big classes"—Marxian and Weberian classes—reemerge rapidly on the political stage. In the state of Wisconsin in 2011, the governor and state legislature introduced legislation to effectively destroy state-sector unions. This triggered massive demonstrations of teachers, nurses, police, firefighters, clerical workers, janitors, and virtually all other categories of state employees, plus many nonstate workers in solidarity, who saw this change in the rules-of-the-game as an assault on their common interests. The many micro-classes embedded in state employment suddenly congealed as a big class. The commonalty of interests *with respect to the rules of game* became more salient than the differentiated interests, education, and experiences connected to the specific occupations. Similarly, the rise of anti-neoliberal left politics in parts of Southern Europe in the face of prolonged austerity, and the victory of Syriza in Greece calling for a change in the rules of the game under which finance is regulated and income and wealth distribution are managed reflects the potential commonalty of class interests beyond the micro-classes of homogeneous "unit occupations." By identifying a common class enemy—finance capital and the state institutions that protect its interests—a broad class alliance is formed over contestation of the rules of the game of capitalism.

Variations across individuals in attitudes, tastes, lifestyles, life chances, friendships, and all of the other things Grusky and Weeden have explored are legitimate objects of class analysis, but by their very nature they are most closely tied to the micro-level of class analysis. If these are the only questions in which one is interested, then at this moment in history in the rich capitalist countries, micro-class analysis identifies the most systematic causal processes. However, if one's explanatory agenda concerns the potential for progressive social change in the rules of the game and emancipatory transformations of the game itself, it is critical to move beyond a primary concern with only the moves in the game. Individuals live their lives in class structures that shape their interests and subjectivity not only over what strategies are immediately optimal for securing their economic interests, but also over the rules of the game and the game itself. What we need is class analysis that moves across these levels of analysis and explores their interconnections.

7

THE AMBIGUITIES OF CLASS IN THOMAS PIKETTY'S *CAPITAL IN THE TWENTY-FIRST CENTURY*

Until quite recently, the only context in which inequality was treated as a "problem" in the mass media was in discussions of opportunities and rights. Equal opportunity and equal rights are deeply held American values, and certain kinds of inequalities were seen as violating these ideals. Racial and gender discrimination are problems because they create unfair competitive advantages for some people and disadvantages for others. They violate the ideal of a "level playing field." Poverty, of course, has for a very long time been publicly viewed as an important problem, but even here the main issue was not the magnitude of the *distance* between the poor and the rich, but the absolute material deprivations of people living in poverty, especially of children, and how this harms their life chances.[1] The War on Poverty led to the creation of an office of economic opportunity, rather than an office for the reduction of inequality. The way poverty constitutes a disadvantage was thus of great concern, but public discussion gave almost no attention to the degree of inequality of resources or conditions of life across the income distribution as such. Inequality was not an important, publicly recognized problem.

Even among scholars, discussions of inequality focused until recently almost entirely on social mobility and the social production

---

1 The concern with poverty as absolute deprivation is reflected in the way the poverty rate is measured in the United States. In most economically developed countries, the poverty rate is defined as the percentage of the population that falls below 50 percent of the median household income (adjusted for the size of the household). In the United States, in contrast, the poverty rate is defined as the percentage of the population falling below some absolute level of income defined as the "poverty line." In other countries, poverty is as much a question of levels of inequality in the bottom half of the income distribution as it is of material conditions of life at the bottom, whereas in the United States the focus is exclusively on the absolute level of income at the bottom.

of advantages and disadvantages. There was a great deal of concern about inequalities in the way people gained access to social positions, and certainly much research on how hard life was for people living below the poverty line, but almost no concern with the magnitude of inequalities among the positions themselves. Inequality was not an important, academically recognized problem.

This absence of discussion of the magnitude of the economic inequality was largely shared by both conservatives and liberals. To be concerned with the distance between the rich and the poor and the "middle class" seemed to reflect envy and resentment. As long as fortunes and high incomes were acquired legally—by playing by the rules—the degree of inequality this generated was unobjectionable. And what's more, as many people continue to argue even today, in the long run the high incomes of the wealthy benefit everyone, since it is out of this high income that new investments are made, and investment is a necessary condition for the proverbial rising tide that lifts all boats. Inequality was not an important, politically recognized problem.

This situation has changed dramatically. Today, talk about inequality in everywhere. The media, the academy, and politicians are giving increasing attention to the problem of inequality in its own right. The slogan of the Occupy Movement exemplifies this: the 1% versus the 99% indicates an antagonism between those at the very top of the income distribution and everyone else. Politicians and pundits speak of the dangers of increasing inequality. And scholars across disciplines have begun to study more systematically the changing contours of inequality.

This is the context in which Thomas Piketty's book *Capital in the Twenty-First Century* appeared, made such a stir, and became such an unlikely best seller.[2] The book is nearly 600 pages long (not counting notes and index and the online appendix) and published by an academic press. While the text is lively in places, it is nevertheless a serious scholarly work and written in a sober academic style—not the sort of book one expects to sell hundreds of thousands of copies. But it has. This success reflects the salience of inequality as an issue of broad public concern.[3]

---

2   Thomas Piketty, *Capital in the Twenty-First Century*, Cambridge, MA: Harvard University Press, 2013. Further citations of this work are given in the text.

3   *Capital in the Twenty-First Century* may also be the premier example of a book that is frequently purchased and rarely read all the way through. The mathematician Jordon Ellenberg has developed an indicator he calls the

Piketty's book is a built around the detailed analysis of the trajectory of two dimensions of economic inequality and their interconnection: income and wealth. Previous research on these issues has been severely hampered by lack of data on the richest people, both because so few people at the top are selected in survey samples, and because of top coding of income and wealth categories in most available data. It has also been impossible to systematically study the historical trajectory of inequality for more than a few decades because of the lack of any good data much before the middle of the twentieth century. Piketty has solved these problems to a significant extent by assembling a massive dataset that goes back to the early 1900s based on tax and estate data.[4]

In what follows I briefly outline the central arguments and conclusions of Piketty's analysis of the trajectories of income and wealth inequality. I then discuss the problematic role that class plays in his analysis.

THE TRAJECTORY OF INCOME INEQUALITY

The central observation that animates much of Piketty's analysis is the by now familiar U-shaped graph of the share of national income going to the top layers of the income distribution. A version of this graph is reproduced in Figure 7.1, showing the percentage of national income in the United States going to the richest 10 percent and 1 percent from 1913 to 2012. The share of the top decile in total national income (which includes capital gains) reached an early peak of 49 percent in 1928, then hovered around 45 percent

---

Hawking Index (named in honor of Steven Hawking's book *A Brief History of Time*), which identifies the five most popular passages in a book highlighted by Kindle book readers and listed on Amazon's "popular highlights" feature. The Hawking Index takes the average of the page numbers on which these occur and divides this by the number of pages in the book. This is a crude indicator of how far people read into a book. The index for many books is around 40 percent. For *A Brief History of Time* the figure is 6.6 percent. For Piketty's book it is only 2.4 percent. For a discussion, see Jordon Ellenberg, "The Summer's Most Unread Book Is . . .," http://www.wsj.com/articles/the-summers-most-unread-book-is-1404417569.

4   This dataset was developed jointly with another economist, Emmanuel Saëz. It is publicly available in a superbly designed public-access website, *The World Top Incomes Database,* http://topincomes.g-mond.parisschoolofeconomics.eu.

until World War II, when it dropped precipitously to around 35 percent and remained at that level for four decades until it began to rise rapidly in the 1980s, reaching a new high of just over 50 percent in 2012. It is worth stating this basic fact again: in 2012 the richest 10 percent of the population received just over half of all income generated in the US economy.

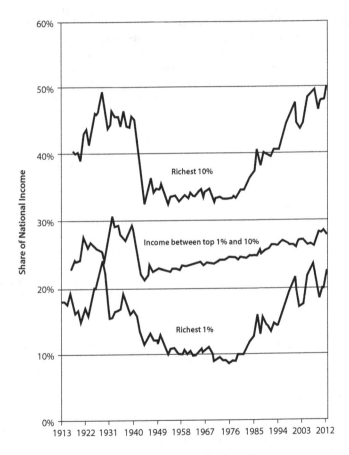

Figure 7.1. Share of National Income Going to Different High-Income Categories

Source: *The World Top Incomes Database*, http://topincomes.g-mond.parisschoolofeconomics.eu

This graph has undoubtedly received the most widespread publicity of any of the findings reported in Piketty's book.[5] But a second finding is of almost equal importance: the sharp rise in income share of the top income decile is largely the result of the dramatic rise in income share of the top 1 percent. Of the 17 percentage point increase in the share of income going to the top decile between 1975 and 2012, 13.6 percentage points (80 percent of the increase) went to the top 1 percent; the share going to the next richest 9 percent of the population only increased by 3.4 percentage points. Income is not merely becoming more concentrated at the top; it is being much more concentrated at the top of the top.

One final general finding on the trajectory of income inequality is important: while in every country studied income concentration at the top of the distribution declined sharply between the first decades of the twentieth century and the middle decades, countries varied considerably in the degree to which concentration increased at the end of the century. These trends are much more pronounced in the United States than in other countries, and quite muted in some.

How does Piketty explain these broad patterns? The crux of Piketty's analysis boils down to two main points. First, the rapid increase in concentration of income since the early 1980s is mainly the result of increases in super-salaries at the top of labor market earnings rather than the result of dramatic increases in income from capital ownership. This reflects the fact that the high income concentration in the early twentieth century had a very different underlying basis than in the present: in the earlier period, "income from capital (essentially dividends and capital gains) was the primary resource for the top 1 percent of the income hierarchy . . . In 2007 one has to climb to the 0.1 percent level before this is true" (p. 301). Second, the universal decline in income inequality in the middle of the twentieth century and the variations across countries in the extent of its increase at the end of the century largely stem from the exercise of power in various ways, not the "natural" workings of the market. Power exercised by the state is especially important in counteracting the inegalitarian forces of the market through taxation, income transfers, and a range of regulations. But

---

5 While I cannot prove it, I also suspect that versions of this graph have become the most widely reproduced statistical graphs in the history of social science. No one I have asked has come up with an alternative that has been disseminated nearly as widely.

also important is the power of what Piketty terms "supermanagers": "these top managers by and large have the power to set their own remuneration, in some cases without limit and in many cases without any clear relation to their individual productivity" (p. 24). The exercise of this power is constrained by social norms, which vary across countries, but is at most very weakly constrained by ordinary market processes.

THE TRAJECTORY OF WEALTH INEQUALITY

Piketty uses the terms "wealth" and "capital" interchangeably. He defines capital in a comprehensive manner as "the sum total of nonhuman assets that can be owned and exchanged on some market. Capital includes all forms of real property (including residential real estate) as well as financial and professional capital (plants, infrastructure, machinery, patents, and so on) used by firms and government agencies" (p. 46). Ownership of such assets is important to people for a variety of reasons, but especially because they generate a flow of income, which Piketty refers to as the return on capital. A fundamental feature of any market economy, then, is the division of the national income into the part that goes to owners of capital and the part that goes to labor.

The story Piketty tells about wealth inequality revolves around two basic observations: first, levels of concentration of wealth are always greater than concentrations of income; and second, the key to understanding the long-term trajectory of wealth concentration is what Piketty calls the capital/income ratio. The first of these observations is familiar: in the United States in 2010 the top decile of wealth holders owned 70 percent of all wealth, and the bottom half of wealth holders owned virtually nothing. As with the income distribution, during the middle of the twentieth century this concentration at the top declined from considerably higher levels in the beginning of the century—the top decile of wealth holders in the United States owned 80 percent of all wealth in 1910—but the rise in wealth concentration in recent decades has been more muted than the rise in income concentration. Still, the main point is that wealth concentration is always very high.

The second element of Piketty's analysis of wealth, the capital/income ratio, is less familiar. The capital/income ratio is a way of measuring the value of capital relative to the total income generated by an economy. In developed capitalist economies today, this ratio for privately owned capital is between 4:1 and 7:1, meaning that the value of capital is typically 4 to 7 times greater than the annual total income in the economy. Piketty's basic argument is that this ratio is the structural basis for the distribution of income between owners of capital and labor: all other things being equal, for a given return on capital, the higher this ratio, the higher proportion of national income will go to wealth holders.

A substantial part of Piketty's book is devoted to exploring the trajectory of the capital/income ratio and its ramifications. These analyses are undoubtedly the most difficult in the book. They involve discussion of the interconnections among economic growth rates, population growth, productivity, savings rates, taxation, and other factors. Without going into details of this analysis, a number of Piketty's conclusions are worth noting:

- As economic growth in the rich countries declines, the capital/income ratio is almost certain to rise unless counteracting political measures are taken.

- Over time, the rise in the capital/income ratio will increase the weight of inherited wealth among wealth holders, so concentrations of wealth, which have risen only modestly since the 1970s, should begin to rise more sharply in the course of the twenty-first century, perhaps even reaching the levels of the early twentieth century.

- Given the presence of unprecedented high concentrations of earnings among people who also receive considerable income from capital ownership, in the course of the coming decades concentrations of income are likely to exceed the levels of the nineteenth century.

The implication of these arguments is sobering: "The world to come may well combine the worst of the two past worlds: both very large inequality of inherited wealth and very high wage inequalities justified in terms of merit and productivity (claims with very little factual basis, as noted). Meritocratic extremism can thus lead to a race between supermanagers and rentiers to the detriment of those who are neither" (p. 417). The only remedy, Piketty argues, is political intervention to counteract these economic processes, since "there is no natural, spontaneous process to prevent destabilizing inegalitarian forces from prevailing permanently" (p. 21). His preferred policy solution is the introduction of a global tax on capital, but even if one is skeptical about that specific proposal, the basic message remains convincing: so long as market dynamics are left largely unhindered, the polarization of the extreme concentration of income and wealth is likely to deepen even further in the future.

AMBIGUOUS CLASS ANALYSIS

At first glance, *Capital in the Twenty-First Century* is all about class. The title, after all, deliberately invokes Marx's *Capital*, and much of the book talks about "capital" and "labor," which are expressions closely connected to the idea of the class relations binding together capitalists and workers. What is more, in the opening gambit on the first page of chapter 1 of the book, Piketty tells the story of the bloody class struggle between miners and owners in the Marikana platinum mine in August 2012, in which thirty-four miners were killed by police. He uses this conflict to announce an overarching question:

> This episode reminds us, if we need reminding, that the question of what share of output should go to wages and share to profits—in others words, how should the income from production be divided between labor and capital?—has always been at the heart of distributional conflict.

And later, he concludes the discussion of these events by writing:

> For those who own nothing but their labor power and who often live in humble conditions (not to say wretched conditions in the case of eighteenth-century peasants or the Marikana miners), it is difficult to accept that the owners of capital—some of whom have inherited at least part of their wealth—are able to appropriate so much of the wealth produced by their labor. (p. 49)

This is solid class analysis: the income generated in production is divided between antagonistic classes, capital and labor, and the part that goes to capital constitutes the appropriation of wealth produced by labor. Classes are understood relationally, and these relations involve domination and exploitation systematically connected to production.

This relational understanding of class largely disappears after the opening of the first chapter.[6] When the term "class" is used at

---

6 Occasionally in the book a shadow relational class analysis appears. In one place, for example, Piketty invokes the idea of a *transfer* of income when he writes: "[I]t is important to note the considerable transfer of US national

all, it is treated as simply a convenient way of talking about regions of the distribution of income or wealth—a top, upper, middle, and bottom. The owners of capital receive a "return on capital"; they are not described as exploiting the labor of workers. The distribution of income reflects a division of the national income pie into "shares"; it is not a real transfer from one class to another.

There is much of value in Piketty's empirical research and in his theoretical arguments about the long-term trajectory of income and wealth inequality that does not depend on a relational class analysis. But the absence of a sustained class analysis of the social processes by which income is generated and appropriated obscures some of the critical social mechanisms at work.

Let me elaborate this point with two examples, one from the analysis of income inequality and one from the analysis of returns on capital.

Income Inequality

One of Piketty's important arguments is that the sharply rising income inequality in the United States since the early 1980s "was largely the result of an unprecedented increase in wage inequality and in particular the emergence of extremely high remunerations at the summit of the wage hierarchy, particularly among top managers of large firms" (p. 298). This conclusion depends, in part, on precisely what is considered a "wage" and what is "capital income." Piketty adopts the conventional classification used by economists and treats all of the earnings of top managers as "income from labor," regardless of the form the earnings take—whether ordinary salary, bonuses, or stock options—or the specific mechanisms by which the level of earnings is determined. This is obviously the correct way to classify these elements of earnings for purposes of tax law and the theories of conventional economics in which a CEO is just a well-paid employee. But this way of treating the earnings of CEOs becomes less obvious when

---

income—on the order of 15 points—from the poorest 90 percent to the richest 10 percent since 1980 . . . [T]his internal transfer between social groups . . . is nearly four times larger than the impressive trade deficit the United States ran in the 2000." (pp. 297–8). But even here the "transfer" refers to shifts in the distribution of income from the mass of people to the top, not between relationally interacting social categories. "Transfer" here simply indicates a division of the pie more favorable to the top of the distribution, not the actual appropriation of income produced by the labor of one class of people to another.

we think of the position of CEOs (and other top managers) as embedded in class relations.

As already noted, Piketty argues that "top managers by and large have the power to set their own remuneration, in some cases without limit and in many cases without any clear relation to their individual productivity." This is especially true for top executives:

> At the very highest levels salaries are set by the executives themselves or by corporate compensation committees whose members usually earn comparable salaries ... It may be excessive to accuse senior executives of having their "hands in the till," but the metaphor is probably more apt than Adam Smith's metaphor of the market's "invisible hand." (pp. 331–2)

What precisely does this diagnosis of CEO and other top executive salaries mean in terms of a relational understanding of class? Class relations are fundamentally power relations. To say that in the class relations of capitalism capitalists "own" the means of production and workers "sell" their labor power for a wage is to describe a set of power relations binding together the activities of capitalists and workers. Among the powers of capitalists in these relations are the power to offer employment at given wages, to issue orders to employees about what work they must do, and to dispose of the profits—the surplus generated by the firm—for alternative purposes. Other powers can be added to this list, but it should already be clear that what we call the capital/labor relation is actually a very complex multidimensional bundle of power relations.

In the modern corporation many of the powers-of-capital are held by the top executives. This means that they cannot reasonably be described as simply "labor" within the firm that is just much better paid. They occupy what I have called contradictory locations within class relations, meaning that relationally they have some, but not all, of powers of capitalists.[7] This has direct implications for how we should think of the super salaries of CEOs: a significant part of the earnings of top managers and executives should be thought of as an allocation by the executives themselves of profits of the firm to the personal accounts of managers rather than a wage in the ordinary sense. They exercise their capitalist-derived power within the class relations of the firm to appropriate part of the corporation's profits for their personal accounts. If this is correct, a substantial part of

---

7 For my approach to these issues, see *Classes* (London: Verso, 1985) and *Class Counts* (Cambridge: Cambridge University Press, 1997).

their earnings should be thought of as a return on capital, albeit of a different form from dividends derived from ownership of a stock.

It would, of course, be extremely difficult to figure out how to divide the earnings of top managers into a component that was functionally a return on capital and another that was functionally a wage. This is quite similar to the problem, which Piketty recognizes, of dividing the income of the ordinary self-employed into a wage component and a capital component, since the income generated by the economic activity of self-employed people inherently mixes capital and labor. A relational class analysis of the capitalist corporation suggests that this is equally a problem for the earnings of managers who have the kinds of powers described by Piketty. The implication for Piketty's overall analysis of the trajectory of income inequality in recent decades is that more of this increase should be attributed to the capital share of total income than is conventionally calculated through national income accounts. And this claim, if accepted, also calls into question one of Piketty's key conclusions: "This spectacular increase in inequality largely reflects an unprecedented explosion of very elevated incomes from labor, a veritable separation of the top managers of large firms from the rest of the population" (p. 24). To be sure, the increase of inequality does represent the explosion of very high incomes of top managers, and this certainly does create a "separation of the top managers of large firms from the rest of the population," but this should not be treated as entirely due to increasing inequality in incomes *from labor*. A significant part constitutes a form of income from capital.

Returns to Capital

The absence of a relational class analysis is also reflected in the way Piketty combines different kinds of assets into the category "capital" and then talks about "returns" to this heterogeneous aggregate. In particular, he combines residential owner-occupied real estate and capitalist property into the aggregate category "capital." This is an important issue, for residential real estate comprises between about 40 and 60 percent of the value of all capital in the countries for which Piketty provides this breakdown. Combining all income-generating assets into a single category is perfectly reasonable from the point of view of standard economic theory, in which these are simply alternative investments for which a person receives a return. But combining these two kinds of economic processes into a single category makes much less sense if we want to identify the social mechanisms through which this return is generated.

Owner-occupied housing generates a return to the owner in two ways: as "housing services," which are then valued as a form of imputed rent, and as capital gains if the value of the real estate appreciates over time. In the United States in 2012 about two-thirds of the population were homeowners, and roughly 30 percent of these owned their homes "free and clear," while another 51 percent have positive equity but were still paying off their mortgages.[8] The social relations in which the economic returns are linked to these patterns of home ownership are completely different from those within capitalist production relations. There are, of course, important social and moral issues linked to home ownership and access to affordable housing, and so inequalities in this form of "capital" matter. But they don't matter for the same reasons that inequalities in capitalist property matter, and they don't operate through the same causal processes. As a result, the social struggles that are unleashed by inequality in home-ownership on the one hand and by inequality in the ownership of capitalist capital on the other are fundamentally different. And, crucially, the public policies that would help remedy the harms generated by these different kinds of "returns to capital" would also be different. Piketty's proposed global tax on capital is a plausible element in a policy designed to respond to the inequalities linked to the global mobility of capital, but this seems to have little relevance to the harms generated by inequality in returns to ownership of residential real estate.

Thomas Piketty and his colleagues have produced an extraordinary dataset on income and wealth inequality that includes data on the wealthiest of the wealthy. And by making these data publicly available in such an accessible, user-friendly way they have performed a wonderful service to the academic community. But Piketty's analysis ends up obscuring crucial processes by treating capital and labor exclusively as factors of production that earn a return. If we want to really understand the disturbing trends in income and wealth inequality, and especially if we want to transform the power relations that generate these trends, we must go beyond the conventional categories of economics to identify the class relations that generate escalating economic inequality.

---

8   See http://www.zillow.com/blog/more-homeowners-are-mortgage-free-than-underwater-108367/.

THE DEATH OF CLASS DEBATE

In the mid- to late 1990s and early 2000s there was a short but lively discussion that came to be known as the "death of class debate."[1] This was not the first time that there had been announcements of the death of class, or at least of the declining relevance of the concept for contemporary social theory and research, but in the context of the capitalist triumphalism at end of the Cold War and the marginalization of Marxism as an explicit framework for social criticism, the argument that class no longer had any explanatory power had particular bite. This attack was perhaps particularly salient for scholars like myself, who continued to anchor their work in the Marxist tradition and who argued that class analysis remained the secure hard core of Marxist theory. If class was irrelevant, then what was really left of Marxism as a social scientific critique of capitalism?

In this chapter I examine the central arguments of two of the forceful exponents of the death of class thesis, Jan Pakulski and Malcolm Waters, as they present their ideas in synoptic form in their essay "The Reshaping and Dissolution of Social Class in

---

1 Contributions to the debate include Jan Pakulski and Malcolm Waters, *The Death of Class*, London: Sage, 1996; and a symposium on the book in the journal *Theory and Society*, 25: 5, October 1996, 717–24, (with contributions by Jan Pakulski and Malcolm Waters; Erik Olin Wright; Jeff Manza and Clem Brooks, and Szonja Szelényi and Jacqueline Olvera); Paul Kingston, *The Classless Society*, Stanford, CA: Stanford University Press, 2000; Takis Fotopoulos, "Class Divisions Today: The Inclusive Democracy Approach," *Democracy & Nature* 6: 2, July 2000, 211–52; Ulrich Beck, "Beyond Class and Nation: Reframing Social Inequalities in a Globalizing World," *British Journal of Sociology* 2007 58: 4, 2007: 679–705; Will Atkinson, "Beck, Individualization and the Death of Class: A Critique," *British Journal of Sociology* 58: 3, September 2007, 349–66.

Advanced Society."[2] While the core arguments they present are not new, as they themselves emphasize, they marshal those arguments in a more systematic way than in most critiques of class analysis, and they defend a particularly stark conclusion—that contemporary class analysts "manufacture class where it no longer exists as a meaningful social entity."[3] Defenders of class analysis should engage these arguments in the spirit of a healthy and serious interrogation of foundational concepts and their empirical relevance. Just as feminists need to take seriously, rather than dismiss out of hand as absurd, the claim that gender oppression is withering away, so class analysts of both Marxist and Weberian inspiration need to take seriously the arguments that we are moving rapidly towards a classless society, or at least a society within which class has "dissolved" as a salient explanatory category. I hope to show here that Pakulski and Waters' arguments and evidence are not persuasive, but I believe a dialogue with their arguments can be productive for clarifying the nature of class analysis, the status of its explanatory claims, and the tasks it faces.

As often happens in debates over theoretical ideas connected to ideological commitments, there is a tendency for the rhetoric to become more extreme and polarized than perhaps the authors actually believe. Statements of the form "social class is in the process of dissolving" tend to drift into statements like "social class has dissolved." This kind of slippage occurs frequently in the Pakulski and Waters paper. For example, they argue that the downward shift in the distribution of property "blurs traditional class divisions"—which suggests that the division is still present, but less sharply drawn—while immediately after they state that the "downward distribution of property . . . makes impossible the establishment of any boundary between classes on the basis of property"—which suggests not simply that the class division is blurred, but that it has disappeared entirely.[4] The temptation in defending class analysis against their arguments is to focus on these extreme statements. It is, after all, much easier to find evidence that simply demonstrates that class divisions exist and have consequences than to show that these divisions remain causally powerful. In my judgment, the heart of their argument is not in these most extreme formulations, but resides instead in the weaker claim that

2   This article appeared as the lead essay in the symposium on class in the journal *Theory and Society* 25: 5, 1996, 667–736.

3   Pakulski and Waters, *Death of Class*, 667.

4   Ibid., 662.

class is no longer a powerful or salient explanatory category. It is on the weaker claim that I will therefore focus in this discussion.

In the following section I briefly discuss four general propositions that Pakulski and Waters argue define the core commitments of class analysis. As I try to show, their characterization of most of these commitments amounts to insisting that class analysis requires a generalized belief in class primacy, whereas I will argue that class primacy is not an essential component of class analysis. In the final section I then examine a range of empirical evidence that indicates the enduring importance of class relations for understanding contemporary capitalist societies.

FOUR PROPOSITIONS

The central target of Pakulski and Waters's critique is class analysis rooted in the Marxist tradition, but many of their arguments also apply to any form of class analysis that defines class in terms of the ownership and control over economic assets. They build their case around four general propositions that, in their words, "can be abstracted from the literature on class."[5] They refer to these as the proposition of economism, the proposition of group formation, the proposition of causal linkage, and the proposition of transformative capacity. To facilitate the discussion I number the sentences in their statement of each proposition.[6]

The Proposition of Economism

1. Class is fundamentally an economic phenomenon.

2. It refers principally to differences in the ownership of property, especially productive property with an accumulation potential, and to differential market capacity, especially labor market capacity.

3. Moreover, such economic phenomena as property or markets are held to be the fundamental structuring or organizing principles in societal organization

Statements 1 and 2 in this proposition are on target. While some class analysts argue that class is as much a cultural and political

---

5 Ibid., 662.
6 The synoptic statements of these for propositions are all in ibid., 670.

concept as it is an economic concept, the core of both the Marxist and Weberian traditions of class analysis revolves around the economic dimension of the concept. The problem in this proposition enters with the third statement, specifically with the use of the definite article "the" before "fundamental." While class analysts may in general subscribe to the view that class is *a* fundamental structuring principle, no Weberian would consider class to be *the* fundamental principle, and many contemporary Marxists would also shy away from such a categorical claim, especially when it is specified with respect to an explanandum as vague and encompassing as "societal organization." To be sure, there is a strand of classical Marxism revolving around the "base/superstructure" metaphor in which the "base" is identified with class structure, the "superstructure" is everything else in society, and the base is seen as explaining the superstructure. Many, perhaps most, Marxists engaged in class analysis today reject such explanatory pretensions.[7] In any case, for class analysis to constitute a research program worth pursuing it is sufficient that it identify important causal mechanisms; it is not necessary that class be the most important or fundamental determinant of social phenomena.[8]

The Proposition of Group Formation

1. Classes are more than statistical aggregates or taxonomic categories.

---

7   As G. A. Cohen has convincingly argued, even in classical Marxism the idea of the "superstructure" was not so all-encompassing as to include everything other than the base. Instead, historical materialism generally takes the form of what Cohen calls "restricted historical materialism" (as opposed to "inclusive historical materialism"), in which the superstructure consists only of those noneconomic social phenomena that have reproductive effects on the base (i.e., effects that tend to stabilize and preserve the economic structure of society). According to Cohen, the thesis of restricted historical materialism is that superstructural phenomena defined in this way are *functionally* explained by the base. See G. A. Cohen, "Restricted and Inclusive Historical Materialism," chapter 9 in *History, Labour and Freedom*, Oxford: Clarendon Press, 1988.

8   As I have argued in detail elsewhere, it is extremely difficult to establish claims that some cause is the most important or most fundamental unless there is a very clear specification of the explanandum and the range of variation for which the claim applies. See Erik Olin Wright, Andrew Levine, and Elliott Sober, "Causal Aysmmetries," chapter 7 in *Reconstructing Marxism*, London: Verso, 1992.

2. They are real features of social structure reflected in observable patterns of inequality, association, and distance.

3. So deep and fundamental are these cleavages that they form the principle and enduring bases for conflict and contestation.

Again, the first two of these statements correctly identify commitments of most class analysts, at least those of a nonpostmodernist bent. Most Marxists and Weberians are generally "scientific realists," seeing their concepts as attempts at understanding causal mechanisms that exist in the world, and thus both believe that if class relations matter they should generate observable effects. The third statement, however, would be rejected by virtually all Weberian class analysts from Weber himself to the present. Many contemporary Marxist class analysts would also demur from the statement in this unqualified and categorical form. While Marxists generally believe that class relations constitute *an* enduring basis for conflict, much of the thrust of contemporary Marxism has been towards understanding the conditions under which class compromises are formed and class conflict is displaced from center stage. Although most Marxists would argue that even when class formation and class struggle have been contained there will continue to be effects of class relations on other forms of conflict, this does not imply the stronger claim that class cleavages constitute *the* principle *basis* for *all* conflict. To claim enduring and even pervasive effects is not to claim class primacy.

The Proposition of Causal Linkage

1. Class membership is also causally connected to consciousness, identity, and action outside the arena of economic production.

2. It affects political preferences, lifestyle choices, child-rearing practices, opportunities for physical and mental health, access to educational opportunity, patterns of marriage, occupational inheritance, income, and so on.

This proposition is sound, since Pakulski and Waters do not assert here that class must be the primary causal determinant of each of the explananda listed under point 2. The proposition does not even insist that class be a *direct* cause of these explananda since the expression "causally connected to" encompasses indirect and mediated effects of class on phenomena outside of economic production. All the proposition therefore asserts is that access to economically relevant assets has a systematic effect (direct or indirect) on these kinds of phenomena. I would only add one caveat. As specified in this proposition, the list of phenomena for which class is claimed to have effects is almost completely open-ended. Most class analysts would qualify the "proposition of causal linkage" by saying that class matters more for some phenomena than others, and that for certain explananda, class might have negligible effects. Furthermore, the extent to which class matters for various explananda may itself be contingent upon various other variables—i.e., there may be strong interactive effects between the micro-level effects of class location and various macro-level processes. Class analysis would not disappear as a legitimate research program if for some of these explananda it turns out that class determinants were weak.

The Proposition of Transformative Capacity

1. Classes are potential collective actors in economic and political fields.

2. Insofar as they consciously struggle against other classes, classes can transform the general set of social arrangements of which they are a part.

3. Class therefore offers the dynamic thrust that energizes society.

4. Classes are the principal collective actors that can make history.

Statement 1 accurately characterizes most forms of class analysis. Few class analysts deny that class is the basis for *potential* collective action. I would only modify this statement in one respect: Except metaphorically "classes" as such are *never* literally "collective actors." The idea of a collective actor makes some sense when it refers to organizations such as unions and political parties. Such organizations may be deeply connected to people in specific locations in the class structure and may represent the class interests of those people, and thus it may be justifiable to describe them as class formations. But still, it is organizations that act strategically in economic and political fields, not the classes themselves.

The second statement, because of the conditionality of the expression "insofar," would also be acceptable to most strands of class analysis so long as the word "transform" is taken to include something like "modifications in the rules of the game" and not simply "revolutionary ruptures in the game itself."

The third and fourth statements are much more contentious because of the assertion of class primacy. While classical Marxism certainly affirmed the thesis that "class struggle was the motor of history," most contemporary Marxists would qualify such claims by stressing the importance of a variety of enabling conditions that make it possible for collectively organized class forces to have such system-shaping effects. Few Marxists believe that the collective capacity for radical transformations is automatically produced by the "contradictions of capitalism."[9]

Overall, then, Pakulski and Waters do accurately identify some central strands in class analysis in these propositions, but they consistently slide from a reasonable description of propositions that affirm the relevance of class to much stronger and contentious claims about class primacy. Indeed, they seem to believe that without the claim of class primacy, there would be no point at all to class analysis. In commenting on what they describe as weaker forms of class analysis, they state: "In order to distinguish itself from sociological analysis in general, this enterprise must necessarily privilege economically defined class over other potential sources of inequalities and division, as well as accept the principle of causal linkage. There would otherwise be little point in describing the activity as *class* analysis—a class analysis that can find no evidence of class is clearly misnamed."[10] The final clause in this statement is clearly correct: if there were "no evidence of class," there would be no point to class analysis. But the previous sentence is not: class analysis need not universally privilege class over all other social divisions in order to justify its research program.[11] Class analysis is premised on the view that class constitutes a salient causal structure with important ramifications. As I show in the next section, there is abundant evidence to support this claim. It is an additional, and

---

9 For an extended discussion of the conditionality and contingency of the development of the capacity for transformative class struggles, see Wright, Levine, and Sober, *Reconstructing Marxism*, part 1.

10 Pakulski and Waters, *Death of Class*, 671.

11 In the context of their argument, I take the word "privilege" to imply "causally more important." There is a much weaker sense in which class analysis inherently does "privilege" class, namely that it *focuses* on class and its effects. In this sense, an endocrinologist "privileges" hormones over other causal processes, but this hardly implies that endocrinology implies that hormones are universally more important than other factors. If Pakulski and Waters simply mean that class analysis focuses on class, there is nothing contentious about their claims.

much more contingent claim", that class processes constitute the most important cause of particular social phenomena, and a far more contentious (and implausible) claim that they constitute the most important cause of everything.

EVIDENCE

As an explanatory concept, class is relevant both to macro-level analyses of social systems and micro-level analyses of individual lives. In both contexts, class analysis asserts that the way people are linked to economically relevant assets is consequential in various ways. In what follows I examine a range of evidence that such consequences are an enduring feature of contemporary society.

1. Have class boundaries disappeared?

One way of exploring this question is to investigate what I have called elsewhere the "permeability" of class boundaries.[12] Permeability refers to the extent to which the lives of individuals move across different kinds of social boundaries. One can study permeability of any kind of social boundary—race, gender, class, occupation, nationality—and one can study such boundary-crossing permeability with respect to a wide range of life events—mobility, friendship formation, marriage, membership in voluntary associations, etc. In my own research I have focused on three kinds of events—intergenerational class mobility, cross-class friendship formation, and cross-class household composition—and studied the extent to which these events occur across the different kinds of boundaries within a class structure.

The class structure concept I have used in my research sees class relations in capitalist societies as organized along three underlying dimensions—property, authority, and expertise (or skills). For

12 The research discussed here is reported in detail in Erik Olin Wright, *Class Counts: Comparative Studies in Class Analysis,* Cambridge: Cambridge University Press, 1997, 2000. See also Erik Olin Wright, "The Permeability of Class Boundaries to Friendships: A Comparative Analysis of the United States, Canada, Sweden, and Norway," *American Sociological Review*, February 1992; and Erik Olin Wright and Mark Western, "The Permeability of Class Boundaries to Intergenerational Mobility: A Comparative Study of the United States, Canada, Norway and Sweden," *American Sociological Review* 59: 4, June 1994, 606–29.

purposes of empirically studying class boundary permeability, I trichotomize each of these dimensions: the property dimension is divided into employers, petty-bourgeois (self-employed without employees), and employees; the authority dimension into managers, supervisors, and nonmanagerial employees; and the skill/expertise dimension into professionals, skilled employees, and nonskilled employees.[13] I then define permeability as a boundary-crossing event that links the poles of these trichotomies. Friendships between employers and employees, for example, would count as an instance of permeability across the property boundary, but a friendship between a worker and a petty bourgeois or between a petty bourgeois and an employer would not. The empirical problem, then, is to explore the relative odds of permeability events across these three class boundaries, as well as the odds of events between different specific locations within the class structure.

Without going into detail, some of the basic findings of this research are roughly as follows:

1. The property boundary is generally the least permeable of the three boundaries for all three kinds of events (mobility, friendships, and household composition), followed by the skill/expertise boundary and then the authority boundary. With some minor exceptions, this rank-ordering of relative permeability holds for the four countries I have studied—the United States, Canada, Sweden, and Norway.

2. The odds of mobility between a working class location (i.e., a nonmanagerial, nonskilled, employee) and an employer location is about 25 percent of what it would be if the link between these two locations was random; the odds of a close personal friendship between these two locations is about 20 percent of what it would be if these events were random; and the odds of a two-earner household containing an employer married to a worker are about 10 percent of the random association.

3. The odds of events linking workers and the petty bourgeoisie, on the other hand, are generally only modestly different from random for all three kinds of events. The class boundary between workers and petty bourgeois is therefore 3 to 6 times more permeable than the boundary between workers and employers.

---

13 Details of the strategy of analysis and operationalizations can be found in Erik Olin Wright, *Classes*, London: Verso, 1985, chapter 5 and appendix 2.

None of these results demonstrates that class boundaries are the least permeable of all social boundaries in capitalist societies. In the United States racial boundaries are undoubtedly less permeable to household composition than are class boundaries, and in some countries, religious affiliation may be a much less permeable boundary than class for certain kinds of events. But these results unequivocally indicate that class boundaries have not disappeared: the coefficients for events across the property and the expertise/skill boundaries are significantly negative (at $p<.001$ level of statistical significance in nearly all cases) in all countries.

2. Have inequalities in the distribution of capital declined to the point in recent years that it no longer matters much for people's lives?

Pakulski and Waters are correct that compared to a hundred years ago, perhaps, there is a more egalitarian distribution of wealth in most capitalist countries. This does not, however, imply that the distribution has equalized to the point that the basic nexus between class and capital asset-holding has been broken. In 1983, the richest half of 1 percent of American households owned 46.5 percent of all corporate stock, 44 percent of bonds, and 40 percent of net business assets. The next 0.5 percent richest owned 13.5 percent of stock, 7.5 percent of bonds, and 11.5 percent of net business assets. The richest 1 percent of American households therefore owned 50 to 60 times their per capita share of these crucial capitalist assets.[14] This was before the massive increase in wealth concentration that occurred in the last decades of the twentieth century and continued in the twenty-first. By 2012, the top 0.1 percent of households in the United States had as much wealth as the bottom 90 percent.[15]

Of course, unequal ownership of these assets may not matter much for peoples' lives. The claim of class analysis is not simply that there is an unequal distribution of ownership and control of economic assets, but that this inequality in assets is consequential for people. In 1990 the average family income of the top 1 percent of income earners in the United States was just under $549,000. On average over $278,000 of this—more than 50 percent of the total—came directly from capital assets (not including an

14   These data are from Lawrence Mishel and David Frankel, *The State of Working America*, New York: M. E. Shape, 1991, 154.

15   Emmanuel Saez and Gabriel Zucman, "Wealth Inequality in the United States since 1913," NBER Working Paper 20625, October 2014, Table 1.

additional $61,000 from self-employment earnings). In contrast, the average family income of the bottom 90 percent of the population in the United States was only about $29,000 in 1990, of which, on average, less than 10 percent (about $2,400) came from capital assets.[16] These inequalities connected to income generated by capital ownership intensified considerably in the following decades. The inegalitarian distribution of capital assets is clearly consequential.

The direct impact on household income is only one of the salient consequences of unequal distribution of capital assets. Equally important is the way the distribution of ownership rights in capitalist production affects the stability and distribution of jobs. One would be hard pressed to convince a group of newly unemployed workers from a factory that has closed because the owner moved production abroad that their lack of ownership of capitalist assets has no significant consequences for their lives. If the workers themselves owned the firm as a cooperative or if it were owned by the local community, different choices would be made.[17] The same international pressures would have different consequences on the lives of workers if the distribution of capital assets—i.e., the class relations within which they lived—were different.

An objection could be raised that I have grossly exaggerated the levels of inequality in distributions of assets, since pension funds of various sorts are among the biggest holders of stock and other financial assets. Shouldn't those workers covered by pension funds be considered quasi-capitalists by virtue of their connection to these

---

16   Mishel and Frankel, *State of Working America*, 34.

17   In a neoclassical model of the capitalist economy with perfect information and complete markets (including complete futures markets), property rights would make no difference. As Paul Samuelson famously quipped: it doesn't matter whether capitalists hire workers or workers hire capital—the behavior of the firm will be the same. In such a world, if it were profit-maximizing for the capitalist to move a factory abroad then, even if the workers themselves owned the factory, it would be profit-maximizing for them to do the same thing. They would simply chose to unemploy themselves, move the factory abroad and hire workers there. In such a world, workers would not be credit-constrained to obtain loans to buy the firms in which they worked, since with perfect information (including perfect information about the behavior of the workers) banks would not hesitate to make loans to workers. But we do not live in such a world, and it is precisely the pervasive information asymmetries and the absence of perfect futures markets that transform the atomistic domination-free interactions of the Walrasian market into the power-laden, exploitative class relations of real capitalist societies.

assets? Doesn't this effectively erode the class distinction between workers and employers?

The experience of conflict in Sweden over the "wage-earners' fund" in the late 1970s sheds light on the nature of the class relations linked to pension funds. In Sweden, as in many other countries, large pension funds exist for union members. Strict rules govern the nature of these pension fund investments, ostensibly to avoid risky investments and insure the continuing stream of income for future pensioners. In the 1970s a proposal in Sweden known as the Meidner Plan was made, initially by the left of the labor movement and the Social Democratic Party, which would have enabled pension funds to be used by unions to gradually gain ownership control of Swedish corporations. Corporations would have been forced by law to give stock to these funds as part of the benefits package for workers, and over time this would have resulted in a shift of real ownership from the Swedish capitalist class to the unions. All of this would have been done at real market prices, so there was no question of confiscation. The Swedish bourgeoisie massively and vigorously opposed this proposal. The original form of the Meidner Plan represented a fundamental shift from pension funds as a source of forced savings available for investment to those funds being used to transform the governance structure of Swedish industry and thus ultimately the class structure. The turmoil over this proposal lead in part to the defeat of the Social Democratic Party, and in the end, the proposal was watered down to the point where it no longer posed any kind of threat. What this episode reflects is the fact that the various forms of *indirect* "ownership" of assets represented by such things as pension funds do not in fact constitute a significant erosion of the class relations of ownership and control of productive assets. What matters is the way power relations are articulated to formal ownership rights.

3. Is the extraction of labor effort no longer a problem in capitalist firms?

At the core of Marxist conceptions of class is the problem of extracting labor effort from producers who do not own the means of production. This problem has also emerged as a central theme in transactions cost economics under the rubric of principal/agent problems within capitalist firms. The economics version of the argument states that under conditions of information asymmetries (employees have private information about their work effort that is costly for employers to acquire) and a divergence of interests between principals and agents (employers want workers to work harder than the workers voluntarily want to work), there will be a problem of enforcement of the labor contract.

A range of consequences are generated by this principal/agent problem as employers adopt strategies that try to align the behavior of agents to the interests of principals. One of the results is an "efficiency wage" in which workers are paid more than their reservation wage in order to raise the cost of job loss, thus making them more hesitant to shirk.[18] Another consequence will be the erection of an apparatus of monitoring and enforcement within firms. A third consequence is that employers make technological choices partially in terms of the effects of alternative technologies on monitoring and social control. This does not imply, of course, that the class dimensions of technical choice are always the most important, or even that they are always significant, but simply that employers are not indifferent to the effect of alternative technologies on their capacity to monitor and extract labor effort.[19] Considerable empirical evidence exists for each of these effects.

Most economists do not use the language of class analysis in discussions of this principal/agent problem because they take the distribution of property rights within the capitalist firm for granted, yet this distribution of property rights is a central dimension of class structure. Making the class character of the problem explicit has the advantage of focusing attention on the ways in which *variations* in the class relations of production might affect the principal/agent problem. Consider two examples: worker-owned firms and capitalist firms within which it is difficult to fire workers because they have enforceable employment rights.

In the case of cooperatives, Bowles and Gintis have argued that if workers were the residual claimants on the income generated within production (i.e., if they were the owners of the assets), the problem

---

18   For evidence on the costs of job loss, see Samuel Bowles and Juliet Schor, "The Cost of Job Loss and the Incidence of Strikes," *Review of Economics and Statistics* 69: 4, November 1987, 584–92.

19   For an extended discussion of this model of extracting labor effort, see Samuel Bowles and Herbert Gintis, "Contested Exchange: New Microfoundations for the Political Economy of Capitalism," *Politics & Society*, 18: 2, 1990, 165–222. For evidence on the role of monitoring and social control in technical choice, see David Noble, "Social Choice in Machine Design," *Politics & Society* 8: 3/4, September 1978, 313–47; and Samuel Bowles "Social Institutions and Technical Choice," in M. DeMatteo, A. Vercelli, and R. Goodwin, eds., *Technological and Social Factors in Long-Term Economic Fluctuation*, Berlin: Springer Verlag, 1988.

of monitoring and enforcement of work effort would be dramatically transformed.[20] The problem of extracting labor effort would not disappear because there would still be free-rider problems among the worker-owners, but since in worker cooperatives there are stronger incentives for mutual-monitoring than in conventional capitalist firms, and since the motivations of actors are likely to strengthen anti-free-rider norms and identities, the costs of monitoring should go down and thus productivity would increase. Employees in an employee-owned firm are embedded in a different set of class relations than are employees in a conventional capitalist firm, and this variation affects the labor extraction process.[21]

Capitalist firms within which workers have effective rights to their jobs are also a case of a transformation of class relations within production. In this case, workers are not residual claimants to the income of the firm (i.e., they do not "own" the capital assets), but the employers have lost certain aspects of their property rights—they no longer have the full right to decide who will use the means of production that they "own." Such a situation poses specific problems for the employer. On the one hand, by making it harder to fire workers, strong job rights reduce the efficiency of monitoring and make shirking easier. But this constraint on firing also makes the time horizons of workers with respect to their place of employment longer and may make them identify more deeply with the welfare of the firm. Which of these two forces is stronger depends upon the details of the institutional arrangements that regulate the interactions of employers and workers. The research on the implications for cooperation and productivity of strong job rights in Japanese and German capitalism can be considered instances of class analyses of principal/agent problems.[22]

---

20   For an extended discussion of the effects on monitoring and efficiency of cooperative forms of ownership, see Samuel Bowles and Herbert Gintis, *Recasting Egalitarianism: New Rules for Communities, States and Markets*, vol. 3 of the Real Utopias Project, London: Verso, 1998.

21   Numerous studies support the claim that productivity is higher in worker owned firms than in comparable capitalist firms. The most comprehensive study of the effects of worker ownership on productivity and other outcomes, is Joseph Blasi, Richard Freeman, and Douglas Kruse, *The Citizen's Share*, New Haven, CT: Yale University Press, 2013. For an earlier review of the evidence, see David Levine and Lara d'Andrea Tyson, "Participation, Productivity and the Firm's Environment," in Alan Binder, ed., *Paying for Productivity*, Washington, DC: Brookings, 1990, 183–244.

22   David Gordon presents evidence for a strong inverse relation between the degree of cooperation in the labor management relations of a country and the

It is, of course, possible to discuss the effects of worker cooperatives or job rights on principal/agent problems without ever
mentioning the word "class." Nevertheless, the theoretical
substance of the analysis still falls within class analysis if the causally salient feature of these variations in firm organization centers
on how workers are linked to economic assets.

4. Does class location no longer systematically affect individual subjectivity?

Pakulski and Waters are on their strongest ground when they argue
that class is not a powerful source of identity, consciousness, and
action. My own research on class structure, class biography, and
class consciousness in the 1980s indicates that in most of the countries I studied, class-related variables were only modest predictors
of values on the various attitude scales I adopted. However,
"modest" is not the same as "irrelevant." In Sweden, individual
class location by itself explained about 16 percent of the variance in
a class-consciousness scale, while in the United States the figure was
only 9 percent and in Japan only 5 percent.[23] When a range of other
class-linked variables were added—including such things as class
origins, self-employment experiences, unemployment experiences,
and the class character of social networks—this increased to about
25 percent in Sweden, 16 percent in the United States, and 8 percent
in Japan. In all three countries these class effects were statistically
significant, but not extraordinarily powerful.

What should we make of these results? First, at least in the United
States and Sweden, the explained variances in these equations are not
particularly low by the standards of regressions predicting attitudes.
In general, it is rare for equations predicting attitudes to have high
explained variances unless the equations include other attitudes as

---

weight of its administrative-managerial employment: the correlation between
an index of cooperation and the percentage of administrative and managerial
employment was −.72 for 12 OECD countries. Cooperative labor management
relations are closely linked to strong job rights and other arrangements that
increase the effective rights of workers within production. See David Gordon,
*Fat and Mean: Corporate Bloat, the Wage Squeeze and the Stagnation of Our
Conflictual Economy*, New York: Free Press, 1996.

23 The class-consciousness scale combined a number of simple strength of
agreement/disagreement items concerning people's attitudes towards class
conflict, corporations, employee participation in decision-making, strikes, and
related matters. For details, see Erik Olin Wright, *Class Counts*, Cambridge:
Cambridge University Press, 1997, chapter 14.

independent variables (for example, using self-identification on a liberalism/conservatism scale as a way of predicting attitudes towards specific public policies). Part of the reason for this is undoubtedly the pervasive problem in adequately measuring attitudes; a significant part of the total variance in measured attitudes may simply be random with respect to any social determinants. And part of the reason for the low explained variance in attitude regressions is that the causes of individual attitudes are often irreducibly idiographic— it is hard to imagine a multivariate regression rooted in social structural variables that would "predict" that Engels, a wealthy capitalist, would be a supporter of revolutionary socialism. In any case, class often performs as well or better than many other social structural variables in predicting a variety of aspects of attitudes.

The second thing to note in these results is the very large cross-national variation in the explanatory power of class variables for predicting individual attitudes. What is more, on a more fine-grained inspection, there are interesting variations in the specific ways class location and attitudes are linked in the three countries. Without going into detail here, if we define "ideological coalitions" as sets of class locations that are more like each other ideologically (as measured by these attitude questions) than they are like other locations, we find three quite distinct patterns in these three countries in the 1980s (when I did this research). In Sweden, the class structure is quite polarized ideologically between workers and employers, and there is a fairly large "middle class coalition" that is ideologically quite distinct from the bourgeois coalition and from the working class coalition. In the United States, the class structure is less ideologically polarized and the bourgeois ideological coalition extends fairly deeply into the structurally defined "middle class": managers and professionals are firmly part of this coalition. In Japan there is a third configuration: ideological polarization is much more muted than in either of the other two countries, and the ideological divisions that do occur fall mainly along the expertise dimension rather than the authority dimension of the class structure.

These patterns of variation demonstrate that the linkage between class location and individual subjectivity is heavily shaped by the macro-social context within which it occurs. Class locations do not simply produce forms of subjectivity; they shape subjectivity in interaction with a range of other processes—institutional arrangements within firms; political strategies of parties and unions; historical legacies of past struggles, etc. These complexities certainly do undercut any simple-minded class analysis that asserts something like "class determines consciousness."

But they do not undermine the broader project of investigating the ways in which class, in interaction with other social processes, has consequences.

COMPLEXITY VS DISSOLUTION

If the evidence discussed in the previous sections is correct, it certainly seems premature to declare the death of class. Class may not be the most powerful or fundamental cause of "societal organization," and class struggle may not be the most powerful transformative force in the world today. Class primacy, as a generalized explanatory principle across all social explananda, is implausible. Nevertheless, class remains a significant and sometimes powerful determinant of many aspects of social life. Class boundaries, especially the property boundary, continue to constitute real barriers in people's lives; inequalities in the distribution of capital assets continue to have real consequences for material interests; capitalist firms continue to face the problem of extracting labor effort from nonowning employees; and class location continues to have a real, if variable, impact on individual subjectivities.

In denying the significance of these kinds of empirical observations, Pakulski and Waters seem to be mistaking the increasing *complexity* of class relations in contemporary capitalist societies with the *dissolution* of class altogether. While it was never true that a simple, polarized, two-class model of capitalism was sufficient to understand the effects of class on consciousness and action in concrete capitalist societies, there were times and places when perhaps this was a reasonable first approximation. For most purposes this is no longer the case, and a variety of forms of complexity needed to be added to class analysis:

- "Middle class" locations need to be given a positive conceptual status, for example by treating them as "contradictory locations within class relations."

- The location of individuals within class structures needs to be defined not simply in terms of their own jobs (direct class locations) but also in terms of the ways they are linked to mechanisms of exploitation through family structure (mediated class locations).

- Class locations have a specific temporal dimension by virtue of the ways in which careers are organized. This temporal dimension means that to the extent that career trajectories have a probabilistic character to them, some class locations may have an objectively indeterminate character.

- The diffusion of genuine ownership of capitalist assets among employees, if still relatively limited, creates additional complexity in class structures, since some people in managerial class locations, and even some in working class locations, can simultaneously occupy locations in the capitalist class as rentiers. This constitutes a special form of "contradictory location within class relations."

Class analysis needs to incorporate these, and other, complexities. The reconstruction of class analysis in these ways, however, does not imply the dissolution of the causal processes that class theory identifies. The relationship of people to the pivotal economic assets of the capitalist economy continues to shape life chances and exploitation, and these in turn have wide ramifications for other social phenomena. These complexities may lead to a conceptual framework that is less tidy, and that perhaps evokes less fiery passions. But in the end, the contribution of class analysis to emancipatory projects of social change depends as much on its explanatory capacity to grapple with the complexity of contemporary capitalist society as on its ideological capacity to mobilize political action.

9

IS THE PRECARIAT A CLASS?

From time to time in theoretical discussions in sociology and related disciplines, the question arises whether a particular social category should be considered "a class." We have already encountered this issue in the discussion of David Grusky and Kim Weeden's proposal that fine-grained occupational categories are "micro-classes." In this chapter I explore the problem of when a category is a class in the case of what has come to be known as "the precariat." This concept has its origins in discussions of the increase in economic insecurity and precariousness of employment (also called "precarity") in the 1980s and 1990s, but in those earlier discussions this was treated mainly as a condition faced by workers rather than as a distinct class within a class structure. The importance of these trends has been broadly accepted by analysts of contemporary capitalism. The reconceptualization of these trends from *precarity as a condition* to *the precariat as a class* is much more controversial. In what follows I interrogate the arguments for this view by its most influential advocate, Guy Standing, in his two books, *The Precariat* and *The Precariat Charter*.[1]

I begin by outlining Guy Standing's basic analysis of the precariat and his arguments for why it should be considered a class. I then examine the place of the precariat within a broad understanding of class analysis. I argue that while the precariat can be situated within class analysis, it is not useful to treat it as a distinct class in its own right.

---

1 Guy Standing, *The Precariat: The New Dangerous Class*, London: Bloomsbury, 2011; and *The Precariat Charter: From Denizens to Citizens*, London: Bloomsbury, 2014.

Standing grounds his arguments that the precariat is a class in a quite complex three-dimensional definition of class: "Class can be defined as being determined primarily by specific 'relations of production,' specific 'relations of distribution' (sources of income), and specific relations to the state. From these arises a distinctive 'consciousness' of desirable reforms and social policies."[2]

The explicit inclusion of relations to the state is quite distinctive here. While many class analysts see the relationship of classes to the state as an important issue, few build this into the very definition of class structures. Standing does so because he believes that one of the pivotal aspects of the lived reality of the position of the precariat in contemporary capitalism centers on the increasing marginalization of many people from the rights normally associated with citizenship. It is really the intersection of economic precarity with political marginality that most sharply creates a boundary dividing the precariat from the working class.

On the basis of the three dimensions of relations—relations of production, relations of distribution, and relations to the state—Standing identifies seven classes that comprise the class structure of contemporary capitalist societies:

1. *The elite or plutocracy.* This is a true ruling class in the classical Marxist sense. In Standing's words: "They are not the 1 per cent depicted by the Occupy movement. They are far fewer than that, and exercise more power than most people appreciate. Their financial strength shapes political discourse, economic policies and social policy."[3]

2. *The salariat.* This class is defined as people in "stable full-time employment, some hoping to move into the elite, the majority just enjoying the trappings of their kind, with their pensions, paid holidays and enterprise benefits, often subsidized by the state. The salariat is concentrated in large corporations, government agencies and public administration, including the civil service."[4]

---

2 Standing, *Precariat Charter*, 13.
3 Ibid., 13.
4 Standing, *The Precariat*, 12.

3. *Proficians.* This is a term that "combines the traditional ideas of 'professional' and 'technician' but covers those with bundles of skills that they can market, earning high incomes on contract, as consultants or independent own-account workers."[5]

4. *The old "core" working class (proletariat).* This class is "defined by its reliance on mass labour, reliance on wage income, absence of control or ownership of the means of production, and habituation to stable labour that corresponded to its skills."[6]

5. *The precariat.*

6. *The unemployed.*

7. *The lumpen-precariat (or "underclass").* Standing specifies this category as "a detached group of socially ill misfits living off the dregs of society."[7]

Standing's objective is not to provide careful, analytically rigorous definitions of each of these classes. He is really only concerned with differentiating the precariat from the rest of the class structure, especially from the working class. He therefore provides only a vague set of demarcations and rationales for some of these categories. For example, it is not at all clear from his analysis how nonmanagerial white collar and credentialed employees in stable jobs in the state and private sectors should be treated. They do not seem part of the core working class, which Standing identifies with manual labor, but they also do not fit comfortably into his definition of the salariat, since that category also includes top corporate executives "hoping to move into the elite," nor do they fit into his category of proficians, who are highly mobile educated own-account workers. This lack of precision would be a problem if Standing were attempting to generate a general class map of contemporary capitalism, but that is not his aim. His goal is to defend the concept of the precariat and provide a fine-grained account of the characteristics that distinguish it from the working class.

He does this by contrasting workers and the precariat in terms of the three dimensions of class relations.

---

5 Ibid., 12–13.

6 Standing, *Precariat Charter*, 15.

7 Standing, *The Precariat*, 13.

Distinctive relations of production. In identifying the criteria that differentiate the precariat from the proletariat, Standing does not explicitly give any one of the three dimensions of class relations more weight than others. Still, the first of these—the relations of production—seems to be the most fundamental in anchoring the concept and giving the concept its name. In terms of the relations of production, he writes, "The precariat consists of people living through insecure jobs interspersed with periods of unemployment or labour-force withdrawal (misnamed as 'economic inactivity') and living insecurely, with uncertain access to housing and public resources." Standing sees these relations of production as sharply differentiating the precariat from the proletariat:

> The precariat was no part of the "working class" or the "proletariat." The latter terms suggest a society consisting mostly of workers in long-term, stable, fixed-hour jobs with established routes of advancement, subject to unionization and collective agreements, with job titles their fathers and mothers would have understood, facing local employers whose names and features they were familiar with.[8]
>
> The working class was expected to supply stable labour, even if its members were subject to unemployment. The term that character-ized their working lives was proletarianization, habituation to stable full-time labour ... Whereas the proletarian norm was habituation to stable labour, the precariat is being habituated to unstable labour.[9]

Standing elaborates this core idea of insecurity by arguing that the precariat lacks "the seven forms of labour-related security" that characterized the working class following World War II: *labor market security* (adequate income-earning opportunities); *employment security* (protection against arbitrary dismissal, regulations on hiring and firing, etc.); *job security* (the ability and opportunity to retain a niche in employment); *work security* (protections against accidents and illness at work); *skill reproduction security* (opportu-nity to gain skills through apprenticeships); *income security* (assurance of adequate stable income); *representation security* (possession of a collective voice in the labor market through inde-pendent trade unions with a right to strike).[10] The absence of the first five of these forms of security are aspects of the distinctive form of relations of production of the precariat.

---

8   Ibid., 10.
9   Standing, *Precariat Charter*, 15, 17.
10   Standing, *The Precariat*, 17.

Distinctive relations of distribution. Income, Standing notes, comes in a wide variety of forms: "own-account production, income from producing or selling to a market, money wages, enterprise non-wage benefits, community and solidarity benefits, state benefits, and income from financial and other assets."[11] The distinctive characteristic of the precariat is that it lacks access to all of the nonmoney wage sources of income:

> During the twentieth century, the trend was away from money wages, with a rising share of social income coming from enterprise and state benefits. What distinguishes the precariat is the opposite trend, with sources of income other than wages virtually disappearing ... The precariat lacks access to non-wage perks, such as paid vacations, medical leave, company pensions and so on. It also lacks rights-based state benefits, linked to legal entitlements, leaving it dependent on discretionary, insecure benefits, if any. And it lacks access to community benefits, in the form of a strong commons (public services and amenities) and strong family and local support networks.[12]

The critical issue here, I think, is the increased vulnerability people face when their material standard of living comes entirely from money wages, with no social safety net, community backup, or other sources of benefit. The standard of living of the working class, in this account, remains underwritten by forms of income other than money wages, even though these may be declining in the era of austerity. For the precariat, those benefits have largely disappeared. The combination of employment instability and income vulnerability defines the economic precarity of the precariat.

Distinctive relations to the state. While the various aspects of economic precarity may be the most obvious factors that contribute to the precariat being constituted as a class, Standing also feels that its distinctive relations to the state are critical in creating a real boundary between it and the working class. He builds his analysis around the contrast between "citizens" and "denizens": citizens are people with full rights granted by the state; "denizens" are mere residents who live under the jurisdiction of the state, but with much more limited rights.[13] "The precariat," Standing writes, "lacks

---

11 Standing, *Precariat Charter*, 18.
12 Ibid., 18–19.
13 Included in this discussion of rights are political rights ("the precariat is

many of the rights provided to citizens in the core working class and salariat. Members of the precariat are denizens."[14] Traditionally, noncitizen migrants were denizens in this sense: they had permission to live somewhere, but with a much more limited set of politically guaranteed rights. This condition, Standing argues, has now been extended to a significant number of people who formally remain citizens. In contrast, for the working class these rights remain largely intact.

The precariat is thus defined by three overarching criteria: *precariousness* within the relations of production, *vulnerability* within the relations of distribution, and *marginality* within the relations to the state. While some segments of the working class may share some of these characteristics, taken together they constitute the precariat as a distinct class.[15]

This does not mean that there are no divisions within the precariat. In the second decade of the twenty-first century, Standing argues, the precariat in the developed capitalist world is internally divided into three main subcategories. The first are people who were previously firmly within the working class but have been marginalized by the trajectory of capitalist development. They are "people bumped out of working class communities and families. They experience a sense of relative deprivation. They, their parents or grandparents belonged to working class occupations, with status,

---

relatively disenfranchised"), civil rights ("the precariat is losing rights to due process"), cultural rights ("governments are demanding more conformity to societal norms and majoritarian institutions, intensifying cultural marginalization of minorities"), and economic and social rights ("the precariat is losing social and economic rights, notably in the sphere of state benefits and the right to practice an occupation"). Standing, *Precariat Charter*, 20–21.

14   Ibid., 20.

15   In addition to the distinctive properties of the precariat with respect to the three relations that are part of his definition of class, Standing also argues that the precariat has a number of other distinctive features that demarcate it from the working class: the collapse of occupational identity; lack of control over time; detachment from labor; low social mobility; overqualification; uncertainty; and poverty and poverty traps. The logical status of these additional attributes is unclear in the analysis, since they do not constitute part of his explicit definition of the concept of class, and he acknowledges that some of them also apply to segments of the working class. Some of these might be thought of as further elaborations of aspects of the relations of production and relations of distribution, and some of them might be thought of as effects of the primary conditions defining the precariat.

skill and respect."[16] The second variety "consists of traditional denizens—migrants, Roma, ethnic minorities, asylum seekers in limbo, all those with the least secure rights anywhere. It also includes some of the disabled and a growing number of ex-convicts."[17] And the third variety, which Standing feels is the dynamic core of the precariat, "consists of the educated, plunged into a precariat existence after being promised the opposite, a bright career of personal development and satisfaction. Most are in their twenties and thirties. But they are not alone. Many drifting out of a salariat existence are joining them ... They are not doing what they set out to do, and there is little prospect of doing so."[18]

All three segments experience a deep sense of deprivation, a painful gap between the lived realities of their lives and their life expectations, but the focus of this gap is different in each case: "The first part of the precariat experiences deprivation relative to a real or imagined past, the second relative to an absent present, an absent 'home,' and the third relates to a feeling of having no future."[19] These different subjective experiences of deprivation linked to precarity generate serious divisions that undermine the capacity of the precariat to act collectively as class. "The precariat is divided to such an extent," Standing writes, "that one could describe it as a class at war with itself."[20] And yet in spite of this he believes that it has the potential to become a "dangerous class" much more capable than the working class of challenging "the mainstream political agendas of the twentieth century, the neo-liberalism of the mainstream 'right' and the labourism of social democracy."[21]

2. THE PRECARIAT'S PLACE IN CLASS ANALYSIS

There is little doubt that precariousness along a number of dimensions has increased as a condition of life in developed capitalist countries. The question remains how this phenomenon should be understood conceptually. Guy Standing's proposal is that the precariat is a class in the same sense that the working class is a class. He refers to the precariat as a class-in-the-making in deference to

---

16 Standing, *Precariat Charter*, 29.
17 Ibid., 29.
18 Ibid., 30.
19 Ibid., 30–31.
20 Ibid., 29.
21 Ibid., 31.

the fact that it does not yet act as a unified collective actor—it is not yet a class-for-itself in traditional Marxist terms—but nevertheless it is a distinct class location in terms of its structural location within the class structure of capitalism, differentiated from the working class and the other classes in his inventory.

Standing's basic strategy for defending this claim is to argue that there is a set of distinctive conditions that differentiate the lives of the precariat from those of the traditional working class. He acknowledges that there is an overlap between the precariat and parts of the working class if these conditions are taken one by one, but he argues that taken as a whole these characteristics generate a real boundary of demarcation: "In sum, the precariat is defined by ten features.[22] Not all are unique to it. But taken together, the elements define a social group, and for that reason we may call the precariat a class-in-the-making."[23]

Standing is quite dismissive of scholars who disagree that the precariat is a class. In particular, he is critical of Marxists, whose "desire to compress the precariat into old notions of 'the working class' or 'the proletariat' distract us from developing an appropriate vocabulary and set of images to guide twenty-first century analysis."[24] The question before us, then, is whether or not sharing this set of socio-economic characteristics elaborated by Standing is sufficient to describe a social category as a class? What, precisely, are the criteria by which we can answer this question?

The most basic criterion, used in both the Marxist and Weberian traditions of class analysis, is *material interests*. There is a poster from around 1979 that shows a working class woman leaning on a fence. The poster reads: "Class consciousness is knowing which side of the fence you are on. Class analysis is figuring out who is there with you."[25] This is a claim about material interests: two people within a given class have greater overlap in their material interests than do two people in different classes. So, to claim that the working class and the precariat are distinct classes is to claim that they have distinct material interests.

This claim, of course, merely displaces the original question, for now we need a clear criterion for what constitutes "material

---

22 These ten features are the three dimensions of class relations plus seven other characteristics. See footnote 15 above.

23 Ibid., 28.

24 Ibid., 31.

25 Poster published by Press Gang Publishers, Vancouver, B.C.; undated.

Class consciousness is knowing which side of the fence you're on.

Class analysis is figuring out who is there with you.

interests." This is a perennial problem in social theory and raises a host of tricky theoretical issues.

Perhaps the biggest disagreement in discussions of interests is the issue of *objective* versus *subjective* interests. Some people argue that the idea of interests is legitimate only when it refers to the subjective states of actors concerning their own understanding of their interests. Others insist that it also makes sense to talk about objective interests. In the first view, the idea of interests is closely connected to preferences. In the second view, it is intelligible to say to someone who is about to do something: "You are mistaken. That is not in your interests," which means that interests should not be collapsed into preferences. The concern expressed in this disagreement is that claims about the "objective interests" of the working class can easily slide into an elite telling the masses what is "good for them." Claims about objective interests have historically been used as a weapon to defend policies imposed by authoritarian parties and states, so there is good reason to be wary of invocations of objective interests. Being wary, however, need not mean dispensing with the idea of objective interests altogether; it just means treating claims about objective interests as propositions rather than authoritative edicts.

In any case, class analysis in both the Marxist and Weberian traditions makes claims about a particular domain of objective interests, which can be identified as "material interests." For any given person it is possible to identify actions and social changes that would improve or harm their material conditions of life. Sometimes the term "material" is used narrowly to simply mean income; sometimes it is used expansively to include many aspects of a person's economic situation, including working conditions, opportunities, leisure, economic stability, control over time use, and much more. In both cases, the claim is that it is possible to objectively assess the range of strategies and alternatives that will affect these aspects of a person's economic situation.[26]

If we accept the idea that objectively definable material interests are a legitimate criterion for differentiating class locations, the next question becomes how to specify these interests with respect to the class

---

26 Once a complex array of dimensions are included in "material interests" it will generally be the case that people face trade-offs in improving one or another of these dimensions. For example, strategies and social changes that improve economic security may be at odds with those that improve income. To claim that people have objective material interests is not to also claim that they have an objective interest in favoring one or another of the dimensions of those interests where there are trade-offs. The objectivity of material interests in these more complex situations is the objectivity of the trade-offs faced by people. To say that two people have the same objective material interests, then, is to say that they face the same basic trade-offs. To talk about objective material interests is also not to claim that people have some overarching objective interest in actually pursuing their material interests, as opposed to some other kind of interest. Frederick Engels, after all, was the son of a capitalist and devoted his time and energy to supporting Marx and the workers movement. The idea that class interests are "objective" in this case means that when Engels supported revolutionary socialism he was acting against his objective material interests.

structure of contemporary capitalism. This will help us answer the question of whether the precariat and the working class are distinct classes. For this task it will be helpful to use the game metaphor introduced in the discussion of the Grusky-Weeden model of micro-classes in chapter 6. The objective material interests of any location in a capitalist economic system can be specified at the level of the game itself, at the level of the rules of the game, and as moves within the game.

At the level of *the game itself*, the Marxist question is this: How would the material interests of people differently located within capitalism be affected by a change of the game from capitalism to socialism?[27] This question, needless to say, is deeply controversial. Many people reject the whole idea of socialism of any variety as a viable alternative to capitalism, or they argue that while socialism is possible, almost everyone would be worse off in socialism, and so there is no class differentiation within capitalism *at the level of the game*. This claim means, in effect, that all class locations within capitalism have shared material interests against socialism. Others, who do believe that a positive alternative to capitalism is possible, disagree sharply on precisely what "socialism" means, and depending on how socialism is conceived, the terrain of interests within capitalism with respect to the alternative will vary.

In spite of these difficulties, the connection between the class structure within capitalism and the possibility of socialism is the defining question of Marxist class analysis. Unless one retains some coherent idea of there being an alternative to capitalism, a Marxist class analysis loses its central anchor. These issues pose a serious challenge for contemporary Marxist work on class. Given the obvious complexity of contemporary class structures, how can we clearly specify the interests of people located within the existing economic structure with respect to an alternative as abstract as "socialism"? It is one thing to define these interests with a simple, binary view of the class relations of capitalism as consisting only of capitalists and workers. It is quite another to locate the interests connected to locations in the complex class structures of capitalism analyzed at more concrete levels of analysis.

---

27 There are actually two connected questions here: the interests of people connected to different class positions within capitalism in living in a socialist society, and the interests in the transition from a capitalist to a socialist society. Depending on one's view of the likely transition costs of social transformation, one can have unequivocal interests in socialism in the first sense and still not have an interest in trying to achieve socialism. And, of course, such interests in both cases depend on precisely what one means by "socialism."

Trying to solve this problem has been the central preoccupation of my work on class. Without going into any detail here, I have proposed the concept of "contradictory locations within class relations" as a way of connecting the complexity of class structures within capitalism to the alternative of socialism. The basic idea was to identify a series of locations within the class relations of capitalism that were in some sense simultaneously in more than one class. More specifically, with respect to relations of domination and exploitation, some locations can be simultaneously dominated and dominating or exploiting and exploited.[28] In the present context, this implies that with respect to material interests defined in terms of the games of capitalism versus socialism, such locations have contradictory interests—interests pointing in opposite directions.

At the level of *the rules of the game*, the problem of class interests concerns which set of rules governing capitalism are optimal for different locations within capitalism, given that the people in those positions will continue playing the game of capitalism. Is it better for manual industrial workers to be playing the Game of American Capitalism or the Game of Danish or German Capitalism? What about highly educated workers like doctors or engineers? Do different rules of the capitalist game confer particular advantages and disadvantages on people in different locations in the system? These questions can be asked for the large-scale variations in the rules of capitalism—for example, neoliberal capitalism with a thin safety net and weak provision of public goods versus capitalism with an expansive welfare state and broad provision of public goods and public services—or for second-order variations in the rules. The point is that we can define material interests, and thus the nature of the locations of people in a class structure, with respect to such variations in the rules of capitalism and not simply over the game of capitalism itself.

Finally, at the level of *the moves in the game*, the problem of class interests concerns the optimal strategies people face in securing and improving their material interests, given that the rules themselves cannot be changed. People occupy specific positions in the socio-economic system. The problem each person faces is this: in terms of my material interests, what should I do, given that I am in my present position? Should I try to move into a different kind of position (become a different kind of player)? Should I get more training to improve my bargaining position in my current location? Should I move to a different place? Should I join with other people like me in

28 For details on this conceptualization, see Erik Olin Wright, *Classes*, London: Verso, 1985; and *Class Counts*, Cambridge: Cambridge University Press, 1997.

a collective action for mutual improvement, and if so, who are the other people "like me" for this task? This is quite different from asking the question about what sorts of changes in the rules would make my life better, let alone asking if I would be better off in a wholly different game. In chapter 6 I argued that the Grusky-Weeden model of occupationally based micro-classes can be interpreted as an analysis of class at this level of moves in the game.

Using this metaphor of capitalism as a game, we can now turn to the question of whether the precariat is a distinct class from the working class. How different are the material interests of people in the precariat, as defined by Guy Standing, and in the working class with respect to the game itself, the rules of the game and moves within the existing game?

At the level of the game itself, if one believes that a democratic socialist alternative to capitalism is possible—even if not achievable in current historical circumstances—then the precariat and the working class clearly occupy the same location within the class structure. The material conditions of life for people in both locations within capitalism would be enhanced in an alternative economy built around various forms of social ownership, democratic empowerment over broad investment priorities, an expansive sector of decommodified public goods, a cooperative form of market relations, and the other components of democratic socialism.[29] However, since the collective struggle for such an alternative is not presently on the political horizon, class divisions at the level of rules of the game and moves in the game may be more immediately relevant to the question "Is the precariat a class?"

In terms of the rules of the game, it is certainly clear that under the existing rules—broadly speaking, the rules of neoliberal capitalism—the material conditions of life of most people in all three segments of the precariat are worse than most people in the working class. Precariousness itself, after all, is a significant harm. But does this mean that the changes in the rules of the game that would significantly improve conditions for the precariat would adversely affect the material interests of workers? And are there significant

29 For an exploration of the contours of this conception of democratic socialism as an alternative to capitalism, see Erik Olin Wright, *Envisioning Real Utopias*, London: Verso, 2010, chapters 5–7, and Robin Hahnel and Erik Olin Wright, *Alternatives to Capitalism: Proposals for a Democratic Economy*, New Left Project, 2014, available as an ebook at www.newleftproject.org/index.php/site/article_comments/ alternatives_to_capitalism_proposals_for_a_democratic_economy.

changes in the rules that would benefit workers but would worsen conditions for the precariat? Are they on the same side of the fence or opposite sides when the fence is defined by struggles over the rules of the game withing capitalism?

Let's first look at changes in rules that would benefit the precariat. In *The Precariat Charter*, Standing proposes a general inventory of demands for improving the conditions of the precariat. This charter contains 29 Articles:

Article 1: Redefine work as productive and reproductive activity.
Article 2: Reform labour statistics.
Article 3: Make recruitment practices brief encounters.
Article 4: Regulate flexible labour.
Article 5: Promote associational freedom.
Articles 6–10: Reconstruct occupational communities.
Articles 11–15: Stop class-based migration policy.
Article 16: Ensure due process for all.
Article 17: Remove poverty traps and precarity traps.
Article 18: Make a bonfire of benefit assessment tests.
Article 19: Stop demonizing the disabled.
Article 20: Stop workfare now!
Article 21: Regulate payday loans and student loans.
Article 22: Institute a right to financial knowledge and advice.
Article 23: Decommodify education.
Article 24: Make a bonfire of subsidies.
Article 25: Move towards a basic income.
Article 26: Share capital via sovereign wealth funds.
Article 27: Revive the commons.
Article 28: Revive deliberative democracy.
Article 29: Re-marginalize charities.[30]

These are all solid, progressive proposals, and if instituted would certainly make a tremendous difference in the lives of people in the precariat. Some of these are quite narrowly directed at the distinctive conditions faced by the precariat, such as *Article 4, Regulate flexible labour*. Some apply to very specific categories of people, such as *Article 19, Stop demonizing the disabled*. Some of these proposals refer to very narrow rules of the game of contemporary capitalism, such as *Article 21, Regulate payday loans and student loans*. And some refer to transformations of rules that, if implemented in a serious way, would prefigure an emancipatory

---

30   The details of these articles are presented in *The Precariat Charter*, 151ff.

alternative beyond capitalism, such as *Article 25, Move towards a basic income; Article 26, Share capital via sovereign wealth funds; Article 27, Revive the commons;* and *Article 28, Revive deliberative democracy.* While some of the proposals certainly seem less pressing then others—reforming labour statistics is not as pressing an issue as eliminating poverty traps and precarity traps—all of them are in the material interests of people in the precariat.

The question at hand, however, is not simply whether these proposals serve the interests of the precariat, but whether they provide grounds for claiming that the precariat is a distinct class from the working class. Is there a divide in material interests between the precariat and the working class with respect to this charter of proposed changes in the rules of the game of capitalism? The answer, I think, is no: none of these proposed changes in the rules of the game goes against the material interests of the working class, and nearly all of them would significantly advance the interests of workers. While these proposals may matter more for the lives of people in the precariat than for those still in the stable working class, they are in the interests of both kinds of locations within the class structure of capitalism. This is, however, not true for everyone in capitalism. For the plutocratic elite, as defined by Standing, enactment of the articles in this charter would certainly impinge on their power, wealth, and autonomy. The same would be true for much of the salariat, especially for the well-paid segments of the corporate hierarchy. For proficians some of the articles in the charter would be innocuous, but many would interfere with their advantages. If we use the 29 Articles of the Precariat Charter as a diagnostic test of class locations with respect to the rules of the game, the precariat and the working class are parts of the same class.

The diagnosis becomes somewhat more complicated when we ask if there are other significant changes in the rules of the game that would advance the interests of most people in the working class but that would be harmful for the precariat. For example, would changes in employment law that would increase job protections for workers by making it harder for workers to be laid off have the side effect of harming the precariat? What about legal changes in the United States that would make unionization easier by restricting the antiunion strategies of employers? There are some real ambiguities here, for these kinds of changes in the rules could have the side effect of deepening the dualism in the labor market and making it harder for people in precarious positions to move into more stable jobs. It is also possible, depending on the details of such changes, that they could increase the number of precarious jobs relative to stable jobs.

These ambiguities are a basis for considering the precariat to be a distinct *segment* of the working class at the level of the rules of the game. Different segments of a class share the same general interests over the optimal rules of the game within capitalism, but differ in the relative priority of potential changes in the existing rules and may have opposing interests over specific rules in certain historical contexts.

Another possibility is to argue that these tensions between the precariat segment of the working class and some of the rest of the working class reflect a specific kind of *contradictory location within class relations* in twenty-first-century capitalism. The idea here would be that those workers who still actually have enforceable rights to their jobs—the most secure, if dwindling, part of the working class—have a kind of limited property right that normally is associated with owning the means of production: the right to fire an employee. They can quit, but they cannot be fired. Fully proletarianized workers lack such rights, much like the mid-nineteenth-century factory workers of the industrial revolution who lacked all rights and job protections. Those workers with such quasi-property rights in their jobs are thus in a distinctive kind of contradictory location within class relations.[31] In this way of framing the problem, much of the precariat is firmly in the working class, while the most securely protected workers occupy a privileged contradictory class location.

What about class locations defined with respect to the *moves* in the game? In chapter 6 we saw that the micro-classes proposed by Grusky and Weeden could be considered distinguishable locations within a class structure when class is specified exclusively in terms of the optimal moves to realize material interests under existing rules of the game. Perhaps the precariat and the working class are distinct classes when class is specified in this way. Two problems arise with this proposal. First, the working class itself ceases to be "a" class if we restrict the specification of class to moves in the game. The material interests of workers located in different sectors and occupations can easily diverge sufficiently to create lines of demarcation so long as interests are defined with respect to moves in the game rather than rules of the game. Second, the precariat itself is internally divided into distinct categories at this level of

---

31   A contradictory location within class relations is simultaneously in more than one primary class. Workers with these strong rights to their jobs in a sense partially "own" their jobs, and thus are like the petty bourgeoisie. The idea that enforceable job security is a form of property rights was suggested by Philippe van Parijs in his essay "A Revolution in Class Theory," in Erik Olin Wright, ed., *The Debate on Classes*, London: Verso, 1989, 213–41.

analysis, as Standing himself acknowledges. Again, while people in all subcategories of the precariat may share common interests embodied in the Precariat Charter, they do not share common interests defined by available strategies of action under the existing rules of neoliberal capitalism.

What we are left with, then, is that the precariat is either a part of the working class, if class is analyzed in terms of the basic rules of the game of twenty-first-century developed capitalism; or it is itself an aggregation of several distinct class locations, if class is defined narrowly in terms of homogeneous interests defined by moves in the game. The precariat, as a rapidly growing segment of the working class and the bearer of the sharpest grievances against capitalism, may have a particularly important role to play in struggles over the rules of capitalism and over capitalism itself, but it is not a class in its own right.

One response to this is "so what?" Who cares? The salience of precariousness as part of the condition of life for millions of people in the world today does not depend on whether people in such positions are viewed as being in a distinct class. What matters is the reality of the conditions they face and what can be done about them. It is also certainly the case that in some rhetorical contexts calling the precariat a class could help elevate the status of the issues connected to precariousness and serve as a way of legitimating and consolidating a program of action. This is, I think, what Standing intends by his Precariat Charter. But if class analysis is to help us develop a coherent, consistent way of theoretically understanding social cleavages and the possibilities of transformation, the concepts we use should have precise meanings that illuminate the nature of shared and conflicting interests and potential collective capacities. And for these purposes, treating the precariat as a class—even as a class-in-the-making—obscures more than it clarifies.

PART 3

Class Struggle and Class Compromise

10

BENEFICIAL CONSTRAINTS: BENEFICIAL FOR WHOM?

There is, perhaps, no idea more fundamental to economic sociology than the claim that all seemingly voluntaristic economic practices presuppose the existence of noneconomic social practices and relations. The idea of a genuinely "free market" constituted solely by the voluntary choices of interacting individuals is a myth; no market is possible without a complex set of social conditions. Durkheim announced this principle in his famous discussion of the "noncontractual bases of contract." Sometimes these "noncontractual" bases are conceived in largely cultural and normative terms; at other times in terms of institutions of power, coercion, and domination. But whatever the specific content given to these social foundations of economic activity, the central sociological thesis is that without these social foundations, economic activity would, at best, function in highly suboptimal ways, and at worst would scarcely be possible.

In an important essay published in the mid-1990s, "Beneficial Constraints: On the Economic Limits of Rational Voluntarism," Wolfgang Streeck builds on this foundational idea of economic sociology to propose a theory of the variability in the effectiveness of economic performance in market societies.[1] His basic claim is that the economic performance of a market economy is enhanced where there exist effective, socially embedded constraints on self-interested, rational economic action. This claim is stronger than the conventional acknowledgment by economists that unfettered markets will sometimes generate "failures," such as the underprovision of public goods. Rather, Streeck insists that even the

---

1 Wolfgang Streeck, "Beneficial Constraints: On the Economic Limits of Rational Voluntarism," in *Contemporary Capitalism: The Embeddedness of Institutions*, ed. J. Rogers Hollingsworth and Robert Boyer, Cambridge: Cambridge University Press, 1997.

mundane, routine transactions of a market economy—buying and selling goods, hiring workers, working in a labor process, etc.—will not be effectively carried out if they are governed by unconstrained, individualistic rational economic action. In the absence of trust, legitimacy, responsibility, and other forms of "obligation," market interactions will generate highly suboptimal levels of economic performance. Streeck describes this corrective to the conventional understanding of economists as a "Durkheimian perspective on economic action." I would like to add a Marxian flavor to Streeck's Durkheimian cake.

In what follows I make three basic points: first, Streeck's Durkheimian view of market economies tends to marginalize the variability in the meaning of "good economic performance" for different classes in a market economy, especially for classes with antagonistic class interests; second, in general the level of economic constraints that is optimal for the interests of capitalists will be *below* the level of constraints that is optimal for workers; and third, the level of constraints on markets not only affects economic performance but also the relative power of workers and capitalists, and this further complicates the problem of optimal constraints for particular classes.

Streeck's Durkheimian view is represented graphically in Figure 10.1. Societies vary in the degree to which market interactions are constrained by institutional regulations and normative arrangements.[2] At one extreme is an ideal-type world of highly atomized markets lacking any effective regulatory institutions with very weak normative constraints. Such an economy generates very low levels of economic performance. Opportunism is rampant, the noncontractual bases of contract are weak, trust is in very limited supply, prisoner's dilemmas and collective action failures abound. At the other extreme is an economy with massive institutional regulations and pervasive normative constraints. This too would, in general, produce low levels of performance because of excessive

---

2   It is, of course, a considerable simplification to treat this problem primarily as one of the *level* of institutional/normative constraint rather than the *kind* of constraint. The qualitative properties of the constraints on market interactions may matter more than the sheer degree of constraint. Nevertheless, in this discussion I will generally refer only to the levels of constraints in order to keep the graphical representation of the argument simple. I do not believe that the central argument of this paper is affected by this simplification.

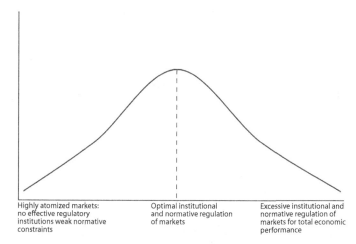

Figure 10.1. Effects of Socially Embedded Institutional and Normative Market Constraints on Economic Performance

inflexibilities that block adaptiveness.[3] What is needed is some intermediate level of constraint, sufficient to create a cohesive, well-integrated society, but not so strong as to undermine the efficiency-enhancing properties of market competition. This level of constraint can be referred to as the *social optimum for enhancing comprehensive economic performance.*[4]

---

3 If, following the arguments of Jens Beckert, we characterize the problem of social embeddedness of economic practices in terms of the conditions for solving problems of cooperation, uncertainty, and innovation, the atomized economy has substandard performance primarily because of failures of cooperation and high levels of uncertainty, while the hyperregulated economy has substandard performance because of failures of innovation. Jens Beckert, "What Is Sociological about Economic Sociology? Uncertainty and the Embeddedness of Economic Action," *Theory and Society* 25: 6, 1996, 803–40.

4 The expression "comprehensive economic performance" is meant to identify a broad, multidimensional evaluation of economic outcomes, not simply a narrow "bottom line" definition of efficiency or productivity in terms of market-registered rates of profit. Thus, for example, when firms are able to impose negative externalities on citizens in the form of pollution or other public bads, this would constitute a negative component of comprehensive economic

In this Durkheimian world, if a society's institutions fall to the left of the optimal level of constraint, it is in *everyone's* interests to try to create new institutional solutions. This might require enlightenment, since people may be duped by laissez-faire ideologies and believe, incorrectly, that a further unfettering of the market would improve poor economic performance. Furthermore, as Streeck points out, it is often a very tricky business to deliberately engineer the deepening and expansion of such normative/institutional regulation, since institutions that are designed exclusively to enhance the normative foundations for high economic performance will be unlikely to accomplish this goal. Nevertheless, it is in nobody's real economic interests to operate to the left of the socially optimal level of institutional constraints.

This Durkheimian vision is certainly an improvement over the standard neoclassical view of market economies. However, it shares with standard neoclassical models the implicit assumption that there are no classes with fundamentally antagonistic economic interests within these economies.[5] The key criterion for evaluating the outcomes of an economy is "economic performance," not the extent to which the material interests of different classes are realized. The possibility that the optimal level of institutional constraint (let alone the qualitative form of such constraints) might be systematically different for different categories of actors is not entertained.

Let us suppose, for the sake of argument, that there exist fundamental antagonisms of this sort between capitalists and workers. This opens up a potential wedge between the level (or form) of normative/institutional constraint that is optimal for overall economic performance and the level (or form) of such constraints that are optimal for the interests of capitalists, as illustrated in Figure 10.2.[6] If capitalists were exclusively concerned with comprehensive economic performance, the two curves would of course

---

performance even if doing so increased growth and profits. Similarly, relatively intangible things like the quality of life, job security, and work satisfaction should be treated as components of comprehensive economic performance.

5   More precisely: Streeck's analysis is silent on the question of class divisions and how they relate to the problem of "good economic performance" and "beneficial constraints."

6   It is also possible that the optimal level of institutional and normative constraint on the market for the interests of workers (defined as a subset of noncapitalists) might be different from the level that maximizes comprehensive economic performance. I will not consider this possibility in these comments.

overlap. But they are not. They are concerned with the rate of profit (and related economic issues like growth, market share, etc.). The conditions that maximize profits, even long-term profits, will in general be different from those which maximize comprehensive economic performance, at least if things like "quality of life," negative externalities paid by consumers, and economic security are included in the concept of economic performance.[7]

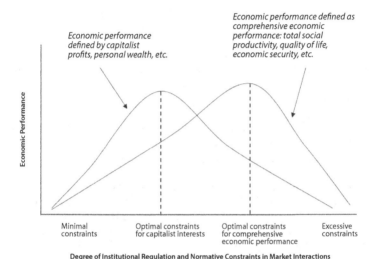

Figure 10.2. Effects of Socially Embedded Institutional and Normative Market Constraints on Economic Performance and on Capitalist Interests

The model in Figure 10.2 argues that the level of normative/institutional constraints needed to maximize comprehensive economic performance will generally be *greater* than the optimal level for realizing the interests of capitalists. This means that, contrary to the pure Durkheimian assumption, capitalists will

---

7 It is important for the argument at hand that comprehensive economic performance not be identified simply with profitability, bottom-line productivity, or even competitiveness. If it is, then the distinction between the interests of capitalists in profits and growth and comprehensive economic performance dissolves. What is good for General Motors becomes, *definitionally*, what's good for America.

prefer a level of normative and institutional constraint to the left of the social optimum. Note, however, that if the curves in Figure 10.2 are drawn approximately correctly, capitalists faced with the binary choice of having a level of institutional constraint set at the social optimum for comprehensive economic performance or at the minimal level of highly atomized markets, they would prefer the social optimum (i.e., in Figure 10.2, the social optimum level of institutional constraints corresponds to a higher level of realization of capitalist interests than does the extreme lefthand part of the curve). This is the kind of choice posed in many sociological discussions of these issues: the Hobbesian state of nature (pure atomization) of unregulated "free" markets governed by pure economic rationality is compared to an optimally cohesive and integrated society. Capitalists would certainly have their interests better served in the latter. However, in real social worlds the alternatives are not binary, and capitalists would generally prefer a level of constraints between atomization and the social optimum. There is thus a basic conflict of interest between capitalists and those who would gain from the social optimum.

When a conflict of interest of this sort occurs, the relative power of contending forces will at least partially determine the actual level of institutional and normative constraints. For simplicity let us consider only the balance of power between capitalists and workers. (For present purposes, "workers" can stand for the set of social actors whose interests are advanced by the socially optimum level of institutional and normative constraints on the market). Once we introduce power into the equation, the analysis gets considerably more complicated. The problem is that the balance of power between capitalists and workers is not exogenous to the institutions that generate constraints on markets. In general, institutional and social structural arrangements that impose significant normative constraints on market interactions will also tend to increase the power of workers. There are two general possibilities, as illustrated in Figure 10.3. In the lower curve, the relative power of workers rises slowly as institutional and normative constraints are imposed on the market. This means that at the level of constraints that is optimal for realization of capitalist interests, the balance of political power is still heavily weighted towards the capitalist class. In the upper curve, on the other hand, the power of workers rises rapidly as institutional/normative constraints on markets increase, so that at the capitalist optimum the balance of power has shifted strongly towards workers. In such circumstances, workers would potentially be powerful enough to further push for the elaboration of institutional constraints, perhaps even to the socially optimum level. Under this power function, in other words, *the capitalist optimum is not a stable institutional equilibrium*: it cannot be dynamically sustained, since it empowers those actors whose interests are better served by an even higher level of institutional constraint.

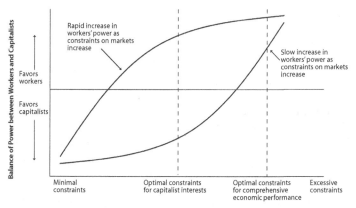

Figure 10.3. Effects of Socially Embedded Institutional and Normative Market Constraints on the Balance of Power between Capitalists and Workers

This dynamic instability of the capitalist optimum might well underwrite a preference on the part of capitalists for a level of institutional constraints that is to the left of the capitalist optimum itself: that is, to prevent the empowerment of challengers to their interests, capitalists may prefer a set of economic institutions that are suboptimal on strictly economic grounds *even for their own interests*. This is one way of interpreting neoliberalism and the mania for excessive deregulation in the past two decades: the zeal to dismantle the regulatory machinery of capitalism since the early 1980s was driven by a desire to undermine the conditions for empowerment of interests opposed to those of capitalists—even if doing so meant underregulating capitalism from the point of view of long-term needs of capital accumulation.

I do not know which—if either—of these power functions is more realistic. The shape of these curves certainly depend on a range of other factors not included in this discussion. But I do think that these power dynamics illustrate an important source of complexity that needs to be added to the Durkheimian perspective on economic systems. The push for deregulation and the erosion of those institutions that sustain strong normative commitments and constraints on markets may not simply reflect myopia on the part of elites or a lack of understanding on their part about the essential role that trust and obligation play in the effective functioning of a capitalist market economy. The ideology of the unfettered, unregulated market may be an effective weapon in a battle over the optimal level of provision of such constraints, a battle driven by real conflicts of interests and resolved through the exercise of power. Capitalists may also, of course, have short time horizons and be vulnerable to "pressure for detailed cost accounting" that lead them to destroy institutional arrangements that are in their own long-term interests.[8] But I do not think that this is the main story. Enlightenment of the capitalist class to their long-term interests in a strong civic culture of obligation and trust is not enough; the balance of power also needs to be changed. And since this shift in balance of power will be costly to those in privileged positions, it will only occur through a process of mobilization and struggle.

8   Streeck, "Beneficial Constraints," 206.

11

WORKING CLASS POWER, CAPITALIST CLASS INTERESTS, AND CLASS COMPROMISE

The concept of "class compromise" invokes three quite distinct images. In the first, class compromise is an illusion. Leaders of working class organizations—especially unions and parties—strike opportunistic deals with the capitalist class that promise general benefits for workers but, in the end, are largely empty. Class compromises are, at their core, one-sided capitulations rather than reciprocal bargains embodying mutual concessions.[1]

In the second image, class compromises are like stalemates on a battlefield. Two armies of roughly similar strength are locked in battle. Each is sufficiently strong to impose severe costs on the other; neither is strong enough to definitively vanquish the opponent. In such a situation of stalemate the contending forces may agree to a "compromise": to refrain from mutual damage in exchange for concessions on both sides. The concessions are real, not phony, even if they are asymmetrical. Still, they don't constitute a process of real cooperation between opposing class forces. This outcome can be referred to as a "negative class compromise."

The third image sees class compromise as a form of mutual cooperation between opposing classes. This is not simply a situation of a balance of power in which the outcome of conflict falls somewhere between a complete victory and a complete defeat for either party. Rather, here there is a possibility of a non-zero-sum game between workers and capitalists, a game in which both parties can improve their position through various forms of active, mutual cooperation. This outcome can be called a "positive class compromise."

This chapter explores the theoretical logic of positive class compromises and proposes a general model of the conditions

---

1 Parts of this chapter overlap with pp. 338–61 of my *Envisioning Real Utopias*, London: Verso, 2010.

conducive to them in developed capitalist societies. I do not attempt a systematic empirical investigation, although I use empirical illustrations to clarify elements of the model. My premise is that so long as capitalism in one form or another is the only historically available way of organizing an economy, a positive class compromise—if it is achievable—will generally constitute the most advantageous context for the improvement of the material interests and life circumstances of ordinary people. If one is interested in advancing such interests, therefore, it is important to understand the conditions that facilitate or hinder the prospects for positive class compromise.

The central argument I make is that the possibilities for stable, positive class compromise generally hinge on the relationship between the *associational power* of the working class and the *material interests* of capitalists. The conventional wisdom among both neoclassical economists and traditional Marxists is that in general there is an inverse relationship between these two variables: increases in the power of workers adversely affect the interests of capitalists (see Figure 11.1). The rationale for this view is straightforward for Marxist scholars: since the profits of capitalists are closely tied to the exploitation of workers, the material interests of workers and capitalists are inherently antagonistic. Anything that strengthens the capacity of workers to struggle for and realize their interests, therefore, negatively affects the interests of capitalists. The conventional argument by neoclassical economists is somewhat less straightforward, for they deny that in a competitive equilibrium workers are exploited by capitalists. Nevertheless, they see working class associational power as interfering with the efficient operation of labor markets by making wages hard to readjust downward when needed and by making it harder for employers to fire workers. Unions and other forms of working class power are seen as forms of monopolistic power within markets, and like all such practices generate monopoly rents and inefficient allocations. As a result, unionized workers are able to extort a monopoly rent in the form of higher wages at the expense of both capitalists and nonunionized workers.

This chapter explores an alternative understanding of the relationship between workers' power and capitalists' interests: instead of an inverse relationship, this alternative postulates a curvilinear *reverse-J* relationship (see Figure 11.2).[2] As in the conventional

2 The reverse-**J**-shaped relationship between working class power and capitalist interests was first suggested to me in a 1990 paper by Joel Rogers,

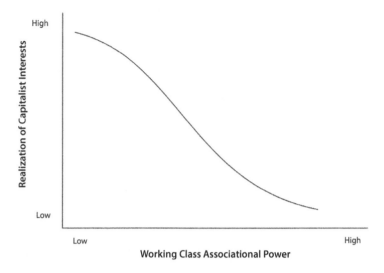

Figure 11.1. Conventional View of the Relationship between Working Class Associational Power and Capitalist Interests

wisdom, capitalist class interests are best satisfied when the working class is highly disorganized, with workers competing with each other in an atomized way and lacking significant forms of associational power. As working class power increases, capitalist class interests are initially adversely affected. However, once working class power crosses some threshold, working class associational power begins to have positive effects on capitalist interests. As we shall see in more detail below, these conditions allow for significant gains in productivity and rates of profit due to such things as high levels of bargained cooperation between workers and capitalists, rationalized systems of skill upgrading and job training, enhanced capacity for solving macro-economic problems, and a greater willingness of workers to accept technological change given the relative job security they achieve because

---

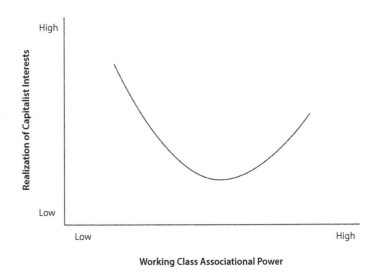

Working Class Associational Power

Figure 11.2. Curvillinear Relationship between Working Class Associational Power and Capitalist Interests

of union protections. The upward-bending part of the curve, where increases in working class power have positive effects on capitalist class interests, generates conditions for positive class compromise. The goal of this chapter, then, is to elaborate a general theoretical model of the causal processes underlying the relation presented in Figure 11.2.

Section 1 briefly defines the core concepts used in the analysis and discusses a number of methodological issues. Section 2 situates the problem of positive class compromise within a broader literature on interclass cooperation, labor relations and economic governance. Section 3 then frames the problem of class compromise in terms of various possible game theory models of the interactions of workers and capitalists. With this game theoretic background, section 4 elaborates a general theoretical model and underlying mechanisms for the reverse-**J** model of positive class compromise.

I. CORE CONCEPTS AND METHODOLOGICAL ISSUES

None of the concepts used in this analysis have transparent meanings. In particular, the concepts of class, interests, and power are all highly contested. I will not attempt to elaborate analytically complete definitions of these concepts here, but some brief clarifications are necessary.

Class

Class and its related concepts—class structure, class struggle, class formation, class compromise—can be analyzed at various levels of abstraction. For some purposes it is important to deploy a highly differentiated class concept that elaborates a complex set of concrete locations within class structures. My work on the problem of the "middle class" and "contradictory locations within class relations" would be an example of such an analysis.[3] For some problems the causal processes cannot be properly studied without specifying a range of fine-grained differentiations and divisions within classes on the basis of such things as sector, status, gender, and race. For other purposes, however, it is appropriate to use a much more abstract, simplified class concept, revolving around the central polarized class relation of capitalism: capitalists and workers. This is the class concept I use in this chapter.

In a stylized Marxian manner, I define capitalists as those people who own and control the capital used in production and workers as all employees excluded from such ownership and control. In this abstract analysis of class structure I assume that these are mutually exclusive categories. There is thus no middle class as such. No workers own any stock. Executives, managers, and professionals in firms are either amalgamated into the capitalist class by virtue of their ownership of stock and command of production, or they are simply part of the "working class" as employees. This is of course unrealistic. My claim, however, is that this abstract, polarized description of class relations in capitalism can still be useful to clarify real mechanisms that actual actors face and is thus a useful point of departure for developing a theory of class compromise.[4]

---

3 Wright, *Classes*, London: Verso, 1985; *Class Counts: Comparative Studies in Class Analysis*, Cambridge: Cambridge University Press, 1997.

4 The claim that this abstract polarized concept of class is analytically useful

Interests

Throughout this chapter, I focus on what can be narrowly termed the "material interests" of people by virtue of their class location, or what I refer to in shorthand as "class interests."[5] In general, I make two radical simplifying assumptions about the nature of these interests: first, that class interests can be reduced to a single quantitative dimension, so that one can talk about the extent to which the interests of the members of a class are realized; and second, that all people in a given class location share the same class interests. Both of these assumptions are problematic when we study concrete capitalist societies, but, as in the adoption of a simple polarized class structure concept, they are useful simplifications for the present analytical purposes.

Power

Like the term "interests," "power" is used in many different ways in social theory. In the context of class analysis, power can be thought of as the *capacity of individuals and organizations to realize class interests.* Insofar as the interests of people in different classes—workers and capitalists in the present analysis—are opposed to each other, this implies that the capacity of workers to realize their class interests depends in part on their capacity to counter the power of capitalists. Power, in this context, is thus a relational concept.

In this chapter my concern is mainly with what I term working class "associational" power—the various forms of power that result from the formation of collective organizations of workers.

---

may be controversial. Given that actual capitalist firms engaging in complex strategies and bargaining with their employees encounter considerable heterogeneity, and this heterogeneity in fact does matter for the optimal profit maximizing strategy of the firm, it may seem illegitimate to bracket such complexity in favor of a simple model of capital and labor. As in many attempts at elaborating theoretical models, the appropriate level of abstraction is a matter of contestation.

5   When I speak of "class interests" I always mean the interests of people determined by their location in the class structure. I do not believe that classes as collective entities have "interests" in a literal sense. Of course, individuals may have interests in the strength of the collective organizations of classes, and the class interests of individuals may be contingent upon the security of the interests of other members of the same class, but this still does not mean that classes-*qua*-collectivities have interests.

These organizations include unions and parties, but may also include a variety of other forms, such as works councils or forms of institutional representation of workers on boards of directors in schemes of worker co-determination, or even, in certain circumstances, community organizations. Associational power contrasts with what can be termed "structural power"—power that results simply from the location of workers within the economic system. The power of workers as individuals that results directly from tight labor markets or from the strategic location of a particular group of workers within a key industrial sector are thus instances of structural power. While such structural power may itself influence associational power, associational power is the focus of analysis here.

The models I examine do not directly concern the role of associational power of capitalists in the formation of class compromise. As the literature on neocorporatism has pointed out, there are certain institutional settings of class compromise in which the associational power of employers plays a pivotal role,[6] and I refer in my analysis to the role of such associations. My concern, however, is not with capitalist associational power as such, but with the ways in which working class associational power has potential impacts on the interests of capitalists.

There is no implication in the analysis that workers' associational power is entirely exogenous to the processes investigated. While I concentrate on the ways in which increases in workers' power can positively benefit capitalist interests, it may also be the case that part of the explanation for the level of workers' associational power is precisely the existence of this beneficial effect, and conversely, that the erosion of such beneficial effects may itself contribute to the decline of workers' power. To the extent that the intensity of resistance by capitalists, individually and collectively, to workers' attempts to create and sustain associational power itself partially depends on the potential benefits to capital of such

6 Wolfgang Streeck and Philippe Schmitter, "Community, Market, State—and Associations? The Prospective Contribution of Interest Governance to Social Order," *European Sociological Review* 1:2, September 1985, 119–38; Wolfgang Streeck, *Social Institutions and Economic Performance: Studies of Industrial Relations in Advanced Capitalist Economies*, Newbury Park, CA: Sage, 1992; Jonas Pontusson, "Between Neo-Liberalism and the German Model: Swedish Capitalism in Transition," in *Political Economy of Modern Capitalism: Mapping Convergence and Diversity*, Colin Crouch and Wolfgang Streeck, eds., Thousand Oaks, CA: Sage, 1997.

power, the extent of workers' power will in part be a function of capitalist interests. In any case, this chapter does not attempt to develop a dynamic theory of the causes of working class power, but focuses instead on the effects of workers' power on capitalist interests.

Sites of Class Compromise

Class struggle and compromise do not occur within an amorphous "society," but within specific institutional contexts—firms, markets, states. The real mechanisms that generate the reverse-J curve in Figure 11.2 are embedded in such institutional contexts. Three institutional spheres within which class struggles occur and class compromises are forged are particularly important:

> *The sphere of exchange.* This sphere concerns above all the labor market and various other kinds of commodity markets, but in some situations financial markets may also be an arena within which class conflicts occur and class compromises are forged.

> *The sphere of production.* This sphere concerns what goes on inside firms once workers are hired and capital invested. Conflicts over the labor process and technology are characteristic examples.

> *The sphere of politics.* Class conflict and class compromise also occur within the state over the formation and implementation of state policies and the administration of various kinds of state-enforced rules.

There is a rough correspondence between each of these institutional spheres of class conflict and class compromise and characteristic kinds of working class collective organizations: *labor unions* are the characteristic associational form for conflict/compromise in the sphere of exchange; *works councils* and related associations are the characteristic form within the sphere of production; and *political parties* are the characteristic form within the sphere of politics.

The central task of our analysis, then, is to examine the mechanisms that enable these different forms of working class associational power—unions, works councils, parties—to forge *positive* class compromises within the spheres of exchange, production, and politics.

2. SITUATING THE CONCEPT OF CLASS COMPROMISE

In the most abstract and general terms, class compromise—whether positive or negative—can be defined as a situation in which some kind of *quid pro quo* is established between conflicting classes in which, in one way or another, people in each class make concessions in favor of the interests of people in the opposing class.[7] The "compromise" in class compromise is a compromise of class-based interests—members of each class give up something of value. Class compromise is thus always defined against a counterfactual in which such concessions are not made. Typically this is a situation in which the use of threats, force, and resistance plays a prominent active role in class interactions.

Defined in this way, the idea of class compromise is closely linked to Gramsci's concept of hegemony.[8] Gramsci uses hegemony to distinguish two general conditions of capitalist society. In a *non*hegemonic system, capitalist class relations are reproduced primarily through the direct, despotic use of coercion. In a hegemonic system, in contrast, class relations are sustained in significant ways through the *active consent* of people in the subordinate classes. Coercion is still present as a background condition—hegemony is "protected by the armor of coercion" in Gramsci's famous phrase—but it is not continually deployed actively to control people's actions. To quote Przeworski, "A hegemonic system is, for Gramsci, a capitalist society in which capitalists exploit with consent of the exploited."[9] For hegemony to be sustained over time, there must be, in Przeworski's apt expression, "material bases of consent." This, in turn, requires some sort of class compromise: "The fact of hegemony presupposes that account be taken of the interests and the tendencies of the groups over which hegemony is to be exercised, and that a certain compromise equilibrium should be formed—in other words, that

---

7   Although the actual term "class compromise" appears mainly within the Marxian tradition of social theory, the substantive idea has much broader currency. I will not limit the discussion here to instances where the term is explicitly deployed.

8   Antonio Gramsci, *Selections from the Prison Notebooks*, ed. and trans. Quintin Hoare and Geoffrey Nowell Smith, New York: International Publishers, 1971.

9   Adam Przeworski, *Capitalism and Social Democracy*, Cambridge: Cambridge University Press, 1985, 136.

the leading group should make sacrifices of an economic-corporate kind."[10]

Gramsci developed the concept of class compromise in only a sketchy and fragmented form. The scholar who has most systematically and rigorously elaborated this concept in a manner relevant to the issues in this chapter is Adam Przeworski. Przeworski makes the central quid pro quo of class compromise explicit:

> Given the uncertainty whether and how capitalists would invest profits, any class compromise must consist of the following elements: workers consent to profit as an institution, that is, they behave in such a manner as to make positive rates of profit possible; and capitalists commit themselves to some rate of transformation of profits into wage increases and some rate of investment out of profits.[11]

Przeworski's formulation here is close to what I have called "negative class compromise" insofar as he emphasizes the abstention of workers from levels of militancy that would interfere with the production of profits in exchange for material concessions by capitalists. Elsewhere, he explores the positive face of class compromise in his analysis of how Keynesianism, backed by organized labor and social democratic parties in the advanced capitalist countries in the post–World War II period, expanded aggregate demand in ways which ultimately benefitted capital as well as labor.[12] The model of class compromise which I develop in this chapter can be viewed as an extension and reformulation of Przeworski's core idea through the elaboration of this positive side of class compromise.

Before examining the details of this model, it will useful to situate it within a broader array of alternative treatments of the problem of cooperation and compromise among class actors. Table 11.1 organizes this conceptual space along two dimensions: first, whether the strategic basis of class compromise is primarily *individual strategies* or *associational power*; and second, whether the form of class compromise is primarily *negative* or *positive*. The four categories generated by these two dimensions constitute distinctive ways in which interclass cooperation and compromise can be generated.

---

10   Gramsci, *Prison Notebooks*, 161.

11   Przeworski, *Capitalism and Social Democracy*, 182.

12   Ibid., 205–11.

Form of Class Compromise

Strategic Base of Class Compromise		Negative	Positive
	Individual strategies without associational power	Effort-promoting efficiency wages	Loyalty-promoting internal labor markets
	Associational power	Collective bargaining as mutual concessions	Positive-sum social pacts: Keynesianism, neocorporatism

Figure 11.1. The Conceptual Space of Class Compromise

The paradigmatic case of negative class compromise grounded in individual strategies is so-called "efficiency wages."[13] As already noted in chapter 7, an efficiency wage is a wage premium—a wage above the equilibrium "market-clearing wage"—paid by an employer as part of a strategy to reduce shirking on the part of employees. As elaborated by Bowles and Bowles and Gintis, employers face a problem of the "extraction of labor effort" from workers—getting workers to work harder than they want to do spontaneously—since the labor contract is neither transparent nor costlessly enforceable.[14] Employers face a trade-off between spending more money on improving the effectiveness of monitoring or paying higher employment rents. Such efficiency wages are a form

---

13   There are some treatments of efficiency wages which treat them more as a form of *positive* than of *negative* class compromise. For example, Akerloff sees such arrangements less as a concession in response to a form of individual resistance—shirking—and more as a way of improving generalized morale through a kind of normatively grounded "gift exchange." The implication is that efficiency wages underwrite active cooperation. George Ackerlof, "Labor Contracts as Partial Gift Exchange," *Quarterly Journal of Economics* 97:2, 1982: 543–69.

14   Samuel Bowles, "The Production Process in a Competitive Economy: Walrasian, Neo-Hobbesian, and Marxian Models," *American Economic Review* 75: 1, March 1985, 16–36; Samuel Bowles and Herbert Gintis, "Contested Exchange," *Politics & Society* 18: 2, June 1990, 165–222; Samule Bowles and Herbert Gintis, *Recasting Egalitarianism: New Rules for Communities, States and Markets*, vol. 3 in *The Real Utopias Project*, ed. Erik Olin Wright, London: Verso, 1990, 36–9.

of negative class compromise insofar as the higher wages are an alternative to more purely coercive strategies by employers in the face of strategies of resistance (shirking) by individual workers.[15]

Positive class compromises can also emerge out individual strategic interactions between employers and workers. Internal labor markets are perhaps the best example.[16] Although, as in the case of efficiency wages, internal labor markets may increase the effectiveness of negative sanctions by employers, since workers within internal labor markets have more to lose if they are disciplined or fired,[17] most analyses of internal labor markets emphasize the ways they are designed to elicit active cooperation rooted in loyalty and commitment of the individual to the interests of the organization. This is one of the central themes in the extensive literature on

---

15 Investigations of institutional arrangements such as efficiency wages, especially by economists, generally do not explicitly analyze them in class terms. From the point of view of standard neoclassical economics, such arrangements are simply profit-maximizing strategies of employers designed to minimize the transactions costs associated with the inherent human tendency, in Oliver Williamson's expression, for people to be "self-interest seeking with guile." (Williamson, *The Economic Institutions of Capitalism*, New York: Free Press, 1985, 47.) Bowles and Gintis, in contrast, firmly situate the problem of efficiency wages in the class relations of capitalist production, arguing that in firms where workers were also owners mutual monitoring would significantly replace the need for efficiency wages. I would further amend the standard efficiency wage argument by saying that where workers were also owners, the normative conditions for unmonitored reciprocity would also be enhanced.

16 Some discussions of internal labor markets treat them primarily as examples of negative class compromise, emphasizing the ways in which internal labor markets are used to divide the working class, weaken unions and in other ways enhance capitalist control over labor. See, for example, David M. Gordon, "Capitalist Efficiency and Socialist Efficiency," *Monthly Review* 28: 3, 1976, 19–39; and Richard Edwards, *Contested Terrain: The Transformation of the Workplace in the Twentieth Century*, New York: Basic Books, 1979. Others treat internal labor markets strictly as an issue of solving problems of internal efficiency, typically linked to information costs and the problem of retaining skilled employees, without systematic reference to the class character of these efficiency considerations. See, for example, Peter Doeringer and Michael Piore, *Internal Labor Markets and Manpower Analysis*, 2d edn., Lexington, MA: D.C. Heath, 1985; Bruce Greenwald, *Adverse Selection in the Labor Market*, New York: Garland Press, 1979; Michael Waldman, "Job Assignments, Signaling, and Efficiency," *Rand Journal of Economics* 15: 2, 1984, 255–67.

17 Randall Bartlett, *Economics and Power*, Cambridge: Cambridge University Press, 1989, 135–7.

Japanese work organization,[18] but has also figured in the broader analysis of the internal organization of capitalist firms,[19] and even some more abstract analyses of class relations as such.[20]

Most discussions of class conflict and class compromise pay relatively little attention to these forms of interclass compromise, positive or negative, generated by the strategies of individuals. Rather, they focus on the ways class compromises are forged through class struggles rooted in class-based associational power. Analyses of negative class compromise emerging from class struggle are particularly prominent in the Marxist tradition.[21] If the interests of workers and capitalists are inherently antagonistic and

---

18   Ronald Dore, *British Factory, Japanese Factory: The Origins of National Diversity in Industrial Relations*, Berkeley: University of California Press, 1973; W. G. Ouchi, *Theory Z: How American Business Can Meet the Japanese Challenge*, Reading, MA: Addison-Wesley, 1981; Masahiko Aoki, *Information, Incentives, and Bargaining in the Japanese Firm: A Microtheory of the Japanese Economy*, Cambridge: Cambridge University Press, 1988.

19   Oliver Williamson, *The Economic Institutions of Capitalism*, New York: Free Press, 1985; F. K. Foulkes, *Personnel Policies in Large Non-Union Companies*, Englewood Cliffs, NJ: Prentice Hall, 1980; Aage Sörensen, 1994. "Forms, Wages and Incentives," in *Handbook of Economic Sociology*, ed. Neil Smelser and Richard Swedberg, Princeton, NJ: Princeton University Press, 504–28.

20   John Goldthorpe's concept of the service class revolves around the problems employers face when their employees sell a "service" rather than simply "labor." (Goldthorpe, "On the Service Class," in *Social Class and the Division of Labor*, Anthony Giddens and Gavin Mackenzie, eds., Cambridge: Cambridge University Press, 1982, 162–85.) The creation of career ladders built around prospective rewards which create a longer time horizon of commitment for such employees is at the core of his analysis of this employment relation. My analysis of "loyalty rents" for managerial class locations (Wright, *Class Counts*, 21) also emphasizes the problem of creating deeper commitments for certain categories of employees by anchoring their jobs in career ladders. In both of these treatments of class relations, internal labor markets are created as responses to the strategies of individuals within firms.

21   Such views, however, are not restricted to Marxists. John R. Commons's conception of collective bargaining, for example, is essentially a conception of negative class compromise insofar as he felt it was necessary to avoid mutually destructive "class war." Unions might be in the general "public interest," but Commons does not claim that unionization and collective bargaining as such are directly beneficial to capitalists: "The unions and administrative commissions were organized to restrain corporations, also in the public interest, from abuse of their corporate power over individuals." John R. Commons, *The Economics of Collective Action*, Madison: University of Wisconsin Press, [1950] 1970, 132.

polarized, whatever compromises emerge from class struggle would appear to simply reflect balances of power between contending forces.[22]

The idea of positive class compromise generated by organized class struggle sits less comfortably within the Marxist tradition, but is at the core of the large literature on social democracy and neocorporatism,[23] and considerable work in economic sociology that focuses on the problem of the economic performance of different capitalist economies.[24] As Rogers and Streeck put it: "The democratic left makes progress under capitalism when it improves the material well-being of workers, solves a problem for capitalists that capitalists cannot solve for themselves, and in doing both wins sufficient political cachet to contest capitalist monopoly on articulating the 'general interest.'"[25]

The classic form of this argument is rooted in the Keynesian strand of macroeconomic theory. Full employment, insofar as it implies high levels of capacity utilization and higher aggregate demand for the products of capitalist firms, potentially serves the interests of capitalists. But it also risks a profit squeeze from rapidly rising wages and spiraling levels of inflation. Keynes himself recognized this complication: "I do not doubt that a serious problem will arise as to how wages are to be restrained when we have a combination of collective bargaining and full employment."[26] The emergence and consolidation in a number of countries of strong,

22 For an illustrative example, see David Kotz, "Interpreting the Social Structure of Accumulation Theory," in *Social Structures of Accumulation*, eds. David Kotz, Terrance McDonough, and Michael Reich, Cambridge: Cambridge University Press, 1994, 55.

23 Walter Korpi, *The Democratic Class Struggle*, London: Routledge and Kegan Paul, 1983; David Soskice, "Wage Determination: The Changing Role of Institutions in Advanced Industrialized Countries," *Oxford Review of Economic Policy* 6:4, 1990: 36–61; Gøsta Esping-Andersen, *Three Worlds of Welfare Capitalism*, Princeton, NJ: Princeton University Press, 1990.

24 Streeck and Schmitter, "Community, Market, State"; Lane Kenworthy, *In Search of National Economic* Success: *Balancing Competition and Cooperation*, Thousand Oaks, CA: Sage, 1995; David M. Gordon, *Fat and Mean: The Corporate Squeeze of Working Americans and the Myth of Managerial "Downsizing,"* New York: Free Press, 1996; Crouch and Streeck, *Political Economy of Modern Capitalism*.

25 Joel Rogers and Wolfgang Streeck, "Productive Solidarities: Economic Strategy and Left Politics," in David Miliband, ed. *Reinventing the Left*, Cambridge, MA: Polity Press, 1994.

26 Andrew Glynn, "Social Democracy and Full Employment," *New Left Review* 1:211, May/June 1995, 37.

centralized unions capable of imposing wage restraint on both workers and employers was perhaps the most successful solution to this problem in the second half of the twentieth century. In this sense, a powerful labor movement need not simply constitute the basis for a negative class compromise, extracting benefits for workers through threats to capital. If a labor movement is sufficiently disciplined, particularly when it is articulated to a sympathetic state, it can positively contribute to the realization of capitalist interests by helping to solve macroeconomic problems.

The best-known empirical study to explore the curvilinear relationship between workers' power and capitalist interests is Calmfors and Driffill's 1988 study of the effects of union centralization on economic performance.[27] Following Mancur Olson's suggestion that "organized interests may be most harmful when they are strong enough to cause major disruptions but not sufficiently encompassing to bear any significant fraction of the costs for society of their actions in their own interests,"[28] they demonstrate that among eighteen OECD countries during the period 1963–85, economic performance measured in a variety of ways was best among those countries with *either* highly centralized *or* highly decentralized wage bargaining structures, and worst in the intermediary countries. A similar result, using different kinds of indicators, is found in Hicks and Kenworthy's study of the impact of various forms of cooperative institutions on economic performance.[29] They observe

---

27 Strictly speaking, Calmfors and Driffill study the relationship between workers' power and various measures of general economic performance rather than capitalists' interests as such, but in the context of their arguments this can reasonably be taken as an indicator of capitalists' interests. Lars Calmfors and J. Driffill, "Bargaining Structure, Corporatism and Macroeconomic Performance," *Economic Policy* 6, April 1988, 13–61. See also Matti Pohjola, "Corporatism and Wage Bargaining," in *Social Corporatism: A Superior Economic System?*, eds. Jukka Pekkarinen, Matti Pohjola, and Bob Rowthorn, Oxford: Clarendon Press, 1992; Richard Freeman, "Labour Market Institutions and Economic Performance," *Economic Policy* 6, 1988, 64–80; Lars Calmfors, "Centralization of Wage Bargaining and Macroeconomic Performance—a Survey," *OECD Economic Studies* 21, Winter 1993, 161–91; Geoffrey Garrett, *Partisan Politics in the Global Economy*, Cambridge: Cambridge University Press, 1998; Bob Rowthorn, "Corporatism and Labour Market Performance," in Pekkarinen, Pohjola, and Rowthorn, *Social Corporatism*.

28 Calmfors and Driffill, "Bargaining Structure," 15.

29 Alexander Hicks and Lan Kenworthy, "Cooperation and Political Economic Performance in Affluent Democratic Capitalism," *American Journal of Sociology* 103: 6, 1998, 1631–72.

a strong curvilinear relationship between union density and real per capita GDP growth for the period 1960–89 in eighteen OECD countries, indicating that countries with either low or high union density had higher growth rates during these three decades than countries with middling levels of union density.

The rest of this chapter will attempt to elaborate theoretically this curvilinear model of positive class compromise. I begin, in the next section, by framing the problem through a game theoretic perspective on strategic conflicts between workers and capitalists and then turn to the problem of the mechanisms which generate the curvilinear relationship between workers' power and capitalist interests.

3. STRATEGIC GAMES AND CLASS COMPROMISE

In order to analyze the relationship of working class associational power to capitalist class interests and class compromise, we must first more rigorously understand the strategic contexts for the conflicts of interests of workers and capitalists. We can do this by exploring a series of stripped-down game theory models based on a highly simplified picture of class conflict in which workers and capitalists each face a binary strategic choice: to *cooperate* with the other class or to actively *oppose* its interests. Because the actors in this game have qualitatively different roles in the system of production, the meaning of "cooperate" and "oppose" are different for each.

As summarized in Table 11.2, for workers, cooperation with capitalists requires that they work hard and diligently in order to maximize the capitalists' rate of profit. Workers rely primarily on labor market mechanisms (changing jobs) as a way of expressing dissatisfaction with pay or working conditions. While they may have collective associations (unions), they do not engage in active struggles to collectively pressure capitalists for improvements, nor do they engage in political struggle to advance workers' interests against those of capitalists. To oppose capitalists is to struggle against them, individually and collectively, in order to raise workers' incomes and enhance the extent to which workers control their own labor effort, and thus to minimize the extent to which capitalists exploit and control workers. This includes political struggles to expand workers' rights and their capacity to organize collective associations. For capitalists, cooperation with workers means paying workers as much as possible, compatible with maintaining a rate of profit sufficient to

Workers

		Cooperate with capitalists	Oppose capitalists
Capitalists	Cooperate with workers	C,C	O,C
	Oppose workers	C,O	O,O

Meaning of Cooperate and Oppose for Different Classes	
Workers:	
Cooperate:	Work hard and diligently to maximize the profits of capitalists.
Oppose:	Minimize the extent to which capitalists exploit and dominate workers.
Capitalists:	
Cooperate:	Pay workers as much as possible and treat them fairly in the workplace; accept workers' organizations.
Oppose:	Pay workers as little as possible and get as much work out of them as possible; resist workers' organizations.

Table 11.2. Strategic Options for Workers and Capitalists

reproduce the firm; accepting workers' organizations (unions and parties); responding to workers' demands over working conditions; and moderating their own consumption in favor of employment-generating investment. To oppose workers' interests means paying them as little as possible, given the market and technological constraints capitalists face; getting as much labor as possible out of workers; and resisting worker organizations. As in the case of workers, such opposition includes political action, such as opposing unemployment benefits and welfare safety nets that raise the reservation wage and supporting restrictive labor laws that impede unionization. Taking these two alternatives for each class yields the four possible configurations of class conflict presented in Table 11.2. In terms of these alternatives, "positive class compromise" constitutes the situation in which both classes agree to cooperation (C,C).[30]

Figure 11.3 presents the pay-offs to workers and capitalists of alternative strategic combinations in a variety of strategic games. These games can be thought of as either reflecting different underlying power relations and rules of social interaction for workers and capitalists or as reflecting different theories about the nature of the strategic environment faced by workers and capitalists. Model 1 can be called a *unilateral capitalist domination game.* Here, the best outcome for capitalists is C,O: workers cooperate with capitalists (working hard, not organizing, etc.), and capitalists oppose workers (pay them only what the market dictates, oppose collective organization, etc.). The second best outcome for capitalists is mutual opposition (O,O). In this game, capitalists are sufficiently powerful relative to workers that they can punish workers at relatively little cost to themselves when workers organize against them. Workers are thus worse off under O,O than under *unilateral* workers' cooperation (C,O). Struggle doesn't pay. In this game, therefore, C,O will be the equilibrium outcome: capitalists are always better off opposing workers, and given that capitalists always oppose workers, workers are better off cooperating with capitalists.

---

30   Obviously, the options in the real world are much more complex than this stark contrast—not only are there various degrees of opposition and cooperation, but a variety of qualitatively distinct forms of both. Nevertheless, for purposes of developing a general inventory of strategic contexts for class compromise in which mutual cooperation occurs it will be useful to abstract from such complexity and examine games in which members of each class (considered either as individuals or as members of associations) make such simple, dichotomous choices.

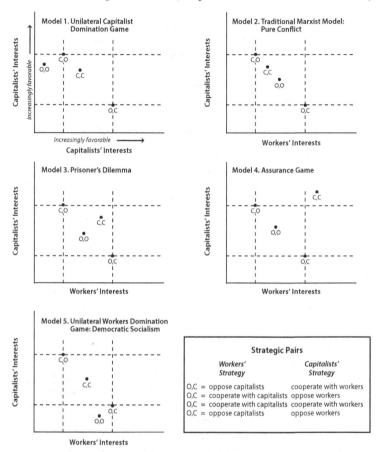

Figure 11.3. Possible Strategic Games and Payoffs for Workers and Capitalists

Model 2 represents the standard Marxist view of class conflict in which the interests of workers and capitalists are treated in a purely inverse relation as a zero-sum *pure conflict game*. The optimal situation for capitalists is to oppose the interests of workers while workers cooperate with them (C,O). The second best situation for capitalists is mutual cooperation (C,C). This, however, is *less* advantageous for workers than is mutual opposition (O,O). In the traditional Marxist view, because the interests of workers and capitalists are strictly polarized, it is always better for workers to struggle against capitalists—to actively oppose capitalist interests—than to willingly cooperate. The C,C solution, in effect, is an illusion: "cooperative" capitalists, the argument goes, treat workers only marginally better than capitalists who actively oppose workers, but cooperative workers are much less able to force their employers to make concessions than are oppositional workers. Above all, when working class associations actively cooperate with capitalists they weaken their capacity for mobilization, and their weakness ultimately invites capitalists to oppose workers interests, thus leading C,C to degenerate into C,O. The O,O option, therefore, generally promises a better long-term pay-off for workers than does the C,C option. As a result of such struggles there will be moments when capitalists indeed do make concessions to workers as a result of these struggles—grant them pay raises, improve working conditions, etc. These concessions are at best a negative class compromise—concessions in the face of struggle. For both classes in this game, opposition is better than cooperation regardless of what the other class does, and thus the equilibrium will be mutual opposition (O,O)—active forms of class struggle.[31] The class struggle is much more like trench warfare with occasional victories and defeats for each combatant, and perhaps periods of relatively stable balances of forces underwriting a *negative* class compromise.

Model 3 is the standard *prisoner's dilemma* game. This is a game with symmetrical payoffs for the two classes: C,C is the second best outcome for each class and O,O is the third best outcome. Unlike in Model 1, mutual opposition is now costly to capitalists. This implies that workers have sufficient power to punish capitalists within class struggles. Unlike Model 2, however, workers are better off in mutual cooperation than in mutual opposition. Both classes are thus better off if they cooperate with each other than if they mutually oppose each other. However, if this were a one-shot game, in standard prisoner's dilemma fashion the equilibrium outcome would be O,O, since both classes could improve their pay-offs by defecting from the mutual cooperation outcome. If this is a repeated game, as it would be in the real world of class interactions, the outcome is less determinate. As Axelrod and many others have shown, in an iterated prisoner's dilemma, mutual cooperation can be a stable solution depending on the ways that opposition in future rounds of the game is used to punish players for noncooperation in

---

31 Even though mutual opposition is the equilibrium solution, Model 2 is not a prisoners' dilemma for workers since in a prisoner's dilemma actors prefer mutual cooperation to mutual opposition.

earlier rounds.[32] As the possibility of a stable C,C solution occurs, then *positive* class compromise also becomes possible.

Model 4 is a standard *assurance game*: for both classes the optimal solution is mutual cooperation and unilateral cooperation is worse than mutual opposition. Unless there is reasonable confidence that the other class will cooperate, therefore, mutual cooperation is unlikely to occur. If class conflict was an assurance game, failures of cooperation would primarily reflect a lack of enlightenment on the part of actors—they simply don't know what's good for them. This corresponds to the views of a certain kind of naïve liberalism, where conflict is always seen as reflecting misunderstanding among parties and "win-win" solutions are always assumed to be possible.

A strict assurance game of this form is unlikely in capitalist economies, since a situation in which capitalists can get full cooperation from workers without having to make any concessions—the C,O outcome—is unlikely to offer capitalists inferior pay-offs to mutual cooperation. Nevertheless, there may be situations in which the C,C pay-off moves in the direction of an assurance game, and certainly situations in which the gap for both classes between C,C and O,O becomes very large.

Finally, Model 5, the *unilateral workers' domination game*, is the symmetrical model to Model 1. Here workers are sufficiently strong and capitalists sufficiently weak that workers can force capitalists to unilaterally cooperate, including forcing them to invest in ways that enhance future earnings of workers (thus making O,C preferable to C,C for workers). This corresponds to the theoretical idea of democratic socialism: an economy within which workers effectively dominate capitalists.[33]

Lurking in the background of the models in Figure 11.3 is the problem of power: the balance of power between workers and

---

32 Robert Axelrod, *The Evolution of Cooperation*, New York: Basic Books, 1984.

33 In this theoretical conception of socialism, capitalists, albeit with curtailed property rights, can exist within a socialist economy just as they existed centuries earlier within a feudal society. It is another question how stable and reproducible such a structure of class relations would be. For a formal model of a sustainable socialist society within which capitalists still have some economic space, see Roemer, *A Future for Socialism*, Cambridge, MA: Harvard University Press, 1994; and *Equal Shares: Making Market Socialism Work*, vol. 2 of *The Real Utopias Project*, ed. Erik Olin Wright, London: Verso, 1996.

capitalists can be thought of as determining which of these strategic games is played. As illustrated in Figure 11.4, as working class power increases from extremely low levels (and thus as the ability of workers to impose sanctions on capitalists increases), the O,O alternative in Model 1 shifts downward and then to the right. This shifts the configuration in the direction of Model 2, in which working class militancy becomes sustainable and the possibility of negative class compromise—a class compromise based on the balance of force—emerges. Further increases in working class power begin to move the C,C option to the right, creating the prisoner's dilemma of Model 3. This sets the stage for the possibility of *positive* class compromise. As working class associational power pushes C,C in Model 3 in an upward direction towards the upper-right quadrant, approaching the assurance game in Model 4, the possibility for a *positive* class compromise increases: the gains from stable, mutual cooperation increase.[34]

If it were the case that increases in working class associational power could actually push the C,C payoff into the upper-right quadrant of this pay-off matrix, the overall relationship between workers' power and capitalists' interests would be a **J**-curve, not a reverse-**J**. That is, the highest across-game equilibrium pay-off for capitalists would be the C,C payoff in the assurance game rather than the C,O payoff in the unilateral capitalist domination game, and thus it would be in the interests of capitalists to accept (and even encourage) high levels of workers' power in order to create the conditions for the assurance game to occur. It is a central substantive assumption of the Marxian framework deployed in this chapter that this situation does not occur because of the underlying antagonistic, exploitative character of capitalist class relations. Stable, mutual cooperation can still occur, but it is because with sufficient power the threat of opposition by workers prevents the C,O option from being an equilibrium, not because mutual cooperation is the best of all possible payoffs for capitalists.[35] The two curves in Figure

---

34 As portrayed in Figure 11.4, working class power only affects the O,O and C,C curves; the C,O and O,C curves remain fixed. The critical issue in the shifts across the models in Figure 11.3, of course, is the change in the *relative* location of the four pay-offs, and this in principle could occur because of changes in the location of C,O or O,C as well as the mutual opposition or mutual cooperation pay-offs.

35 It is difficult to find direct empirical evidence that the shape of the curve is a reverse-**J**—i.e., that capitalists are best off in the C,O equilibrium of the unilateral capitalist domination game. The observation that in countries with

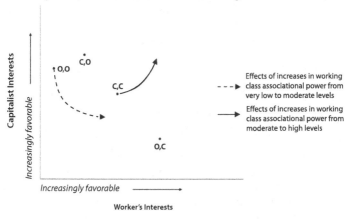

Transformation of the unilateral capitalist domination game into a prisoner's dilemma and towards an assurance game

Effects of increases in working class associational power from very low to moderate levels

Effects of increases in working class associational power from moderate to high levels

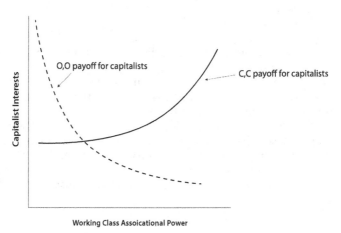

Working class power and the transformation of the O,O and C,C payoffs for capitalists

O,O payoff for capitalists

C,C payoff for capitalists

Figure 11.4. Working Class Power and the Transformation of the Strategic Context of Class Compromise

11.4 are both nonlinear: the O,O curve is convex with a decreasing slope, while the C,C curve is convex with an increasing slope. The nonlinear shape of these relations is important for the proposed reverse-**J** model of class compromise, since if these two curves were each linear they would generate a linear overall relation between workers' power and capitalists' interests. The O,O curve is convex and downward sloping because relatively modest levels of workers' power can do considerable damage to capitalists' interests but are insufficient to generate much sustainable gain for workers. Increases in workers' power from negligible to moderate, therefore, increase the punishment-capacity of workers considerably. Beyond a certain point, however, there are diminishing returns in the additional degree of harm to capitalists generated by additional working class strength. Once workers are sufficiently strong to prevent capitalists from arbitrarily firing workers, for example, being even stronger does not yield additional gains in job security. The C,C curve is nonlinear upward sloping because the positive gains that capitalists can realize by virtue of workers' power result only when workers are sufficiently well organized and solidaristic that their associations can effectively sanction defectors from cooperation both among their own members and among capitalists. Until worker associations are at least moderately powerful, they lack this dual-disciplining capacity and thus generate little positive effect on capitalist interests.

This, then, is the central game-theoretic logic underlying the argument developed in this chapter: as working class power increases, the unilateral capitalist domination game is initially shifted to a pure conflict game, making negative class compromise possible. With further increases in working class associational strength the strategic environment can shift towards an iterated prisoners dilemma, opening the prospect for positive class compromise. The more the game shifts towards an assurance game—even though it is unlikely to actually become one—the more stable the possibility of positive class compromise will become. Underlying this double shift is thus the problem of the relation of working class associational power to the interests of capitalists, a problem to which we now turn.

---

relatively disorganized working classes, such as the United States, the capitalist class and CEOs are personally much richer than in countries with highly organized working classes is consistent with the reverse-**J** argument, but is clearly complicated by many other factors.

4. A CURVILINEAR MODEL OF POSITIVE CLASS COMPROMISE

To the extent that increases in working class power can contribute not merely to the realization of working class material interests, but also to the realization of some capitalist class interests, class compromises are likely to be more stable and beneficial for workers. To the extent that every increase in working class power poses an increasing threat to capitalist class interests, capitalist resistance is likely to be more intense, and class compromises, even if achieved, are likely to be less stable. The intensity of class struggle, therefore, is not simply a function of the relative balance of power of different classes, but also of the intensity of the threat posed to dominant interests by subordinate class power.

If the relationship between workers' power and capitalists' interests were the simple inverse relationship of Figure 11.1, class compromises would always be relatively fragile and vulnerable to attack, for capitalist interests would always be served by taking advantage of opportunities to undermine workers' power. Negative class compromise—the class compromise of a pure conflict game—would be the most one could achieve. If the shape of the relationship is as pictured in Figure 11.2, on the other hand, class compromise can potentially become a relatively durable feature of a set of institutional arrangements. In general, when class conflict is located in the upward sloping region of this curve, class compromises are likely to be both more stable and more favorable for the working class. If the shape of this curve assumes the form of a more **U**-shaped version of a reverse-**J** (i.e., if the upward sloping section becomes more symmetrical), then conditions for class compromise become even more favorable; if the reverse-**J** degenerates into a strictly downward sloping curve, the conditions for class compromise become less favorable.

To more deeply understand the social processes reflected in the reverse-**J** hypothesis of Figure 11.2, we need to elaborate and extend the model in various ways. First I examine more closely the underlying causal mechanisms that generate this curve. Second, I extend the range of the figure by examining what happens at extreme values of working class associational power. Finally, I examine various ways in which the institutional environment of class conflict determines which regions of this curve are historically accessible as strategic objectives.

MECHANISMS UNDERLYING THE REVERSE-**J** RELATION

The reverse-**J** curve presented in Figure 11.2 can be understood as the outcome of two kinds of causal processes—one in which the interests of capitalists are increasingly undermined as the power of workers increases, and a second in which the interests of capitalists are enhanced by the increasing power of workers. These are illustrated in Figure 11.5. In broad terms, the downward sloping curve reflects the ways in which increasing power of workers *undermines the capacity of capitalists to unilaterally make decisions and control resources* of various sorts, while the upward sloping curve reflects ways in which the associational power of workers may *help capitalists solve certain kinds of*

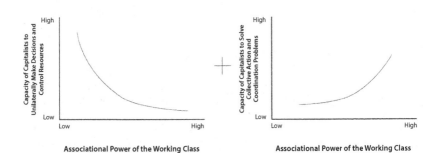

Figure 11.5. Decomposition of the Relationship between
Interests of Capitalists and Associational Strength of Workers

collective action and coordination problems. The specific convex shapes of these curves are derived from the shapes of the curves in Figure 11.4.

The mechanisms that generate the component curves in Figure 11.5 can be differentiated across the three institutional spheres within which class compromises are forged: exchange, production, and politics. These mechanisms are summarized in Table 11.3.

The Sphere of Exchange

Capitalists have a range of material interests within the sphere of exchange that bear on their relationship with the working class: minimizing labor costs; having an unfettered capacity to hire and fire without interference; selling all of the commodities they produce; having a labor force with a particular mix of skills in a labor market that provides predictable and adequate supplies of labor. As has often been argued by both Marxists and non-Marxist political economists, some of these interests contradict each other. Most notably, the interest of capitalists in selling commodities means that it is desirable for workers-as-consumers to have a lot of disposable income, whereas capitalists' interest in minimizing their own wage bill implies an interest in paying workers-as-employees as little as possible.

	Characteristic Forms of Working Class Power	Capitalist Class Interests Threatened by Increasing Working Class Power	Capitalist Class Interests Facillitated by Increasing Working Class Power
Sphere of Exchange	Trade unions	Unilateral ability to hire and fire and make wage offers	Ability to restrain wages in tight labor markets; ability to sell what is producted (Keynesian effects)
Sphere of Production	Works councils	Unilateral ability to control the labor process and job structure	Ability to elicit complex forms of vertical and horizontal cooperation; cheaper solution to information problems in production
Sphere of Politics	Political parties	Unilateral political influence over redistributive policies	Ability to sustain stable tripartite corporatist cooperation

Table 11.3. Decomposition of the Relation between Working Class Power and Capitalist Class Interests in the Spheres of Politics, Exchange, and Production

Increases in working class associational power generally undermine the capacity of individual capitalists to unilaterally make decisions and allocate resources within labor markets. In the absence of unions, capitalists can hire and fire at will and set wages at whatever level they feel is most profitable. Of course, this does not mean that employers set wages without any constraints whatsoever. Their wage offers will be constrained by the tightness or looseness of the labor market, the reservation wages of workers, and, as discussed earlier, the need to pay workers a sufficiently high wage to motivate individual workers to work diligently. Capitalists' decisions are thus always constrained by the actions of individual workers and by general economic conditions. The issue here, however, is the extent of constraint on capitalists imposed by the collective action of workers reflecting their associational power in various forms. Such associational power reduces capitalists' individual capacity to make profit-maximizing decisions on labor markets and thus hurts their material interests.

If capitalists' interests within the sphere of exchange consisted entirely of interests in their individual ability to buy and sell with minimal constraint, something close to the inverse relation portrayed in Figure 11.1 would probably hold. But that is not the case. The material interests of capitalists—their ability to sustain a high and stable rate of profit—depends on the provision of various aggregate conditions within the sphere of exchange, and these require coordination and collective action. The solution to at least some of these coordination problems can be facilitated by relatively high levels of working class associational power.[36]

The classic example is the problem of inadequate aggregate demand for the consumer goods produced by capitalists. This is the traditional Keynesian problem of how raising wages and social spending can underwrite higher levels of aggregate demand and thus help solve underconsumption problems in the economy. Inadequate consumer demand represents a collective action problem for capitalists: capitalists simultaneously want to pay their own employees wages as low as possible and want other

---

36 This does not mean that working class associational power is a necessary condition for the solution to such coordination problems. There may be other devices which may constitute alternative strategies for solving such problems. All that is claimed here is that working class associational power can constitute a mechanism that makes it easier to do so.

capitalists to pay wages as high as possible in order to generate adequate consumer demand for products. High levels of unionization, in effect, prevent individual firms from "defecting" from the cooperative solution to this dilemma. Working class strength can also contribute to more predictable and stable labor markets. Under conditions of tight labor markets where competition for labor among capitalists would normally push wages up, perhaps at rates higher than the rate of increase of productivity and thus stimulating inflation, high levels of working class associational power can also contribute to wage restraint.[37] Wage restraint is an especially complex collective action problem: individual capitalists need to be prevented from defecting from the wage restraint agreement (i.e., they must be prevented from bidding up wages to workers in an effort to lure workers away from other employers, given the relative unavailability of workers in the labor market), and individual workers (and unions) need to be prevented from defecting from the agreement by trying to maximize wages under tight labor market conditions. Wage restraint in tight labor markets, which is important for longer term growth and contained inflation, is generally easier to achieve where the working class is very well organized, particularly in centralized unions, than where it is not.

These positive effects of workers' collective strength on capitalist interests in the sphere of exchange need not imply that capitalists themselves are equally well organized in strong employers' associations, although as the history of northern European neocorporatism suggests, strongly organized working class movements tend to stimulate the development of complementary organization on the part of employers. In any case, the ability of workers' power to constructively help solve macroeconomic problems is enhanced when capitalists are also organized.

Assuming that the positive Keynesian and labor market effects of working class power are generally weaker than the negative wage-cost and firing discretion effects, the combination of these processes yields the reverse-J relationship for the sphere of exchange in Table 11.3.

---

37 See Calmfors and Driffill, "Bargaining Structure"; Andrew Glynn, "Social Democracy and Full Employment," *New Left Review* 1:211, 1995, 33–55; Jonas Pontusson, "Between Neo-Liberalism and the German Model: Swedish Capitalism in Transition," in Crouch and Streeck, *Political Economy of Modern Capitalism.*

The Sphere of Production

A similar contradictory quality of the interests of capitalists with respect to workers occurs within the sphere of production. On the one hand, capitalists have interests in being able to unilaterally control the labor process (choosing and changing technology, assigning labor to different tasks, changing the pace of work, etc.), and on the other hand, they have interests in being able to reliably elicit cooperation, initiative, and responsibility from employees.

As working class associational power within production increases, capitalists' unilateral control over the labor process declines. This does not mean that capitalists are necessarily faced with rigid, unalterable work rules, job classifications, and the like, but it does mean that changes in the labor process need to be negotiated and bargained with representatives of workers rather than unilaterally imposed. Particularly in conditions of rapid technical change, this requirement may hurt capitalist interests.

On the other hand, at least under certain social and technical conditions of production, working class associational strength within production may enhance the possibilities for more complex and stable forms of cooperation between labor and management. To the extent that working class strength increases job security and reduces arbitrariness in managerial treatment of workers, then workers' time horizons for staying in their jobs are likely to increase and along with this their sense that their future prospects are linked to the welfare of the firm. This perception may in turn contribute to a sense of loyalty and greater willingness to cooperate in various ways.

The German case of strong workplace-based workers' organization built around works councils and codetermination is perhaps the best example. Streeck describes how codetermination and works councils positively help capitalists solve certain problems:

> What, then, is specific about codetermination? Unlike the other factors that have limited the variability of employment, codetermination has not merely posed a problem for enterprises, but has also offered a solution. While on the one hand codetermination has contributed to growing organizational rigidities, on the other hand, and at the same time, it has provided the organizational instruments to cope with such rigidities without major losses in efficiency . . .[38]

---

38 Streeck, *Social Institutions and Economic Performance*, 160.

The works council not only shares in what used to be managerial prerogatives, but also accepts responsibility for the implementation and enforcement of decisions made under its participation. This constellation has frequently been described as "integration" or "cooptation" of labor or organized labor, in management; with the same justification, however, it can be seen as "colonization" of management, and in particularly manpower management, by the representatives of the workforce. The most adequate metaphor would probably be that of a *mutual incorporation of capital and labor* by which labor internalizes the interests of capital just as capital internalizes those of labor, with the result that works council and management become subsystems of an integrated, internally differentiated system of industrial government that increasingly supersedes the traditional pluralist-adversarial system of industrial relations.[39]

This tighter coupling of interests of labor and capital with the resulting heightened forms of interclass cooperation helps employers solve a range of concrete coordination problems in workplaces: more efficient information flows within production (since workers have more access to managerial information and have less incentive to withhold information as part of a job-protection strategy); more efficient adjustments of the labor process in periods of rapid technological change (since workers are involved in the decision-making, are thus less worried that technological change will cost them their jobs, and so are more likely to actively cooperate with the introduction of new technologies); more effective strategies of skill formation (since workers, with the most intimate knowledge of skill bottlenecks and requirements, are involved in designing training programs). Most broadly, strong workplace associational power of workers creates the possibility of more effective involvement of workers in various forms of creative problem-solving.[40]

---

39 Ibid., 164.

40 It is possible, under certain social and cultural conditions, for some of these forms of cooperation to emerge and be sustained without strong workplace associational power of workers. This is often the way the relatively cooperative system of employment relations in Japan is described (e.g., Chie Nakane, *Japanese Society*, London: Weidenfeld & Nicolson, 1970), although others have criticized such culturalist views (e.g., Masahiko Aoki, *Information, Incentives, and Bargaining in the Japanese Firm*, Cambridge: Cambridge University Press, 1988, 304ff). In any event, under many conditions high levels of worker cooperation within production are likely to be difficult to sustain if they are not backed by some form of significant associational power.

With so many positive advantages of such cooperative institutions, it might seem surprising that strong workplace associational power is so rare in developed capitalist countries. The reason, as I have argued throughout this chapter, is that such cooperative advantages come at a cost to capital. Streeck recognizes this cost even in the German case:

> Above all, codetermination carries with it considerable costs in managerial discretion and managerial prerogatives . . . Integration cuts both ways, and if it is to be effective with regards to labor it must bind capital as well. This is why codetermination, for all its advantages, is seen by capital as a thoroughly mixed blessing . . . Both the short-term economic costs and the long-term costs in authority and status make the advantages of codetermination expensive for the capitalist class, and thus explains the otherwise incomprehensible resistance of business to any extension of codetermination rights.[41]

Because of these costs, capitalists in general will prefer a system of production in which they do not have to contend with strong associational power of workers in production: thus, the reverse-**J** shape of the functional relation between workers' power and capitalists' interests within production.

The Sphere of Politics

The two components of the reverse-**J** relationship between working class associational power and capitalist interests are perhaps most obvious in the sphere of politics. As a great deal of comparative historical research has indicated, as working class political power increases the capitalist state tends to become more redistributive: the social wage increases and thus the reservation wage of workers is higher; taxation and transfer policies reduce income inequality; and in various ways labor power is partially decommodified. All of these policies have negative effects on the material interests of high-income people in general and capitalists in particular. Working class political power also tends to underwrite institutional arrangements that increase working class power within the sphere exchange and often within the sphere of production as well. Working class associational power in the political sphere, therefore, may also contribute to the downward sloping curves in the spheres of exchange and production.

---

41   Streeck, *Social Institutions and Economic Performance*, 165.

The upward sloping class-compromise curve in the sphere of politics is the central preoccupation of social democracy. The large literature in the 1980s and early 1990s on tripartite state-centered corporatism is, in effect, a literature on how the interests of capitalists can flourish in the context of a politically well-organized working class.[42] Sweden, until the mid-1980s, is usually taken as the paradigm case: the Social Democratic Party's control of the Swedish state facilitated a set of corporatist arrangements between centralized trade unions and centralized employers' associations that made possible a long, stable period of cooperation and growth. The organizational links between the labor movement and the Social Democratic Party were critical for this stability, since it added legitimacy to the deals that were struck and increased the confidence of workers that the terms of the agreement would be upheld in the future. This made it possible over a long period of time for Swedish capitalism to sustain high capacity utilization, very low levels of unemployment, and relatively high productivity growth. State-mediated corporatism anchored in working class associational strength in the political sphere played a significant role in these outcomes.

The inventory of mechanisms in Table 11.3 provides a preliminary set of variables for characterizing the conditions of class compromise within different units of analysis across time and space. Class compromises within the sphere of exchange can occur in local, regional, and national labor markets, or within labor markets linked to particular sectors. Production-level compromises typically occur within firms, but they may also be organized within sectors.[43] Class

---

42 Esping-Anderson, *Three Worlds of Welfare Capitalism*; Philippe Schmitter and Gerhard Lehmbruch, eds., *Trends toward Corporatist Intermediation*, Beverly Hills, CA: Sage, 1979; Philippe Schmitter, "Corporatism Is Dead! Long Live Corporatism! Reflections on Andrew Schonfield's *Modern Capitalism*," *Government and Opposition* 24, 1988, 54–73.

43 In the spheres of production and exchange, there may be considerable heterogeneity in the shape of the class-compromise curves and the degree of working class associational power across firms and sectors. The result is that within a given country the conditions for class compromise may be much more favorable in some firms and sectors than in others. Within the sphere of production, it is easy enough to see how the upward sloping curve can be restricted to a particular sector or even firm, since most of the gains from cooperation are contained within firms. In the sphere of exchange, many of the positive effects of high levels of unionization for capitalists come from aggregate, macroeconomic effects, while some of the positive effects—such as stabilization of labor markets,

compromises in the sphere of politics are especially important within the nation state, but local and regional political class compromises are also possible. The emergence of various forms of meso-corporatism involving local and regional levels of government may indicate the development of political class compromises within subnational units. The reverse-**J** curves that map the terrain of class compromise can therefore be relevant to the analysis of class compromises in any unit of analysis, not simply entire countries.

Different countries, then, will be characterized by different combinations of values on these three pairs of class-compromise curves.[44] In Germany, for example, working class associational power is especially strong within the sphere of production, somewhat less strong in the sphere of exchange, and rather weaker in the sphere of politics. In Sweden—at least in the heyday of social democracy—it has been very strong in the spheres of exchange and politics, and perhaps a bit weaker in the sphere of production. In the United States, working class associational power has dwindled within all three spheres, but is strongest in the sphere of exchange within certain limited sectors. The overall reverse-**J** curve for class compromise within a society is therefore the result of a complex amalgamation of the component curves within each of these spheres.

MAKING THE MODEL MORE COMPLEX: EXTENDING THE THEORETICAL DOMAIN OF VARIATION

The range of variation in Figures 11.2 and 11.5 reflects the typical spectrum of possibilities in contemporary, developed capitalist societies. It will be helpful for our subsequent analysis to consider what

---

rationalized skill formation, and wage restraint in tight labor markets—may be concentrated in specific sectors or localities. The reverse-**J** curve characterizing a given sphere is therefore itself an amalgamation of the distribution of such curves across firms, sectors, and other less aggregated units of analysis.

44 The actual variation across time and place is, of course, much more complicated than is portrayed here. Countries will vary not simply in where they are located on each of these curves, but also on (1) the relative weights of the various curves in defining the overall configuration for the society; (2) the units of analysis within countries within which class compromises are most rooted; (3) the specific shapes of the component curves themselves. In some times and places, for example, the upward sloping segments of some of the curves might be relatively flat and in other cases, quite steep. My theoretical understanding of these relations is insufficient to say anything very systematic about either of these two sources of variation.

happens when working class power increases towards the limiting case of society-wide working class organization and solidarity simultaneously in all three spheres of class compromise. This corresponds to what might be termed "democratic socialism," where socialism is not defined as centralized state ownership of the means of production but as working class collective control over capital.

What happens to capitalist class interests as working class associational power approaches this theoretical maximum? Figure 11.6 presents the relationship between one crucial aspect of capitalists' interests—their control over investments and accumulation (allocation of capital)—and working class power. The control over investments is perhaps the most fundamental dimension of private ownership of the means of production within capitalism. In most capitalist societies, this particular power of capital is not seriously eroded even as working class power increases. Even with strong unions and social democratic parties, capitalists still have the broad power to disinvest, to choose their individual rate of savings, to turn their profits into consumption or allocate them to new investments, etc. Of course, all capitalist states have capacities to create incentives and disincentives for particular allocations of capital (through taxes, subsidies, tariffs, etc.). And in special circumstances "disincentives" can have a significant coercive character, effectively constraining capitalists' capacity to allocate capital. This happens sometimes during periods of extraordinary emergency such as wars. Still, this fundamental aspect of capitalist property rights is not generally threatened within the normal range of variation of working class power. When working class associational power approaches its theoretical maximum, however, the right of capitalists to control the allocation of capital is called into question. Indeed, this is the heart of the definition of democratic socialism—popular, democratic control over the allocation of capital. This suggests the shape of the curve in Figure 11.6: a relatively weak negative effect of working class power on capitalist interests with respect to control over the basic allocation of capital until working class power reaches a very high level, at which point those interests become seriously threatened.[45]

---

45 The x-axis in Figure 11.6 is working class associational power undifferentiated into the spheres of production, exchange, and politics. It thus represents an under-theorized amalgam of the associational power within the three spheres (which are themselves amalgams of associational power across the various units of analysis that make up each sphere). The underlying intuition is that viable democratic socialism requires high levels of workers associational power within all three spheres, and

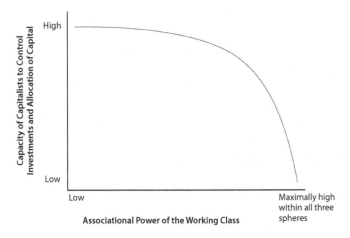

Figure 11.6. Interests of Capital and Power of Workers with Respect to Control of Investment

When Figure 11.6 is added to Figure 11.2, we get the roller-coaster curve in Figure 11.7. There are two local maxima in this theoretical model: the *capitalist utopia*, in which the working class is sufficiently atomized and disorganized to give capitalists a free hand in organizing production and appropriating the gains from increased productivity without fear of much collective resistance; and the *social democratic utopia*, in which working class associational power is sufficiently strong to generate high levels of corporatist cooperation between labor and capital without being so strong as to threaten basic capitalist property rights. These two maxima constitute quite different strategic environments for workers and capitalists. Statically, capitalists should only care about where they sit on the vertical axis of this figure: if you draw a horizontal line through the figure that intersects the curve at three places, capitalists should be statically indifferent among these three possibilities. Understood dynamically, however, capitalists in general will prefer points in the lefthand region of the curve.

---

that a *sustainable* threat to fundamental capitalist property rights under democratic conditions can occur only when such unified associational power occurs. This does not imply, however, that the three spheres are of equal weight in this theoretical gestalt. Traditionally Marxists have argued that working class power at the level of the state is most decisive for challenging capitalist property rights, whereas syndicalists have argued that the pivot is workers' power within production.

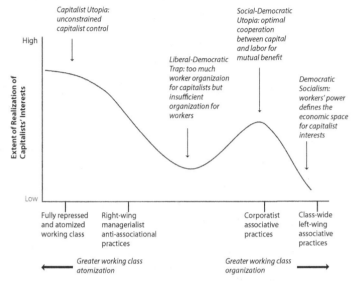

Figure 11.7. Expanded Model of Working Class Associational Power and Capitalist Interests

It is at least in part because of this threat of a society-wide shift in the balance of class power that capitalists might prefer working class associational power to remain to the left of the social democratic "peak" of this curve, even though this peak might be theoretically advantageous to capitalist interests. Arriving at the peak looks too much like a Trojan horse: small additional changes in associational power could precipitate a decisive challenge to capitalists' interests and power. The local maximum of the "social democratic utopia" in Figure 11.7 may thus be a kind of tipping point that is seen by capitalists as too risky a zone to inhabit. This is one interpretation of the strident opposition of Swedish capitalists to the initial formulation of the wage-earners' fund proposal in Sweden in the 1970s. The wage-earners' fund, as initially conceived, was a proposal through which Swedish unions would gain increasing control over the Swedish economy via the use of union pension funds to purchase controlling interests in Swedish firms. From the point of view of economic performance and even the middle-run profit interests of Swedish firms, this plan might be beneficial for Swedish capital, but it raised the possibility of a long-term slide towards democratic socialism by significantly enhancing the power of Swedish labor. The result was a militant attack by Swedish capital against the Social Democratic Party. As Glynn writes: "The policies which the Social Democrats were proposing impinged on the authority and freedom of action of business which was supposed to be guaranteed in return for full employment and the welfare state. This seems to lie at the root of the employers' repudiation of the Swedish model, of which full employment was a central part."[46]

The different regions of this curve correspond to the different game theory models in Figure 11.3. The "Capitalist Utopia" corresponds to the unilateral capitalist domination game in which C,O is the equilibrium solution. The downward sloping region in the center of the figure is the pure conflict game, where, at best, negative class compromise is possible. The upper sloping part of the curve is the iterated prisoner's dilemma, where a stable C,C solution, a positive class compromise, can emerge. The apex of this region of the curve, the "Social Democratic Utopia," is the point that is closest to an assurance game. If in fact it actually became a proper assurance game (i.e., the C,C payoff in Figure 11.3 moved into the upper-right quadrant of the pay-off matrix) the curve in Figure 11.7 would become a **J**-curve rather than a reverse-**J**; the "social democratic utopia" would be higher than the "capitalist utopia" and become a kind of social democratic nirvana in which mutual cooperation between classes was self-reinforcing, no longer resting on a background condition of potential working class opposition. Finally, democratic socialism corresponds to the unilateral working class domination game in which O,C is the equilibrium solution.

WORKING CLASS INTERESTS AND THE CLASS-COMPROMISE CURVE

The models in Figure 11.3 contain both working class interests and capitalist class interests. Figure 11.8 adds working class interests to the class-compromise curve in Figure 11.7. The different regions of these curves can be thought of as specific hypotheses about the effects of marginal changes of working class power on the relationship between workers' interests and capitalists' interests:

---

46   Glynn, "Social Democracy and Full Employment," 53–4.

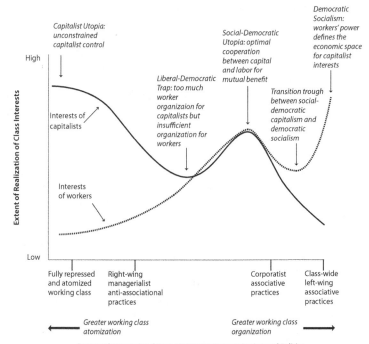

Figure 11.8. Working Class Associational Power, Working Class Interests, and Capitalist Interests

1. The gap between workers' interests and capitalist interests is greatest at the ends of the spectrum: when working class associational power is weakest (the fully atomized working class) or at the maximum strength (democratic socialism).

2. Increases in working class associational power steadily increase the realization of working class material interests up to relatively high levels of associational power. Of course, in actual historical processes of increasing working class power it may well happen that there will be episodes in which the resistance of capitalists results in declines in the realization of working class interests. Nevertheless, in general, increasing workers' power is expected to improve the realization of working class interests.

3. The region of the curve around the "liberal democratic trap" is the region corresponding to the shift from the mutual opposition (O,O) pay-off in Model 2 to the prisoner's dilemma in Model 3, Figure 11.3: workers effectively oppose capitalist interests and capitalists effectively oppose workers interests.

4. There is one region of the curve where the functional relation between workers' power and class interests has the same general shape for both workers and capitalists: the upward sloping section to the right of the liberal democratic trough. This is the region of maximally stable positive class compromise.

5. As working class power extends beyond corporatist associative practices, the immediate realization of working class interests again decline. This region of the curve defines the "transition trough" between capitalism and socialism discussed by Adam Przeworski. Capitalists respond to the threat of losing control over the allocation of capital by disinvesting, shifting investments to other places, or by more organized forms of a "capital strike." This response has the effect of provoking an economic decline that hurts workers' material interests. It is only when workers' associational power increases to the point at which investments can be effectively allocated democratically (in the sense of democratically imposed direction or allocation) that the working class interest curve once again turns upward. Once there is a full realization of hypothetical democratic socialism, the interests of workers and capitalists are once again maximally divergent.

ONE MORE COMPLEXITY: ZONES OF UNATTAINABILITY

In the practical world of real capitalist societies, not all values within this theoretically defined range are historically accessible. There are two different kinds of exclusion-mechanisms that have the effect of narrowing the range of real possibilities. These can be termed *systemic* exclusions and *institutional* exclusions.

Systemic exclusions define parts of the curve that are outside the limits of possibility because of the fundamental structural features of the social system. Specifically, the presence of a *constitutionally secure democracy* removes the fully repressed and atomized working class part of the curve from the historical stage, and the presence of *legally secure capitalist property rights* removes the democratic socialism part of the curve. This does not mean that there are no historical circumstances in which these zones of the curve might become strategically accessible, but getting there would require a fundamental transformation of the underlying social structural principles of the society.

Institutional exclusions refer to various kinds of historically variable institutional arrangements, formed within the limits determined by the systemic exclusions, which make it difficult or impossible to move to specific regions of the curve. For example, restrictive labor law can make it difficult to extend working class associational power towards the corporatist associative practices part of the curve.[47] On the other hand, generous welfare state provisions which render workers less dependent on capital and strong associational rights which facilitate unionization may make it difficult to move towards the right-wing managerialist region. Such institutional exclusions, of course, are themselves the outcomes of historical conflicts and should not be viewed as eternally fixed. But once in place, they help to define the range of feasible strategy immediately open to actors, at least until the time when actors can effectively challenge these institutional exclusions themselves.

These two forms of exclusion are illustrated in Figure 11.9. The central region of the curve defines the space that is immediately accessible strategically. To use the game of metaphor Alford and Friedland discussed in chapter 6, this is the domain of ordinary politics, of interest group conflict over "plays" within a well-defined set of institutional rules of the game. The other regions of the curve become the objects of politics only episodically. Reformist versus reactionary politics are struggles over the rules of the game that define institutional exclusions; revolutionary versus counter-revolutionary politics are struggles over the systemic constraints that define what game is being played.

In Figure 11.9, the "zones of unattainability" defined by the systemic and institutional exclusions symmetrically span the tails of the theoretical curve of possibilities. There is no reason, of course, to believe that the real world is this neat. Indeed, one of the reasons for introducing this complexity is precisely to provide tools for understanding forms of variation across time and place in these exclusions. This historical variability is illustrated in Figure 11.10, which compares the United States and Sweden in the periods of most stable Swedish social democracy and American liberal democracy.

---

47 Rogers, "Divide and Conquer."

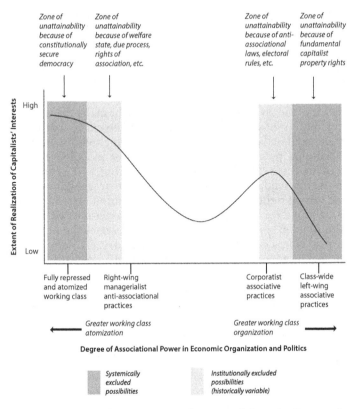

Figure 11.9. Working Class Associational Power and Capitalist Interests in Demographic Capitalism

Systemic exclusions in the United States and Sweden are roughly comparable: both have structurally secure democratic states and capitalist property relations. Where they differ substantially is in the nature of the historically variable institutional exclusions which confront their respective working classes.

In the United States, a variety of institutional rules create a fairly broad band of institutional exclusions to the right of the central trough of the curve. Electoral rules that solidify a two-party system of centrist politics and anti-union rules that create deep impediments to labor organizing all push the boundary of this zone of

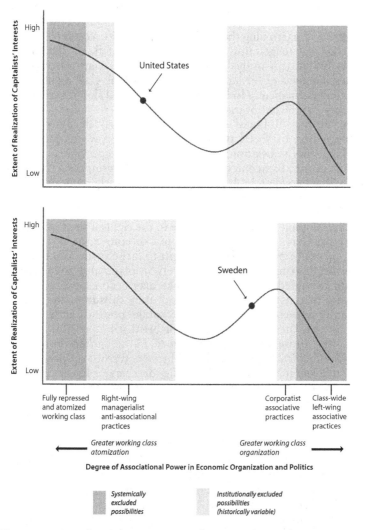

Figure 11.10. Working Class Associational Power and Capitalist Interests in Liberal-Democratic Capitalism (United States) and Social-Democratic Capitalism (Sweden)

institutional exclusion to the left.[48] On the other hand, such things as the weak welfare state, the very limited job protections afforded workers, and laws which guarantee managerial autonomy all have the effect of narrowing the institutional exclusions centered around right-wing managerialist anti-associational practices. The band of accessible strategy in the United States, therefore, affords very little room to maneuver for labor and keeps working class associational practices permanently lodged on the downward sloping segment of the curve to the left of the trough.

Swedish institutional exclusions, particularly during the most stable period of social democracy, all work towards facilitating working class associational power. Labor law is permissive, making it quite easy to form and expand union membership, and the generous welfare state and job protections significantly reduce the scope of right-wing managerialist strategies. The result has been that the Swedish labor movement has for a long time been located on the upward sloping section of the curve to the right of the trough.

Actors living within these systems, of course, do not directly see this entire picture. To the extent that the institutional exclusion mechanisms have been securely in place and unchallenged for an extended period of time, they may become entirely invisible and the parts of the curve which they subsume may become virtually unimaginable. From the vantage point of actors within the system, therefore, the range of "realistic" possibilities may look like those portrayed in Figure 11.11 rather than Figure 11.12. The US labor movement faces a terrain of possibilities that places it chronically on the defensive. Every marginal increase of workers' strength is experienced by capitalists as against their interests, so whenever the opportunity arises, capitalists attempt to undermine labor's strength. Anti-union campaigns are common and decertification elections a regular occurrence. In Sweden, at least until recently, the institutionally delimited strategic environment is much more benign for workers. The central pressure on capitalists has been to forge ways of effectively cooperating with organized labor, of creating institutional spaces in which the entrenched forms of associational power of workers can be harnessed for enhanced productivity. This need not imply that employers actively encourage enhanced working class associational power, but it does suggest less sustained effort to undermine it.

---

48   See Rogers's analysis in "Divide and Conquer."

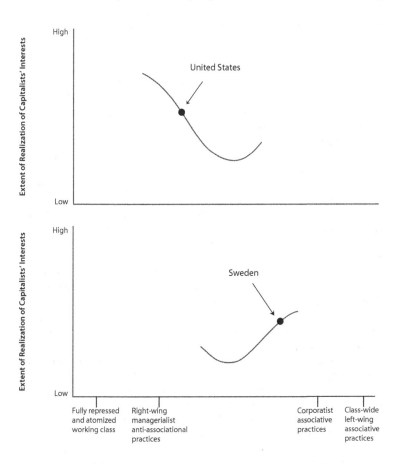

Figure 11.11. **Strategic Environment for Feasible Associational Politics as Seen by the Actors in Social-Democratic Capitalism and Liberal Capitalism**

This chapter has attempted to chart out a general, abstract model of class compromise in capitalist society. The core intuition builds on Gramsci's insight that in democratic capitalist societies the capitalist class is often hegemonic, not merely dominant, and this implies that class conflict is contained through real compromises involving real concessions, rather than brute force. The bottom line of the argument is that the stability and desirability of such compromises depend on the specific configurations of power and interests that characterize the relationship between the capitalist class and the working class: when working class associational power positively contributes to solving problems faced by capitalists, such compromises will be much more durable than when they emerge simply from the capacity of workers to impose costs on capital.

The theory of class compromise proposed here is thus in keeping with the traditional core of Marxist theory in arguing that power and struggle are fundamental determinants of distributional outcomes in capitalist societies. But contrary to traditional Marxist ideas on the subject, the model also argues that the configuration of capitalist and worker interests within the "game of class struggle" is not simply determined by capitalism itself, but depends upon a wide variety of economic, institutional and political factors. Above all, the model argues that class power not only can affect the outcome of class conflict, but the nature of the game itself: whether or not the confrontation of capital and labor takes the form of a sharply polarized zero-sum conflict or an iterated prisoners' dilemma or, perhaps, a strategic context with significant assurance game features conducive to positive class compromise.

In the current era, the prospects for a robust, positive class compromise seem quite dim. The models we have been exploring might have been relevant in an earlier period, but under conditions of crisis, stagnation and austerity, positive class compromise may seem quite far-fetched to many people. It is therefore important to remember that the range of attainable possibilities can change, both as the result of conscious political projects to change institutional exclusions and as the result of dynamic social and economic forces working "behind the backs" of actors. Institutional exclusions are created by victories and defeats in historically specific struggles; they can potentially be changed in a similar fashion. But equally, dynamic changes within economic structures can potentially change the shape of the curve itself. It is to this issue that we now turn in a more speculative manner in chapter 12.

CLASS STRUGGLE AND CLASS COMPROMISE IN THE ERA OF STAGNATION AND CRISIS

In the decades following World War II, social democracy (broadly understood) built and consolidated three main achievements:[1]

1. A system of various forms of publicly supported social insurance to deal with a range of risks people experience in their lives, especially around health, employment, and income.

2. A tax regime sufficient to provide funding by the state for a fairly expansive set of public goods, including basic and higher education, vocational skill formation, public transportation, cultural activities, recreational facilities, research and development, and macro-economic stability.

3. A regulatory regime for the capitalist economy that curtailed a range of negative externalities and harmful practices of capitalist firms: pollution, product and workplace hazards, predatory market behavior, etc.

These achievements were, at least in part, the result of a *positive class compromise* between the capitalist class and popular social forces.[2] Capitalists were basically left free to allocate capital on the basis of profit-making opportunities in the market, while the state took responsibility for correcting the three principle failures of capitalist markets:

---

1 I use the term "social democracy" to refer to the broad spectrum of progressive political parties within capitalist democracies. This includes New Deal Liberalism in the United States, the Labour Party in Britain, and the various socialist and social democratic parties on the European continent.

2 I use the somewhat vague term "popular social forces" here rather than "the working class" to emphasize that broad popular base of this compromise, which extended beyond the boundaries of the working class as such.

vulnerability of individuals to a variety of risks, underprovision of public goods, and negative externalities of private profit-maximizing economic activity. It would be an exaggeration to say that there was no contestation over these achievements—even in the most robust social democracies there was conflict over the scale and scope of each of these elements—but there was nevertheless a loose consensus that these were legitimate activities of the state and that they were broadly compatible with a robust capitalist economy.

This consensus no longer exists, even in the social democratic heartland of northern Europe. Everywhere there are calls for roll-backs of the "entitlements" connected to social insurance, reductions of taxes and the associated provision of public goods, privatization of many public services, and deregulation of capitalist markets. This assault on the affirmative state has intensified in the face of the economic crisis that has gripped global capitalism in recent years. The rhythm and intensity of the crisis has varied from place to place: in the United States it was most severe in 2008–2009, while in 2012 it was most sharply present in Greece and other countries on the periphery of Europe. The details of this economic turmoil also vary considerably across capitalist countries, but there is near universal sense that economic prospects are bleak, that life under capitalism for most people has become more precarious and is likely to stay that way for some time to come, and that in the wake of this crisis the state must retreat from its earlier expansive role.

So far the political Left has not managed anywhere to mobilize a coherent positive response to the crisis. To be sure, there have been protests, sometimes massive protests, and some of them have unquestionably had an important impact on public debate. Some may even have had a significant impact on elites, impeding their strategies for dealing with the crisis on their own terms. The protests have, however, mostly been defensive in nature—resisting draconian cuts to the social safety net, pensions, health, education, and other public programs—rather than mobilizations around a positive project for overcoming the crisis through a reconstruction or transformation of the economic and political conditions for social democratic ideals.

In this chapter I explore the broad contours of what such a positive project for a new progressive politics might look like. I build the analysis around a contrast between the conditions facing progressive politics in what is sometimes called the "Golden Era" of capitalist development in most advanced capitalist countries in the decades following World War II, during which the social democratic achievements were built, and the conditions in the current era of stagnation and crisis. The central argument, building on the analysis in the previous chapter, is that the Left has had its greatest durable successes when it is able to forge a positive class compromise within capitalism. The question, then, is what it would take—or even whether it is possible—to rebuild such a class compromise in the present.

I begin by comparing the conditions for class compromise in the relatively favorable era of the third quarter of the twentieth century with the much less favorable conditions at the beginning of the twenty-first. I then explore two kinds of responses to the erosion of the conditions for class compromise. The first attempts to restore the material foundations of positive class compromise; the second attempts to make the welfare of popular forces less contingent on the robustness of class compromise.

CONDITIONS FOR CLASS COMPROMISE IN THE GOLDEN AGE AND THE EARLY TWENTY-FIRST CENTURY

Figure 12.1 is a somewhat simplified version of Figures 11.11 and 11.12 in the previous chapter. In this chapter I do not distinguish between systemically excluded and institutionally excluded regions of the curve. I also use the more inclusive expression "popular power" rather than "working class associational power" to indicate the strength of popular democratic power involved in forging class compromises.

The relationships portrayed in Figure 12.1 provide a way of comparing the conditions for class compromise across time and place. A number of things in this figure can vary: the shape of the curve itself can vary, with more or less favorable slopes in the positive class compromise region of the curve; the parts of the curve that are excluded by legal rules and public policy can vary, creating a more or less favorable region of the curve that is historically accessible; and the specific location of a country within that historically accessible region can vary depending on the balance of forces. It is, of course, an extremely demanding research task to give precision to any of these forms of variation. There are no easy metrics for any of the dimensions, nor any way (that I know of) to measure variation over time in things like the shape of the curve or the zones of exclusion. The purpose of the figure, therefore, is to clarify theoretical arguments and provide a way of more systematically formulating claims about changes over time. What follows, then, is a suggestive way of framing the contrast in the central conditions for class compromise in the highly favorable situation

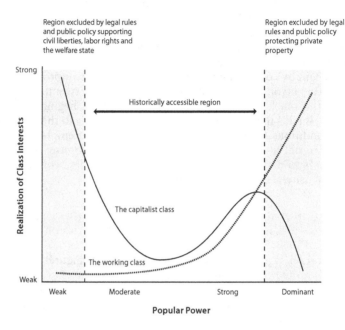

Figure 12.1. The Class-Compromise Curve

of the Golden Age of post–World War II capitalism and the much more difficult context of the current era of neoliberalism, crisis, and stagnation.

Figure 12.2 presents the class compromise curve in the Golden Age for the modal country in the developed capitalist world. Because of the strong institutionalization of labor rights and the stable and relatively generous welfare state promoted by various forms of social democracy, the left region of exclusion was quite broad. So long as these rules of the game were in place, it was relatively easy for the labor movement and other popular social forces to achieve at least moderate levels of popular power. In terms of the shape of the curve, because of relatively positive conditions for capitalist growth and profitability, the upward slopping part of the curve rises to a fairly high level. From the point of view of capitalist interests, therefore, the class compromise part of the curve looks attractive; it is certainly better to be somewhere on the upward

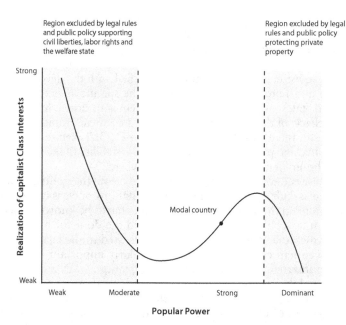

Figure 12.2. Capitalist Class Interests and Popular Power in the "Golden Age" of post-WWII Capitalism in Developed Capitalist Countries

sloping part of the curve than in the valley. While capitalists might still prefer to be well to the left, high on the downward sloping part of the curve, this region is—at least in the short run—strategically inaccessible because of stable institutional rules. So, all things considered, a positive class compromise is a tolerable *modus vivendi*: capitalists make adequate profits; popular power exercised through the state creates public goods that strengthen capitalism and provide employment and income security; and labor movement power in the economy stabilizes employment relations and supports strong productivity growth.

Although the configuration in Figure 12.2 may have been acceptable for capital, it wasn't optimal, or at least, over time, it came to be seen as suboptimal.[3] In the course of the 1960s and early 1970s a series of

---

3   It is a difficult question to resolve whether the kind of class compromise forged in the immediate decades after World War II was optimal for capitalist

contradictions in the regime of accumulation began to intensify and gradually made the positive class compromise less secure, especially in the United States. The welfare state had expanded to the point where it began to absorb too much of the social surplus (from the capitalist point of view); wages were sticky downward and began to create a profit squeeze; global competition intensified with the development of Japan and Europe, which undermined the specific advantages of the United States and the global financial system it anchored. Into this mix, the debacle of the Vietnam War intensified US fiscal problems. And, to top it off, there was the oil price shock in 1973. Taken together these economic and political processes eroded the stability of the Golden Age equilibrium in the United States and elsewhere.

These economic developments helped create the political context for the assault on the institutional foundations of class compromise beginning in the 1980s, an assault that came to be known as neoliberalism.[4] Neoliberalism, in turn, opened the door for a number of other dynamic developments that accelerated in the last decades of the twentieth century. Two are particularly important in the present context: globalization and financialization.

The globalization of capitalism intensified along its many dimensions: trade, foreign direct investment, speculation on currencies, integration of commodity chains and production chains, etc. This meant that the economic conditions in particular places and regions became less autonomously determined by what was happening in those places and more dependent on what was happening elsewhere in the world. Of particular importance was the emergence of a global labor force that included hundreds of millions of very low paid workers in developing countries competing within a relatively integrated global system of production in manufacturing and some kinds of services. Globalization also contributed to the dramatic

---

development from the point of view of capitalist interests, or simply good enough given the constraints. One view, advocated by Peter Swenson in *Capitalists Against Markets: The Making of Labor Markets and Welfare States in the United States and Sweden* (Oxford: Oxford University Press, 2002), is that these postwar arrangements were actually optimal for capital and not really "compromises" at all. They had the *appearance* of compromises in which capitalists made concessions, but this was simply a ploy—in Swenson's view— to enhance their legitimacy.

4   I am using the term "neoliberalism" as a broad umbrella term for the attack on the form of the capitalist state that provided expansive public goods, strong social insurance for ordinary citizens, and systematic regulation against negative externalities, rather than a specific set of policies designed to unfetter markets through deregulation and other policies.

increase in immigration to the developed countries and the increased ethnic heterogeneity of their popular social forces.

The dramatic financialization of capitalist economies in the rich countries meant that capital accumulation became rooted in much more volatile speculative processes and less connected to the development of the real economy than in the past.[5] The globalization of financial markets further intensified the potentially destabilizing effects of the shift of capital accumulation towards the financial sector. The combination of globalization and financialization meant that from the early 1980s the interests of the wealthiest and most powerful segments of the capitalist class in many developed capitalist countries, perhaps especially in the United States, became increasingly anchored in global financial transactions and speculation and less connected to the economic conditions and rhythms of their national bases or any other specific geographical location.

The result of these structural developments was a transformation of the class-compromise curve and the regions of exclusion, as illustrated in Figure 12.3. The critical developments are the following:

• The financialization and globalization of capitalism pushes the righthand peak of the class-compromise curve downward. Basically, the value for many capitalists of a positive class compromise declines as the returns on their investments become less dependent on the social and political conditions of any given place.

• Neoliberalism as a political project shifts the regions of exclusion at both ends of the class-compromise curve. On the one hand, the aggressive affirmation and enforcement of private property rights creates impediments to the enlargement of popular power. On the other hand, the erosion of labor law in some countries (especially the United States), and the partial dismantling of the safety net of the welfare state, reduces the region of exclusion on the downward sloping part of the curve, making more of that region strategically accessible.

---

5 The idea of financialization is somewhat less familiar to many people than globalization. Financialization refers to the shift of the profit-making activities within capitalist economies from the production of goods and services in the real economy to the buying and selling of financial assets of various sorts. Many factors contributed to this change, but the partial deregulation of financial markets certainly played an important role. For an extended discussion of financialization; see Greta Krippner, *Capitalizing on Crisis: The Political Origins of the Rise of Finance*, Cambridge, MA: Harvard University Press, 2011.

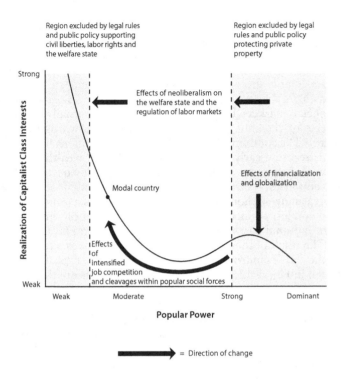

Figure 12.3. Capitalist Class Interests and Popular Power in the Era of Stagnation and Crisis

- In the context of the previous two developments, the level of popular power within the modal country declines as a result of a number of interacting factors: the increasing competition for jobs within the working class as unemployment increases and job security declines; the increasing heterogeneity within popular social forces because of immigration, which erodes mass-based solidarities and opens a political space for right-wing populism; austerity policies that increase the vulnerability of workers and make them more risk-averse; aggressive anti-labor strategies by employers who take advantage of this vulnerability.

Taken together, these forces have pushed the balance of class forces into the adverse downward sloping region of the class compromise curve.

ALTERNATIVE RESPONSES TO EROSION OF CLASS COMPROMISE

I assume that an exit from capitalism is not an option in the present historical period. This is not because of any qualms about the desirability of a break with capitalism as an economic system, but because of a belief in the impossibility of any kind of viable ruptural strategy. This belief is rooted in the central dilemma of revolutionary transformation of capitalist democracies: As Przeworski argued in the 1980s, if a ruptural break with capitalism is attempted under open democratic conditions, it is extremely unlikely, even under the most optimistic of scenarios, that such a socialist political project could survive multiple elections.[6] Because of the disruptions between the election of political forces attempting a break with capitalism and the stabilization of a socialist economy, any plausible transition will be marked by a "transition trough" of sharply declining material conditions of life for most people and considerable uncertainty about future prospects. Under open, competitive democratic conditions, it is implausible that solidarity in the heterogeneous coalition that initially supported the rupture is likely to be sustained over the number of election cycles needed to complete a transition. A ruptural break with capitalism, therefore, can happen only under nondemocratic conditions. But if a rupture with capitalism takes place under nondemocratic conditions it is extremely unlikely that it would create democratic, egalitarian socialism, as suggested by the tragic history of attempts at nondemocratic revolutionary ruptures with capitalism in the twentieth century. The only plausible ruptural scenarios are thus either a nondemocratic rupture with capitalism that results in authoritarian statism rather than democratic socialism, or an attempted democratic rupture with capitalism that is reversed during the extended transition period. For the foreseeable future, therefore, we will be living in an economic system dominated by capitalism, even if we retain revolutionary aspirations for a world beyond capitalism. The question is: living in capitalism on whose terms and in what form?

So long as the working class and other popular social forces live in a capitalist world, a positive class compromise offers the best prospects for securing the material welfare of most people. This

---

6 Adam Przeworski, *Capitalism and Social Democracy*, Cambridge: Cambridge University Press, 1985. The relevance of these arguments for the prospects for democratic socialism in the twenty-first century is discussed in my book *Envisioning Real Utopias*, chapter 9, "Ruptural Transformation."

does not mean that no gains are ever possible without a positive compromise—concessions can sometimes be won through struggles that result in negative compromises. Socialist and social democratic parties can win elections and initiate progressive reforms even in the absence of positive class compromise. But such gains are always more precarious than gains under conditions of positive class compromise, both because they encounter greater initial resistance, and because they are more vulnerable to later counteroffensives. For gains by popular social forces to be stabilized and sustained, therefore, they generally need to be part of a package that includes solutions to problems faced by capitalists and other elites. These solutions need not be *optimal* for capitalist interests, but they need, at least, to be compatible with those interests.

I explore two broad responses to the erosion of conditions for positive class compromise: The first examines strategies that could potentially reverse the trends in Figure 12.3 and reconstruct the favorable conditions in Figure 12.2. The second explores ways of potentially making the welfare of ordinary people living in a capitalist economy less dependent on the prospects for a positive class compromise with the capitalist class.

I. STRATEGIES THAT TRY TO RECREATE CONDITIONS FOR POSITIVE CLASS COMPROMISE

Figure 12.4 presents a rough guide to the kinds of transformations needed to restore conditions for positive class compromise. Here I focus on the problem of the shape of the curve itself: are there plausible strategies and public policies that could affect the shape of the underlying functional relation between popular power and elite interests in ways that would help improve the prospects for stable positive class compromise? Or is the current deterioration of the underlying macroeconomic conditions for class compromise simply the inexorable result of the dynamics of capitalism operating behind the backs of actors and not amenable to strategic intervention?[7] It

---

7 These questions have a family resemblance to a classic concern in discussions of revolutions: do revolutionary movements simply "seize the time" when windows of opportunity for revolutionary action occur—when "the conditions are ripe"—or can they actively contribute to creating those conditions? Of course, the preparation of revolutionary organization ahead of time might itself be important to be able to seize the time, but this is quite different from imagining that revolutionary movements can themselves contribute to creating the critical social structural and economic conditions which make

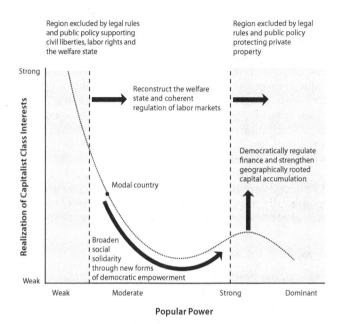

Figure 12.4. Transforming the Conditions for Class Compromise

is possible that the few decades after World War II were a happy historical anomaly in which conditions just happened to be favorable for the positive class compromise that underwrote economic security and modest prosperity for most people in developed capitalist countries. We may now be in the more normal condition of capitalism, in which the best that can be hoped for are occasional periods of negative class compromise, and most people adopt, as

---

possible an effective challenge to the dominant class. Marx almost certainly believed that the laws of motion of capitalism determined the basic dynamic through which revolutionary situations occurred; the critical role for collective action was to take advantage of these opportunities: "History is the judge; the proletariat is the executioner" (quoted by G. A. Cohen in *Karl Marx's Theory of History*). Here our concern is not with strategies that foster revolutionary conditions, but strategies that foster favorable conditions for class compromise.

best they can, individual strategies to cope with the risks and deprivations of life in capitalism.

What I want to explore here is the less pessimistic scenario in which it is possible to forge new structural conditions for a more robust positive class compromise. I do not address the difficult political question of the prospects for actually mobilizing the political forces with progressive ideological commitments necessary for implementing the policies required to create these conditions, but rather the question of what policies could be implemented if progressive political forces were in a position to do so. If my diagnosis in Figure 12.3 is correct that the righthand peak in the class compromise curve has declined because of forces unleashed by globalization and financialization, what is needed are strategies that encourage geographically rooted forms of capital accumulation and that impose effective democratic constraints on financial institutions.[8]

Geographical Rootedness

In terms of the problem of geographical rootedness, one promising line of thought on these issues is Joel Rogers's proposals for what he terms "Productive Democracy" (which he earlier referred to as "high road capitalism").[9] Rogers argues for the importance of concentrating attention on regional economies anchored in metropolitan areas, rather than on the national economy, and especially on the role of the local state in building local public goods capable of supporting high productivity economic activities. The emphasis

---

8 Many discussions of the current period place a great deal of emphasis on the specific ideological currents within the elite and how these have been diffused through specific institutional processes. In the United States, for example, the discussion of the rise of market fundamentalism and the intensifying hostility to the affirmative state has generally emphasized distinctive political processes within the United States, such as the importance of corporate money in elections, the ideological effectiveness of right-wing think tanks, manipulation of racism by the Republican Party, and so on. These processes are obviously of considerable importance in the United States, but do not explain the broad erosion of vigorous support for the affirmative state across a wide range of developed capitalist democracies. It is conceivably the case that other countries have simply been affected by ideological currents generated within the United States, but it is more likely that there is some underlying political-economic process in play throughout developed capitalism which is driving these trends to a significant extent.

9 Joel Rogers, "Productive Democracy," in J. de Munck, C. Didley, I. Ferreras, and A. Jobert, eds., *Renewing Democratic Deliberation in Europe: The Challenge of Social and Civil Dialogue*, Berlin: Peter Lang, 2012, 71–92.

here is on producing a high density of productivity-enhancing infra-structures that create incentives for capitalist firms to become more embedded locally: public transportation, education, research parks, energy efficiency, and much more. Strong local public goods are potentially particularly effective for small and medium-sized firms, which are generally less geographically mobile and whose owners are more likely to have noneconomic roots in the region.

A key element of these local public goods concerns training and skill formation, one of the classic collective action problems faced by capitalist firms (because of the temptation to free-ride on the on-the-job training provided by other firms). Here is where strong unions can play an especially constructive role in the design of training programs and in coordinating skill standards that are essential for the portability of skills. Regional development strate-gies that focus on such public goods and that involve local collective actors (especially unions) in the deliberative problem-solving connected to those public goods could generate local conditions for positive class compromise with locally rooted capital.

Changes in technology may make the anchoring of capitalist production in locally rooted, high-productivity small and medi-um-sized enterprises more feasible. One of the critical features of the era of industrial capitalism was strongly increasing returns to scale in production and distribution, since steep increasing returns to scale give large corporations a competitive advantage. The deep transformation of the technological environment of economic activ-ity in the digital age has significantly reduced these returns to scale in many sectors. Consider publishing. While large publishers still are important, the per unit costs of publishing are much less sensi-tive to scale than they were even a decade ago, especially with the advent of electronic books. New technologies on the horizon for manufacture also suggest the possibility of much weaker returns to scale, which in principle could make small and medium-sized firms much more productive and competitive. All of these developments may increase the prospects a productive democracy underwritten by local and regional public goods.

Public goods, of course, require taxes, and one view is that the taxa-tion capacity of the state is seriously undermined by globalization. If taxes rise, the argument goes, capital moves. This seems even more cogent as an argument against the possibility of local public goods: if local taxes rise to fund local public goods, capitalist firms will simply move out of the jurisdiction levying those taxes. Such arguments assume that taxation must always, directly or indirectly, raise the costs faced by capitalist firms. This, of course, may be the case, especially when the tax is directly levied on profits. But in principle, taxation can simply be a way of dividing the consumption of wage earners between their private consumption and their collective consumption through public goods and have little effect on profits of capitalist firms. Whether workers are willing to accept high or low taxation on wages depends, of course, on the degree of solidarity among wage earners and their confidence that the taxes will in fact be used to finance such public goods. The tax constraints on creating the local public goods needed for a locally rooted productive capitalism are thus much more political and ideological than narrowly economic.

Constraining Finance

With respect to financialization, two things seem especially important to accomplish. The first is to redirect finance from a central preoccupation with speculative activity to investment in the real economy. While there is often no unambiguous line of demarcation between these two faces of the allocation of capital, one of the things that detaches the interests of investors from the conditions of life of ordinary people and thus makes positive class compromise less likely is the disengagement of investment from the real economy. In order to redirect finance towards the real economy, the state has to be able to impose real constraints on investment activity, and this requires at least partially impeding the global flow of capital. So long as capital can easily exit the jurisdiction of a political authority, such regulation will always be precarious. This, then, is the second critical task: reestablishing the capacity of the state to effectively regulate finance and hold it democratically accountable. There are many proposals on the table to move in this direction: breaking up the largest financial institutions, both to undermine their power to manipulate regulatory authority and to remove their willingness to engage in excessive risk because of their "too-big-to-fail" status; explicitly recognizing the public goods aspect of finance as grounds for creating a more vibrant sector of public and cooperative financial institutions—credit unions, cooperative banks, community banks; and new forms of transactions taxes, like the Tobin tax, to impede the smooth global flow of finance for speculative purposes.

Taken together, public policies that help build a locally rooted productive democracy and place more democratic restraints on finance would potentially move the class compromise curve in Figure 12.3 in the direction of the Golden Age curve in Figure 12.4. Such policies, especially the ones that impinge on the power of finance, would certainly meet strong opposition from various elites. The problem, of course, is mobilizing sufficiently strong and resilient political forces to overcome such opposition. Many of the same political-economic structural developments that have generated an unfavorable class compromise curve have also contributed to undermining the power of popular democratic forces needed to push for these kinds of public policies.

2. STRATEGIES THAT STRENGTHEN NONCAPITALIST ECONOMIC DOMAINS

Because of the political difficulty of instituting policies that would change the conditions for the class compromise curve illustrated in Figure 12.4, it is worth exploring the possibility of strategies that respond to the adverse conditions for class compromise by focusing on ways of building alternatives in civil society and the economy itself, rather than by mainly focusing on confronting the state. At the center of my analysis in *Envisioning Real Utopias* of socialist alternatives is the idea that all economies are hybrids of different kinds of economic relations. In particular, I argued that modern capitalist economies should be viewed as hybrids of capitalist, statist, and socialist economic structures. The synoptic description of such a hybrid economy as "capitalism" implies that the capitalist component is "dominant." The idea of positive class compromise is focused on power relations and class interests generated by the capitalist dynamics of the system. One way of approaching the problem of restoring conditions in which at least some of the benefits of positive class compromise can be realized is to strengthen the noncapitalist aspects of the economic structural hybrid. The following sections explore a few examples.

Worker Cooperatives

By their very nature, worker-owned cooperative firms are geographically rooted. The owner-employees in such firms have a stake in where they live, and thus they have a deep interest in creating locally favorable economic conditions and supporting the public goods that make this possible. Although in most existing capitalist economies, worker cooperatives tend to occupy only small niches (in the United States in 2015 there were fewer than 400 worker cooperatives), there are instances of large, successful worker-owned cooperatives, most famously the group of over 100 cooperatives known as the Mondragon Cooperative Corporation.

Of particular relevance in the present context is the fact that in the current economic crisis in Spain, Mondragon has fared much better than most of the rest of the Spanish economy: only one of the cooperatives in the group has had to be dissolved. Many issues are involved in explaining the durability of the Mondragon cooperatives in the face of the crisis. Among other things, the Mondragon structure includes a system of cross-subsidization of less profitable by more profitable cooperatives, which acts as a buffer when times are difficult. The common stakes of workers in the cooperatives and the relatively low level of internal inequality mean that the levels of solidarity and commitment among workers are quite high. The idea that "we are all in this together" is a reality, and thus workers are less resistant to the shared sacrifices needed to weather a crisis. But also, there are nonmember employees in the cooperatives, and lay-offs of these employees also helped.

The existence of Mondragon as a successful, productive, large-scale complex of cooperatives shows that worker cooperatives need not be restricted to small, artisanal firms in marginal parts of the economy. In any case, given the decline in capital intensity in many domains of economic activity (especially because of the development of digital technologies) and the increasing possibilities of modularized forms of production, the scale constraints on worker cooperatives in many sectors are decreasing. One way of fostering a more geographically rooted structure of capital accumulation would be to encourage the development and expansion of worker cooperatives.

Worker cooperatives are founded mainly in two different ways: either by a group of people getting together and collectively starting a firm on a cooperative basis, or by the workers of an established capitalist firm buying out the owners of the firm. The latter strategy is particularly relevant in contexts where aging owners of family firms face a succession crisis in which no one in the younger generation of the family wants to take over the firm. One option in such a situation is for the workers to buy the firm. The problem, however, is that workers generally do not have sufficient savings to do so, and therefore they have to take on debt to buy the firm (if banks are willing to give them loans), which then imposes a significant burden on the subsequent viability of the firm. This problem is intensified in the broader context of macro-level economic stagnation.

In order for small- and medium-sized family firms to be successfully converted into worker cooperatives, therefore, there needs to be some way for workers to assume ownership of firms on a collective basis without taking on excessive debt, which would undermine the future viability of the firm. One possible source for such support might come from the labor movement. Traditionally, unions have been relatively hostile to worker cooperatives, seeing them as rivals for the allegiance of workers. In recent years there are indications of a change in this stance. In the United States, there are new initiatives to create what are coming to be called "union cooperatives"—cooperatives that are incubated and supported by labor unions. Some initial experiments along these lines exist in Cincinnati and a number of other cities. In Cleveland, an initiative to create a cluster of cooperatives facilitated by the city government and other large public institutions has also received support from local unions. In Brazil, unions have also been broadly supportive of cooperatives. Rather than rivals, worker cooperatives may potentially be a complementary basis for collective organization of workers' power. In places where the labor movement remains relatively strong, unions could help mobilize the capital needed for worker-buyouts of small and medium-sized firms.

The state could be another source of potential underwriting of cooperativization, especially local governments. Because an expansion of the cooperative sector could generate strong positive externalities for employment and economic stability, the state at the local or even national level might find it advantageous to create specialized credit institutions for this purpose. New forms of property rights involving partnerships of state and cooperative ownership could also be used to foster a dynamic expansion of cooperative production.

If the problems of credit market failures and undercapitalization of cooperatives were solved, it is possible that over time the number of cooperatives would increase, eventually leading to dense networks of cooperatives, meta-cooperatives (cooperatives-of-cooperatives), and other institutional arrangements of what can be termed a cooperative market economy. On a regional scale this is what the Mondragon Cooperative Corporation has accomplished. Within the Mondragon complex there are a range of institutional devices that increase the viability of each of the individual cooperative enterprises, including specialized research and development organizations; processes for cross-subsidization of profits from higher- to lower-profit cooperatives; and training and education institutions oriented to cooperative management and other needs of the firms in the network. A dense network of cooperatives connected to this kind of elaborated environment of specialized institutions could create a cooperative market economy enclave within the broader capitalist economy.

Employee-Majority Employee Stock Ownership Plans

Employee stock ownership plans (ESOPs) are a hybrid form combining, in varying degrees, capitalist and participatory-democratic elements. There are approximately 4,000 firms in the United States that are 100 percent employee-owned ESOPs.[10] In most firms with ESOPs, especially large firms, the employees own only a minority of shares, and often those shares are concentrated in management. Most 100 percent employee-owned ESOPs are relatively small firms. Actual democratic governance rights also vary across ESOPs, although in 100 percent ESOPs the employees do elect the board of directors of the firm (on a one-share/one-vote basis). Nevertheless, ESOPs with a high percentage of employee shareowners are more geographically rooted than are conventional capitalist firms. ESOPs can be a transitional form between a conventional capitalist firm and a fully democratic worker cooperative (although, of course, worker cooperatives also sometimes convert to ESOPs), but they may also be a stable hybrid form that connects to the development of a substantial cooperative market economy sector much more amenable to the rehabilitation of the democratic affirmative state.

The Social Economy

The social economy constitutes economic activities organized by communities and various kinds of nonprofit organizations directly for the satisfaction of needs rather than for exchange and profit. Most often social economy organizations produce services, but in some contexts such organizations produce goods. The social economy has an ambiguous status with respect to the provision of public goods and reducing vulnerability, for often the social economy mainly serves to fill gaps caused by the retreat of the welfare state. This is one of the reasons why conservatives sometimes applaud the social economy (for example, in the advocacy of "faith-based initiatives" in the United States). But the social economy can also be at the center of building an alternative structure of economic relations, anchored in popular mobilization and

---

10   A technical note on ESOPs: ESOPs are formed in a variety of ways, some of which are more favorable to the interests of worker-employees than others. In the most advantageous ESOPs, workers do not allocate their own savings to purchase shares in the company. Instead, the shares are given as part of a benefit package and distributed to all employees rather than heavily concentrated in the professional and managerial staff of the firm.

community solidarity, especially when it receives financial support from the state. The Quebec social economy is an example of a vibrant social economy involving community-based daycare centers, elder-care services, job-training-centers, social housing, and much more. In Quebec there also exists a democratically elected council, the *chantier de l'economie sociale,* with representatives from all the different sectors of the social economy, which organizes initiatives to enhance the social economy, mediates its relation to the provincial government, and extends its role in the overall regional economy. The *chantier* enhances democratic-egalitarian principles by fostering economic activity organized around needs and by developing new forms of democratic representation and coordination for the social economy.

Solidarity Finance

Another way of strengthening noncapitalist elements within a capitalist economy is by expanding the ways in which popular organizations are involved in allocating capital. Unions and other organizations in civil society often manage pension funds for their members. In effect, this is collectively controlled capital that can be allocated on various principles. An interesting example is the Quebec "Solidarity Fund" initially developed by the labor movement in the 1980s. The purpose of these funds is to use investments deliberately to protect and create jobs rather than simply to maximize returns for retirement. One way the Solidarity Fund accomplishes this is by directly investing in small and medium-sized enterprises, either through private equity investment or loans. These investments are generally directed at firms that are strongly rooted in the region and satisfy various criteria in a social audit. The Solidarity Fund is also involved in the governance of the firms in which it invests, often by having representation on the board of directors. Typically the investments are made in firms with a significant union presence, since this helps solve information problems about the economic viability of the firm and facilitates the monitoring of firm compliance with the side-conditions of the investment. Solidarity finance thus goes considerably beyond ordinary "socially screened investments" in being much more actively and directly engaged in the project of allocating capital on the basis of social priorities.

Solidarity finance can be considered a partial model for enhancing the geographic rootedness of regional market economies by tying investment more closely to people who live there. For this to be done at a scale that would make a significant difference, various kinds of support by the state may be important. The Quebec Solidarity Fund provides generous tax incentives for people who invest through the fund, but a more vigorous form of solidarity finance could involve different kinds of direct subsidies to the fund by different levels of government. Such direct subsidy can be justified on the grounds that geographical-rootedness—rather than free-floating capital mobility—is a public good because of the ways it makes the regulation of negative externalities easier and creates greater space for linking the interests of owners, workers and citizens.

Solidarity funds need not, of course, be restricted to control by labor unions. Other associations in civil society and perhaps even municipalities could also organize solidarity funds. The key idea is to develop decentralized institutional devices that direct investment to those economic activities that are geographically rooted and whose long-term viability depends on the robustness of the regional economy. Solidarity funds can therefore be seen as a complement to the broader menu of regional economic development strategies organized by the state.

Social democracy has, traditionally, not given much weight to strengthening noncapitalist forms of economic organization. Its core ideology was to support the smooth functioning of capitalism and then use part of the surplus generated within capitalism to fund social insurance and public goods. Capitalists were left relatively free to invest as they wished on the basis of private profit-maximizing criteria. The state provided incentives of various sorts to shape investment priorities, and certainly the state tried to create the public goods and regulatory environment that would be congenial to capital accumulation, but it generally did not attempt to nurture noncapitalist sectors and practices. The mainstream Left throughout the developed capitalist world broadly supported these priorities.

It is uncertain whether it will be possible to reconstruct a political-economic equilibrium in which positive class compromise within capitalism could once again govern the terms in which the social surplus is allocated between private returns through capitalist investment and collective returns used to promote well-being through the affirmative state. But even if the conditions for a positive class compromise can be created, given the long-term uncertainties of the trajectory of structural conditions in capitalism, the Left should begin to seriously think about the desirability and possibility of expanding the space for noncapitalist alternatives within capitalist economies.

ACKNOWLEDGMENTS

Nine of the twelve chapters in this book were previously published. They have been edited to remove redundancies and, in a few places, to update specific points, but they have not been substantially revised.

Chapter 1 was originally published as "Understanding Class," *New Left Review* 2:60, November/December 2009, 101–16.

Chapter 2, "The Shadow of Exploitation in Max Weber's Class Analysis," was published in *The American Sociological Review* 67: 6, December 2002, 832–53.

Chapter 3, "Metatheoretical Foundations of Charles Tilly's *Durable Inequality*," was published in *Comparative Studies in Society and History*, 42: 2, April 2000, 458–74.

Chapter 4, "Class, Exploitation and Economic Rents: Reflections on Sørenson's 'Towards a Sounder Basis for Class Analysis,'" appeared as part of a symposium on Sørensen's work in the *American Journal of Sociology* 105: 6, May 2000, 1559–71.

Chapter 7 is based on two published papers, "Class and Inequality in Piketty," *Contexts* 14: 1, Winter 2015, 58–61; and "Stay Classy, Piketty," Books&Ideas.net, November 3, 2014.

Chapter 8 appeared originally as "The Continuing Relevance of Class Analysis" as part of a symposium on the "death of class" in *Theory and Society*, 25: 5, October 1996, 693–716.

Chapter 10, "Beneficial Constraints: Beneficial for Whom?" was published in *Socio-economic Review* 2: 3, 2004, 407–14.

Chapter 11, "Working-Class Power, Capitalist-Class Interests, and Class Compromise," was published in *the American Journal of Sociology* 105: 4, January 2000, 957–1002. Parts of this article were also incorporated into chapter 11 of *Envisioning Real Utopias* (London: Verso, 2010).

Chapter 12 is based on a presentation given at the Nicos Poulantzas Institute, Athens, Greece, in December 2011. A version was subsequently published in *Transform!: European Journal for Alternative Thinking and Political Dialogue* 11/2012, 22–44.

Chapter 5 on Michael Mann's approach to class analysis, chapter 6 on David Grusky and Kim Weeden's theory of micro-classes, and chapter 9 on Guy Standing's analysis of the precariat, appear here for the first time.

INDEX

Printed in the United States
by Baker & Taylor Publisher Services